DEMOCRACY AND RESPONSIBILITY
British History 1880–1965

The Evolution of Western Society

GENERAL EDITOR

PETER BROOKS, Ph.D.

Lecturer in Modern History, University of Kent at Canterbury

OTHER PUBLISHED TITLES IN THIS SERIES

The Emergence of Western Society: European and English History 300–1200
BY COLIN DAVIES

Gathering Pace: Continental Europe 1870–1945
BY MAURICE LARKIN

IN PREPARATION

A British History 1760–1880
BY J. J. TUMELTY

A European and English History 1200–1450
BY COLIN DAVIES

Humanism and Reform: A History of Europe 1450–1650
BY PETER BROOKS

The Bourgeois Century: A History of Europe 1780–1870
BY K. R. PERRY

The Post-War World
BY D. W. HARKNESS

DEMOCRACY
AND RESPONSIBILITY

British History 1880-1965

T. A. NEAL, M.A.

DEPUTY HEADMASTER
BARLBY COUNTY SECONDARY SCHOOL, YORKSHIRE

MACMILLAN

© T. A. Neal 1969

First published 1969 by
MACMILLAN AND CO LTD
Little Essex Street London WC2
and also at Bombay Calcutta and Madras
Macmillan South Africa (Publishers) Pty Ltd Johannesburg
The Macmillan Company of Australia Pty Ltd Melbourne
The Macmillan Company of Canada Ltd Toronto
Gill and Macmillan Ltd Dublin

Printed in Great Britain by
ROBERT MACLEHOSE AND CO LTD
The University Press, Glasgow

Contents

List of Plates

The publishers wish to thank the following who have kindly given permission to reproduce the illustrations: 14: Aerofilms; 15*a*: Barnabys; 3*a*: Birmingham University Library; 15*b*: Electricity Council; 13*a*, 13*b*: G.L.C.; 5*a*, 6*c*, 10*a*: Imperial War Museum; 16*a*: Graham Keen; 10*b*: Keystone; 9*a*, 9*b*: London Express; 1*a*, 1*d*, 2*b*, 3*b*, 4*a*, 4*b*, 5*b*, 6*b*, 7*a*, 7*b*, 8*a*, 8*b*, 11*a*, 11*b*, 12*a*, 12*b*: Radio Times Hulton Picture Library; 2*a*: The Salvation Army; 16*b*: Syndication International.

List of Maps

Acknowledgements

The author and publishers wish to thank the following for permission to quote from their books:

Faber & Faber Ltd and Harcourt, Brace & World Inc., for lines from 'Choruses from 'The Rock' ' and 'The Hollow Men', from *Collected Poems 1909–1962*, by T. S. Eliot, copyright 1936, Harcourt, Brace & World Inc., © 1963, 1964 by T. S. Eliot; and Mr M. B. Yeats and The Macmillan Company, New York, for lines from 'The Rose Tree' and 'Easter 1916', from *The Collected Poems of W. B. Yeats*, copyright 1924 by The Macmillan Company, renewed 1952 by Bertha Georgie Yeats.

A2

General Editor's Introduction

THE EVOLUTION OF WESTERN SOCIETY

FOR some time students have experienced difficulties in getting to grips with more advanced historical study because many textbooks have proved daunting in size and style. Young minds have often been over-burdened with detailed narrative and consequently denied those balanced yet scholarly judgments that can enliven the past and communicate its significance.

In an attempt to combat this trend, *The Evolution of Western Society* consists of a series of volumes specifically designed for those seeking an introduction to relatively advanced work. Written in readable prose, while avoiding gimmicks, these lively studies present a more topical approach to history by expounding a given period in terms of main-point analysis. In a dozen volumes, a team of dons and schoolmasters, who are both authorities in their specialist fields and experienced teachers, will give their readers a wide coverage of British and European history from the decline of the Roman Empire to the conflicts of the contemporary world. Each book contains adequate narrative for those obliged to satisfy the demands of public examinations, but every effort has been made to focus interest upon analysis rather than description, and to convey the spirit of each period by means of selected source quotation and visual material. Full bibliographies are included to guide further reading, and in addition to charts, diagrams and maps, all volumes contain a section devoted to brief lives of important figures, whether artists or churchmen, statesmen or military leaders, scientists or philosophers. Above all, each book is an exercise in three-dimensional history, and presents the reader with the findings of modern scholarship in a comprehensive, comprehensible and stimulating form.

Already the author of a successful history textbook, Mr Terry Neal has had a wide experience of teaching his subject in both grammar and comprehensive Schools. The good schoolmaster was once described by a pillar of the profession as 'he who, given a moment's notice, can teach anything'! But although Mr Neal's competence ranges from cricket to opera, his deep interest in modern English politics makes this the kind of book that will be widely appreciated not only for itself but as the work of a most able teacher of history. I commend his book warmly, and with confidence: it will have a wide appeal.

PETER BROOKS

Preface

THE theme of this study is implicit throughout its pages. The growth of democratic institutions, and the success or failure of government and people in fulfilling responsibilities at home and abroad are distinctive threads in the fabric of modern British history.

I can make no real claim to originality in my selection of material and in many of my judgments. I have attempted a distillation of some of the best modern scholarship on the period, in a form which I hope will prove palatable and provocative to students. I particularly hope that my readers will go on to study more detailed accounts of topics which they find interesting. I gratefully acknowledge my obligations to historians and biographers, which will be at once familiar to readers acquainted with the literature of the subject. Particular debts are recognised in the notes to each chapter.

I am glad of the opportunity to express my thanks to my friends Dr Peter Brooks and Dr John Derry, who have read my book at every stage, and Mr Ronald Chapman, who has read the proofs. All have made most kindly and constructive suggestions. I naturally remain responsible for any errors of fact or of judgement.

My greatest debts are to my wife and son for their patience, understanding and enthusiastic encouragement.

T. A. N.

CHAPTER ONE

Late Victorian England

The later Victorians laid no plans for the future. They were content to meet those demands and to solve those problems the pressure of which was already felt. But within those limits they were more active reformers than their self-satisfied fathers....

G. M. TREVELYAN, *English Social History*

HISTORY is a continuous process which defies convenient packaging for the writers of textbooks. Rigid divisions of time, though important to the mathematician and the scientist, have little significance for the student of history. A study which begins its enquiries in 1880, therefore, plunges into the flowing stream of life in Victorian England.

It is no accident that the whole period takes its epithet from the name of the monarch. England in the late nineteenth century was a monarchy, though of a distinctively parliamentary kind, and the person of the monarch who had been on the throne since 1837 acted as a focus of national and imperial sentiment: when Queen Victoria died in 1901, people were wont to talk of the death of the mother of the nation and the Empire. Her most recent biographer has agreed that 'Her prejudices and her convictions were so exactly those dominant in her age that she seemed to embody its very nature within herself'.[1]

Although the Queen was a controversial figure, her grasp of the emotions of her subjects, particularly towards the end of her reign, was remarkable: 'He always said he wished to die for you', the Queen was told by the widow of one of her soldiers. Her subjects loved her for her domesticity – she was devoted to her family, which extended to most of the royal families of

Europe, whose 'grandmother' she became – for her simplicity, and her patent love of truth, a quality which called forth the admiration of Gladstone, whose patience she sorely tried. Above all, the spirit of the Victorian age which she most clearly and consistently embodied was its devotion to self-improvement, epitomised in Victoria's resolution at the age of eleven that 'I will be good'.

She could, of course, be awesomely reginal and forbidding, and she is frequently remembered for the chilling pronouncement that 'We are not amused'. She combined, though, a high idealism with practical common sense: she revelled in her Imperial title, but her concept of Empire embodied virtue rather than power – 'to protect the poor natives and advance civilisation'.

The death of her beloved consort, Prince Albert, in 1861, had brought out the most morbid aspects of her character, and for fifteen years she lived as a recluse in Windsor. Dependent upon him during his lifetime, she became obsessed with her husband's memory. Disraeli, on his deathbed in 1881, is said to have declined the honour of a visit from the Queen: 'No. It is better not. She'd only ask me to take a message to Albert.'[2] The Queen's withdrawal from public life had seriously jeopardised her popularity; her emergence from her long period of mourning triumphantly restored her prestige, especially during the great Jubilee celebrations of 1887 and 1897.

The Queen was resolved to play the role of a constitutional monarch, but the classic definition of the part by Walter Bagehot – 'to be consulted, to encourage and to warn' – was rather too circumscribed for a Queen determined to do her duty. She was, for instance, shocked by the inflexibility of party, especially as she found it embodied in Gladstone, and she was always hard at work against him behind the scenes. Her distaste for Gladstone bordered on the pathological, and pursued him to the grave: the Prince of Wales incurred his mother's severest displeasure for acting as a pall-bearer at the great man's funeral. Generally speaking, however, her political machinations, though undoubtedly unconstitutional, were innocuous.

The parliament through which the Queen ruled was not yet a democratic institution, and its membership continued to be dominated by the aristocracy and the middle class. Although the reforms of 1832 and particularly 1867 had greatly broadened the franchise, it remained limited. Even after the reform of 1884, two in five men and all women were excluded. By the 1880s, however, there already existed a springboard for the growth of genuine working-class movements in politics.* The growth of democracy, by the extension of the franchise and the opening of new opportunities for talent, is one of the obvious themes of our study. So, too, is the marked development of bureaucracy as governments undertook wider responsibilities and extended the scope of involvement in the everyday lives of citizens. Since Gladstone's reform in 1870, recruitment to the Civil Service which staffed the bureaucracy was by public examination.

The educational facilities which were essential to provide wider opportunities were extended in the later years of the nineteenth century. Education at the elementary level had developed as a responsibility of the state since 1870, but its expansion was bedevilled by sectarian controversy. The gravest weakness of English education continued to be the severe limitation of opportunities for study beyond the elementary stage, although the universities became less exclusive. Since 1871 Oxford and Cambridge had ceased to be the private preserves of Anglicans, and universities on a smaller scale had grown up in Durham and London since the 1830s. An important development was the creation in 1884 of the Victoria University, an amalgamation of colleges in Manchester, Leeds and Liverpool. The Welsh University was created in 1893, and Birmingham in 1900. Education ceased to be a masculine monopoly. By 1880 there was notable progress in the creation of girls' schools, and there were two colleges for women in Cambridge and two in Oxford, where a further two were founded before the end of the century.

The most serious shortcoming in higher education in England was the poverty of its teaching in science, whilst the

* See Chapter Seven, pp. 98–112.

outstanding general need was for the expansion of secondary education. Some contribution towards the solution of both problems was available through the extension of technical education in evening schools, Mechanics' Institutes, and so on, whilst the period was also noteworthy for the extension of public libraries, often through gifts or legacies like those of Andrew Carnegie.

In spite of the ceaseless growth in the activity of the central government, it was still in the local context that government made its most obvious impacts upon the lives of most people. Local government was hindered for too long by excessive pressure from Whitehall, although in the mid-1870s Joseph Chamberlain had shown in Birmingham what could be done at the local level, and notable progress had been made in local government in Manchester and in Liverpool, where municipal stock was first issued in 1880. Municipal building tended to be marked by a lack of aesthetic sense, but an attack on the grievous problems of slum-dwellings was inspired by a star-studded Royal Commission on Housing in 1884.

Rapid progress in the development of local government followed the County Councils Act of 1888 and the District and Parish Coucils Act of 1894, which extended the principle of local government by elected councils, which had existed in municipal boroughs since 1835. The councils came to provide a basis for the administration of education, health, and transport. A particular feature of the expansion of local government was the organisation of London.

In the wider national and international context, the resources of Britain and her Empire were imposing but already vulnerable. Population was still generally regarded as a valid indication of potential strength, both economic and military. The population of the United Kingdom in 1881[3] was 35·2 million (including 5·1 million in Ireland) compared with 50·1 million in the U.S.A., 45·2 million in Germany, and 37·6 million in France. Twenty years later, in 1901,[4] the population of the United Kingdom had risen to 41·9 million (including now only 4·4 million in Ireland, where people were emigrating in large numbers) compared with 75·9 million in

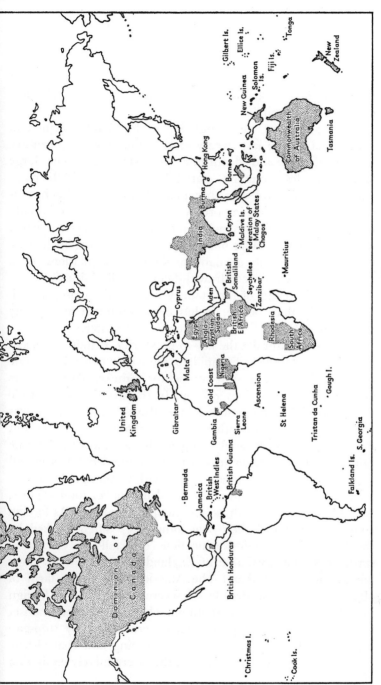

I. The Empire at the death of Queen Victoria, 1901

the U.S.A., 56·3 million in Germany, and 38·9 million in France. Anxiety over the disproportionate expansion of the populations and resources of Britain's rivals was an important factor in Joseph Chamberlain's emphasis upon the resources of the British Empire.

The statistics of the population of the United Kingdom reveal that in the last twenty years of the nineteenth century both birth-rate and death-rate were declining. The large family was less common, particularly in the middle class, where birth-control was becoming fashionable. Such tendencies had, of course, important social repercussions, especially in the accelerated development of a middle-class suburban way of life, with smaller houses and fewer servants; in any case they were less readily available as the rural populations (from which most servants were drawn) themselves diminished.

The total wealth of the country continued to rise, though more slowly than before. It has been computed at £10,037 million in 1885 and £11,393 million ten years later.[5]

Trade was naturally the key to prosperity. Britain's overseas trade in 1880 totalled £698 million, more than twice the volume of the trade of her nearest competitor, France. Twenty years later, the total was £877 million. In the strategic sense trade was secured by the power of the Royal Navy, which was constantly being strengthened by technical advances, but exports were increasingly vulnerable as markets became saturated and foreign competition increased. Nearly all exports were manufactured articles, with textiles predominant. In 1880 textiles accounted for £108 million of total exports, with cotton alone worth no less than £76 million. As foreign countries developed their own industries – often marked by the fruits of a technical education (especially in Germany) superior to that available in England – they built up tariff barriers to protect them. The American McKinley tariff of 1890 introduced a decade of severe protection of foreign industries from British competition. The difficulties were offset for a time by new exports which were essentially stop-gap expedients. Exports of machinery, shipping and coal clearly could not go on indefinitely, since they were merely equipping the industries of Britain's competitors. Whilst 29 million tons of British coal were exported in 1889, the period was marked by significantly increasing imports of foreign steel.

British merchant ships maintained their position in the world's carrying trade but commerce generally was very sensitive to financial weaknesses and to successive booms and slumps. Much British economic influence derived from overseas investment, which totalled £1,302 million in 1885. If banking systems proved suspect, the repercussions could be widespread and disastrous. In 1882, for instance, the collapse of Union Générale in Paris, which had yielded to the alluring temptation to over-speculation, led to a widespread fall in prices which lasted until 1886. In 1890 the great house of Baring in London was in serious trouble through over-speculation in Argentina, and a potential disaster was averted only by the vigorous action of the Bank of England. In 1893 the whole banking system of Australia fell in ruins.

Under such pressures a realistic amalgamation of banks was already taking place. Old-style family banks merged into formidable and stable consortiums. A similar process took place in the organisation of industry. The old family businesses tended often to be weakened by old-fashioned methods, inept sons and a lack of expertise. The amalgamation of capital and the transition from private firms to limited liability companies was an essential tendency, one by-product of which was the growth of the profession of accountancy. Trusts and larger-scale amalgamations were viewed at first with more suspicion, especially by trade unionists who feared a repetition of the worst American practices. The earliest large amalgamations were the Salt Union (1888), the United Alkali Company (made up of no less than 48 firms in 1891) and the English Sewing Cotton Company (1897).

Important advances in transport occurred during the last two decades of the nineteenth century. They were, of course, closely bound up with trade in general. In transport, this was the age of steel and the steamship. In 1881 Britain had a total of 6,695,000 tons of shipping, 3,005,000 tons of which was powered by steam. These were the resources, coupled with notableimprovementsinnautical engines in the 1880s and 1890s, which maintained Britain's share of the world's carrying trade. Internally, the railway-system was virtually completed, with nearly 18,000 miles of track. An outstanding feat of civil engineering was the construction of the Manchester Ship Canal which was opened in 1894. Most of the inventions in transport during the period were made abroad and lethargically taken up in Britain. Electric trams, for example, only slowly made their appearance, but the Central London Railway of 1900 was justly regarded as an outstanding pioneer in underground railways. The latter became a vital factor in transport in an ever-growing metropolis. The most socially significant invention of all was progressing from Daimler's experiments in Germany, but until 1896 motor-cars in Britain were seriously hampered by the law which insisted that they must be preceded on the roads by a man carrying a red flag. One invention which had an amazing social impact was the 'safety bicycle' of 1885, which was made much more comfortable by Dunlop's invention of the pneumatic tyre in 1888.

Yet the greatest transformation in the social and economic life of the period was the ruin of English agriculture. As the technical progress of railroads, shipping and agricultural machinery opened up the great wheatlands of north America, Britain's policy of Free Trade left her wide open to the flood of American wheat. Nature, too, conspired against the farmers: a succession of appalling harvests from 1875 until 1879 was followed by the devastation of flocks from liver-rot in 1879 and of herds by foot-and-mouth disease in 1883.

The disaster to English arable farming is graphically reflected in the falling price of wheat: in 1886 it was as low as 31s a quarter; worse was to come. In 1893 it was down to 26s 4d and in the following year reached rock-bottom at 22s 10d. Between 1880 and 1889, 45 per cent of all cereals in Britain were imported, compared with only 2 per cent half a century earlier. In the last decade of the nineteenth century, half a million acres of wheatlands went out of cultivation. The decline in arable agriculture was not compensated by returns from pastoral farming, for during that period the successful development of refrigeration aboard ship ensured mounting imports of frozen foreign meat.

No comprehensive solution was found despite the creation of the Board of Agriculture in 1889 and the activities of a Royal Commission. The social consequences of the catastrophe to agriculture were widespread. The urbanisation of England was completed. Already in 1881, there were 92,250 fewer labourers on the land than ten years earlier, and between 1871 and 1900 the number of agricultural labourers fell by 43 per cent. In 1901, 77 per cent of the total population lived in towns, but not all those who left the land drifted into the towns: there were nearly a million emigrants from this country in the decade up to 1881 alone. Naturally the number of landowners declined as well: revenues from rents declined from £59 million in 1888 to £42 million in 1901.

The wages and conditions of those who remained on the land improved, partly because there were fewer men employed, but not least through the work of a well-organised trade union, realistically led after 1872 by Joseph Arch. Between 1877 and 1900, despite fluctuations, agricultural wages improved by 120 per cent.

Like all trade unions of the time, however, that of the agricultural workers was particularly susceptible to the effects of boom and slump. Whenever unemployment increased, the authority and effectiveness of the early unions declined in proportion. The legal position of the trade unions had been clarified by Disraeli's legislation in 1875, which had freed the right to strike from possible litigation against conspiracy, and had legalised peaceful picketing. The movement was particularly encouraged by the success of the great London Dock Strike of 1889, and the period is marked by very important developments in tactics and organisation, examined further in our study of the early history of the labour movement.

There is no doubt that the last forty years of the nineteenth century were marked by a general improvement in living standards: between 1860 and 1900, the real value of wages, in terms of their purchasing-power, increased by 77 per cent. As early as 1886, the profits from trade of the Co-operative

Wholesale Society exceeded £20,000. But serious problems remained, as a reading of William Booth's book, *In Darkest England
and The Way Out* (1890), leaves no doubt. Housing remained the
worst feature of working-class life: it simply did not keep pace
with population expansion. Even after the elimination of
the worst slums, appalling and insanitary overcrowding
remained, particularly on Clydeside and Tyneside, but also
in London, Liverpool's dockland, and south Wales. Although
such circumstances brought out the best in social crusaders
like Dr Barnardo and William Booth, voluntary efforts could
make but small inroads into the problem as a whole.

Such conditions coincided with the growth of a more leisured
way of life for the middle class, reflected in suburban homes,
seaside holidays, and a more casual style of dress, at least for
the men. The age of the 'Norfolk jacket' had dawned, and the
frock-coat was on its way out. Women, however, in spite of
the effects of such emancipating influences as the Married
Women's Property Acts of 1882 and 1893, still defied the
judgement of Nature concerning their appropriate shape.
The crinoline slowly went out of fashion, only to be replaced
by the preposterous bustle. Dominating and constricting all
was the whalebone corset, which tortured the Victorian woman
and surely contributed more than anything else to the 'vapours'
to which the poor creature was such a prey.

This was also the beginning of the great age of organised
games which Britain, for good or ill, has presented as one of her
lasting legacies to mankind.

What of the mind of the Englishman within this political,
economic and social context? The great Victorian intellectual
era was already over: Gladstone himself was probably its
last great survivor. The predominance of Evangelical Christian-
ity was crumbling, though many of its legacies remained. Its
very simplicity had been at once the strength and the weakness
of Evangelicalism: 'If one asks', writes R. C. K. Ensor,[6] 'how
nineteenth century English merchants earned the reputation
of being the most honest in the world . . . the answer is:
because hell and heaven seemed as certain to them as tomorrow's
sunrise, and the Last Judgement as real as the week's balance

sheet.' The daily round of prayer and praise, within and beyond the family circle, spread its influences far and wide, from the cloistered ladies' colleges of the formidable Miss Beale and Miss Buss to the mission fields of Africa and China, from the humble dwellings of 'darkest England' to the 10 Downing Street of the High Churchman, Mr Gladstone.

But the same simplicity made Evangelicalism a tender intellectual plant. It withered in face of Anglo-Catholicism within the Church – and all Evangelicalism's assaults could not unseat the saintly Anglo-Catholic Edward King, who was made Bishop of Lincoln in 1885. Free-thinking might be academic and gentle like Matthew Arnold's, or militantly radical like that of Charles Bradlaugh. Nor could Victorian theology withstand the impact of scientific thought of men like Darwin and Huxley, or the development of a genuine historical method, applied to theology no less stringently than to history itself.

By the end of the century, churchgoing had ceased to be an essential ingredient in the lives of many people, partly because of the exhaustion of evangelical fervour, and also because the ritualism of Anglo-Catholicism made only a limited appeal to congregations. The English weekend made inroads into Sunday observance: the National Sunday League, for instance, was prepared to organise railway excursions to the seaside and country instead of to church. The conscious and ostentatious cultivation of luxury became the height of fashion, the pace being set by the Prince of Wales, justly categorised by Kipling as 'a corpulent voluptuary'. Historians are by no means unanimous concerning the extent to which organised vice had played its part throughout the century, beneath the veneer of Victorian respectability. But now there was no doubt, as the 'naughty nineties' openly reflected a marked slackening even of conventional and superficial standards of morality. Yet a man or woman might still be ruined by the divorce court, as prominent and promising politicians like Parnell and Dilke discovered.

The aesthetic standards of the time, bedevilled with the bric-à-brac of affluence, were generally low, and are reflected at their worst and most enduring in architecture. Improved transportation of building materials destroyed many of the regional harmonies of English building and swamped them in brick and slate. Church architecture for the most part remained enslaved to Gothic whilst Westminster Cathedral sought escape in nothing less congruous than a Byzantine style. This is not to say that there were not very good examples of ornate Gothic, whilst there were some memorable experiments, notably E. W. Mountford's Sheffield Town Hall.

The fight against encumbrances which threatened to stifle art and craft was led by William Morris; in spite of a rather self-conscious folksiness he set high design standards for items such as wallpapers. Perhaps his greatest achievement derived from his experiments in fine printing. He preached a most healthy gospel: 'Have nothing in your house except what you know to be useful or believe to be beautiful'.[7]

The advent of photography threw the visual and plastic arts into confusion. Burne-Jones fought off the clinging vestiges of dead realism. Whistler was the precursor of Impressionism, and Sargent helped to make it – in a mild form – respectable. The period did, however, witness a vast extension in the opportunities for looking at pictures: the National Portrait Gallery, the Tate Gallery, and the Victoria and Albert were reflected in the provinces by the opening of galleries in Birmingham, Manchester, Liverpool and elsewhere.

The musical life of England owed much to foreign influences, notably those of the great violinist Joachim, and Robert and Clara Schumann. Hans Richter introduced the marvels and mysteries of Wagner. Parry and Stanford were established, though mediocre, figures, and much of the great promise of Sullivan was dissipated by his association with W. S. Gilbert. But a supreme musical genius was burgeoning. In 1899 Edward Elgar produced his *Enigma Variations*, and in 1900 perhaps the greatest spiritual work of any English composer, *The Dream of Gerontius*. Such was the disappointment of its first performance in Birmingham, where Richter sadly misjudged its difficulties, that it was seriously listened to in England only after it became established in Germany, where Richter made handsome amends.

Much of the literature which was popular at the time has proved ephemeral, like the best-selling *East Lynne* of Mrs Henry Wood, but the novels (and in 1898 the verse) of Thomas Hardy reached a fairly wide public, as did the novels of Stevenson and the short stories of Rudyard Kipling. The novelist who has made the deepest impact upon a later generation of critics, Henry James, exercised a more limited appeal; he was too sophisticated for mass consumption. In poetry, the period was not strong, for the mature work of Yeats lay in the future. Housman's *A Shropshire Lad* was published, but the outstanding poet of the time remained largely unknown: 'Gerard Manley Hopkins', writes W. H. Gardner,[8] 'died in 1889 and rose again as a living poet in 1918', when his poems were published by Robert Bridges.

In the theatre it was the age of the actor-manager, of whom Henry Irving was the last great example. Oscar Wilde (disgraced in 1895) and Shaw (whose best work was yet to come) were probably the outstanding playwrights of the time.

It was a classic age in the writing of history, now feeling the full impact of German scientific methods. Stubbs, Freeman, Gardiner and Lecky, with the brilliant Maitland, remain great authorities; the greatest of all was Acton, who inaugurated the vintage era of Cambridge's historical scholarship, and founded the *English Historical Review* in 1886. Frazer began on his far-ranging intellectual excursion, *The Golden Bough*, in 1890, and the period witnessed the beginnings of two huge and indispensable works of reference, *The Dictionary of National Biography* and *The Oxford English Dictionary*.

Yet perhaps the greatest impact of any legacy of this period has still to be described, for the last years of the nineteenth century witnessed the transformation of the Press in England. Generally speaking, until the 1890s, the historian might still discuss the Press as a branch of literature. Newspapers, often owned by families, were not principally concerned with commercial success but were closely linked with political causes, and reflected essentially upper middle class and masculine attitudes. The most important columns were those devoted to leading articles. Lengthy parliamentary reports occupied most of the newspaper, and what later generations of journalists have learned to call 'human interest' was catered for by the reporting of court cases, for this was the great era of the murderer and the divorcee, and the advocates of the time assumed an aura later accorded to film-stars or matinée idols.[9] Above all, there existed a genuine morality of journalism: the news itself was sacrosanct, and not to be doctored: the leading articles would express the attitudes to the news of individual newspapers. *The Times*, which at 3*d* cost three times as much as most other papers, set the pattern for the others – *The Daily Telegraph*, *The Standard*, and *The Morning Post* (the leading London Conservative dailies), and the Liberal *Daily News* and *Daily Chronicle*.

The reviews, political and literary, retained much of their influence and reached a wider national readership than most of the daily papers. The leading reviews were the *Spectator*, the *Fortnightly Review* (which John Morley edited until 1882) and the intellectual-conservative *Saturday Review*.

The first rumblings of revolution were felt in 1880, when George Newnes issued *Tit-Bits*, a weekly aimed directly at the new readership created by an elementary education which 'taught people to read without teaching them what to read'.[10] The outstanding disciple of Newnes was Alfred Harmsworth, aided by his brother Harold, both of whom were destined to become 'Press Lords' in both the literal and the metaphorical sense. Now commercial enterprise replaced propaganda as the *raison d'être* of newspapers. In 1888, Harmsworth issued *Answers* as a direct competitor with *Tit-Bits*: spiced with racy journalism and with competitions, its readership soared to a quarter of a million. The inevitable next step was Harmsworth's excursion into the world of daily journalism. In 1894 he bought the *Evening News*, which under the editorship of Kennedy Jones, a kindred spirit with Harmsworth, sold at ½*d* a copy and succeeded. Harmsworth's *Daily Mail*, the first example of the tabloid daily, began in 1896 and within three years was selling over half a million copies. Advertisers chased circulation, and Harmsworth's fortune was established: he himself was well on the road to what Baldwin was to stigmatise in 1931 as 'power without responsibility, the prerogative of the harlot through the ages'.

The old-style journalistic ethic went overboard in the insatiable thirst for circulation. No longer was the news sacred: Harmsworth and his reporters and sub-editors did not scruple to invent it if the real thing were not 'readable' enough, regardless of distress which might be caused to individual members of the public. The disruption of personal privacy in the cause of 'human interest' had begun. So, too, had the fruits of the conviction that readers like 'a good hate', which was to give such joy to Harmsworth and his disciples in the Boer War and even more in 1914.

Such were some of the ingredients and changes in English life during the last two decades of the nineteenth century.

CHAPTER TWO

Gladstone and the Frustration of a Mission

> Ireland stands at your bar, expectant, hopeful, almost suppliant – think
> I beseech you, think well, think wisely, think, not for the moment, but for
> the years that are to come.
>
> GLADSTONE, in the great Home Rule debate in the
> House of Commons, 7–8 June 1886

WILLIAM EWART GLADSTONE is a titanic figure in the history of English politics and was a legend in his own lifetime. He was blessed with a remarkable combination of outstanding intellect and prodigious physical strength and his life was the embodiment of all that was best in Victorian piety. No man walked more humbly in the perpetual awareness of the presence of his God. His Christian conviction led him to the towering heights of righteous passion as his oratory assaulted the Turks for their atrocities against their Bulgarian or Armenian subjects; the same humble awareness of Christian duty led him to the very depths of Victorian society in his persistent and potentially ruinous efforts to win for God the souls of London prostitutes. It was utterly characteristic of the man that he should be blissfully unaware that such work might be open to misconstruction and might tarnish his reputation. It was entirely in character, too, that he should have expressed his greatest political ambition, in what are probably his best-known words, in terms of a mission – 'My mission is to pacify Ireland'.

Disraeli was the only contemporary politician whose personality could challenge that of Gladstone, but in terms of political experience Gladstone was unrivalled. Born in Liverpool in 1809, into a family which traced its origins in Scotland, he had been educated at Eton and at Christ Church, Oxford, where he won the supreme distinction of a double First Class in Classics and Mathematics, thus emulating Peel, whose political disciple he became. He entered the House of Commons in 1832 and held office as Under-Secretary for War and the Colonies in Peel's 'Hundred Days' ministry in 1835. When Peel formed his great ministry in 1841 he made Gladstone Vice-President of the Board of Trade, promoting him to the Cabinet in 1843 as President of the Board of Trade. Two years later Gladstone became Secretary for War and the Colonies resigning his previous post on characteristically conscientious grounds.

After the ruin of Peel's ministry over the repeal of the Corn Law in 1846, Gladstone moved, as Peel might well have done had he lived beyond 1850, towards the Whig–Liberal policies of Palmerston and his followers. Gladstone was Chancellor of the Exchequer under Lord Aberdeen from 1852 to 1855, and under Palmerston from 1859 to 1865. Some historians see this as his greatest period. His budgets, particularly under Palmerston, were masterly, progressive, and devoted to the cause of Free Trade.

His great conflicts with Disraeli had already begun when Gladstone became Prime Minister for the first time in 1868. The ministry was undoubtedly a reforming one, but was controversial and in some respects disappointing, and Disraeli's real opportunity came in 1874 when he took over from what he contemptuously dismissed as 'a row of extinct volcanoes'. In 1880 Disraeli (now Lord Beaconsfield) went to the country, and to his surprise and chagrin was defeated.

Gladstone was not in fact the leader of the Liberal Party in 1880. Five years earlier he had retired to 'a position of greater freedom and less responsibility' – a Gladstonian formula of which he and his followers were frequently and ironically reminded in the years ahead. In 1876, however, the atrocities committed by the Turks against their rebellious Christian subjects irresistibly aroused Gladstone's righteous indignation

and led to a bitter controversy with Disraeli: *Punch* depicted
the two great statesmen as urchins hurling mud at each other.
In 1878 Gladstone was still thinking primarily of his own
retirement from public life, but the will of God and the reorganisation of the Liberal Party in Scotland overcame his personal
wishes, and he became the Liberal candidate for Midlothian.

Gladstone's first campaign in Midlothian lasted a fortnight
in November 1879. His method – the concentrated tour of
the constituency, making frequent speeches to massive audi-
ences – was unconventional to the point of being revolutionary,
but Gladstone was realistic enough to understand that such
an undertaking had become necessary in the context of the
extended franchise of 1867; of course it has been a commonplace of political technique ever since – at least until the comfort
of the fireside chair and the television set superseded the public
hall. Disraeli scornfully wrote off the Midlothian campaign as
'a pilgrimage of passion', but the predominant passion which
Gladstone aroused in his hearers was the noble fervour for
liberty. Though he might disclaim the mantle, he was the
prophet of democracy.

Few statesmen have ever surpassed Gladstone's passion and
conviction, and probably none – not even Lloyd George – has
matched his popular appeal. The crowds who flocked to hear
Gladstone in Midlothian in 1879 and again in the second
campaign of March 1880 were largely composed of citizens
still not enfranchised, who looked to Gladstone as a political
oracle. His castigations of Disraeli's 'pestilent' imperialism
and of the Imperial title in India as 'bombast' were blistering.
His crusading clarion-call was awe-inspiring:

> I am sorry to say we cannot reckon upon the landed
> aristocracy! We cannot reckon upon the clergy of the
> Established Church either in England or Scotland!
> . . . We cannot reckon upon the wealth of the county,
> nor upon the wealth of the country! . . . In the main these
> powers are against us . . . We must set them down among
> our most devoted foes! But, gentlemen, above all these,
> and behind all these, *there is the nation itself*. And this great
> trial is now proceeding before the nation. The nation is

a power hard to rouse, but when roused harder still and more hopeless to resist.[1]

Beaconsfield had misjudged the situation when he called for the dissolution of Parliament in March 1880, led astray, as politicians and political tipsters are still liable to be, by deceptively favourable by-election results. The electorate returned 347 Liberals, 240 Conservatives and 65 Irish Nationalists.

The nominal leaders of the victorious Liberal Party were the Marquess of Hartington (son of the Duke of Devonshire) in the House of Commons and Lord Granville in the House of Lords, but the Midlothian campaigns had reasserted Gladstone's predominance beyond all ambiguity. The Queen viewed the situation with unconcealed distaste, and talked of abdication: she invited Beaconsfield to write to her privately, and that wily old campaigner helped to confuse the issue by pressing the claims of Hartington. Gladstone predictably declined subordinate office to an embarrassed Hartington and finally both Hartington and Granville had to tell the Queen unequivocally that she must send for Gladstone.

Queen Victoria's hostility to 'that half-mad firebrand' was only one of the complications which beset a ministry which has understandably been nicknamed 'the ministry of all the troubles'.

Gladstone was already showing signs of the cantankerousness of old age which was to confuse his relations with his colleagues. Until 1882 he combined the Chancellorship of the Exchequer with the office of Prime Minister because of his openly expressed lack of confidence in any of his colleagues to do the job! H. C. E. Childers was an obvious choice for the Exchequer, and Gladstone made way for him in 1882. The fundamental weakness of Gladstone's Cabinet was the one-sided way in which he set about reconciling the divergent interests within the party. Mr Henry Pelling has cogently pointed out that, in the absence of any real organisation of the party outside of Parliament, 'Gladstone's role in politics can be better appreciated if he is regarded as the leader of a 'connexion' of the old eighteenth-century type rather than as the manipulator

B

of a modern political machine.'[2] The elements of the 'connexion' which Gladstone led in 1880 were the old Whigs, the Radicals, and the Nonconformists. Gladstone's choice of colleagues in 1880 was paradoxical: the Midlothian campaigns had been essentially radical in tone and technique, yet in his Cabinet the Whig aristocrats heavily predominated. Joseph Chamberlain, President of the Board of Trade, and the venerable figure of John Bright as Chancellor of the Duchy of Lancaster, were the only really Radical members. Younger Radicals, flushed with their popularity in the country and with the apparent promise of the Midlothian campaigns, were frustrated: the talents of Charles Dilke and George Otto Trevelyan had to wait.

Inside Parliament, the Government's first embarrassment was a painful and rather distasteful one which centred round the person of the Radical atheist M.P. for Northampton, Charles Bradlaugh, who claimed the right to affirm his allegiance rather than to subscribe to what was for him a meaningless oath. Permission was refused, and although Bradlaugh at once offered to swear in the prescribed form, he was expelled from the House. The affair dragged on for six years, prolonged by the ineptitude of the Speaker and by the callous exploitation of the situation by Lord Randolph Churchill, whose activities were thrown into vivid relief by the weakness of the formal Leader of the Opposition, Sir Stafford Northcote, an eminently respectable but undemonstrative man thoroughly under the spell of Gladstone.

The Gladstone administration reaped the whirlwind which had been sown in the wind of Disraeli's imperial policy. Gladstone had, however, himself added to his difficulties in dealing with South Africa. The Boers were unanimous for the independence of the Transvaal, and had confidently expected that Gladstone in office would speedily carry out the implications of his anti-imperialist speeches whilst in opposition. Gladstone hedged until it was too late. The Boers took matters into their own hands and on 27 February 1881 the British General Sir George Colley was killed and his troops routed at Majuba Hill by a force of Boers brilliantly led by Piet Joubert. Gladstone was passionately opposed to the forceful annexation of the Transvaal by Britain and he now found himself in a humiliating and compromising position. He was compelled to yield to force concessions which should have stemmed from his own conscience: by the Convention of Pretoria in 1881 the independence of the Transvaal (subject to British suzerainty) was recognised. In 1884 the Convention of London made some adjustments in the settlement, and clouded the whole issue by not specifying the British claim to suzerainty. The events of 1881 merely deferred a cataclysm in South Africa. There can be no doubt that the comparative ease with which their resort to force had led to the Convention of Pretoria made the Boers over-confident: in Paul Kruger, who became President of the Transvaal Republic in 1883, they found a leader who would exploit any suggestion of British weakness to the utmost.

The Liberal government carried out plans made by the previous administration for the evacuation of Afghanistan. Kandahar, which it had been intended to garrison, proved untenable, and was relieved by an epic march from Kabul by a British force under General Roberts. British influence in Afghanistan for the rest of the century was maintained indirectly, by protection and subsidy, rather than by any direct pressure from within.

In foreign policy the administration was at its least happy. Gladstone harboured a misguided and outdated view of the concert of Europe, and never really understood that the hostility of France made British good relations with Germany eminently desirable. Gladstone was to some extent encouraged in his illusions by an early diplomatic success, but its basis was really bluff, and it was with the greatest relief that the Foreign Office saw Turkey fulfil the obligations imposed upon her by the Treaty of Berlin (1878) in Greece and Montenegro.

Foreign policy and imperial designs conspicuously overlapped in northern Africa, and especially in Egypt, where Britain and France had established a joint influence in the 1870s after the French construction of the Suez Canal and with Disraeli's spectacular purchase in 1875 of the shares in the Canal Company owned by the improvident Khedive Ismael.

Late in 1881 there was a nationalist revolt in Egypt led by Colonel Arabi. In June 1882 foreign property in Alexandria was roughly handled, fifty foreign residents were killed and the British consul was injured. Arabi mounted guns on the fortresses guarding Alexandria, apparently as an open threat to the Royal Navy. After an ultimatum, the Royal Navy bombarded Alexandria on 11 July 1882, and a month later British troops under Sir Garnet Wolseley landed at Port Said. On 13 September 1882 Arabi's revolt was destroyed at the battle of Tel-el-Kebir, and Gladstone excitedly ordered celebratory salutes of guns in Hyde Park.

Although most of the public shared Gladstone's high spirits, much Radical opinion was understandably scandalised, and John Bright resigned over Alexandria in protest at an action which he stigmatised as 'simply damnable – worse than anything ever perpetrated by Dizzy'. Historians and biographers since have sought to explain the bombardment of Alexandria, which was certainly an action wildly out of keeping with Gladstone's high principles and convinced anti-imperialism. Mr A. J. P. Taylor finds it not inconsistent with his assessment of Gladstone as a 'statesman demagogue' – 'Sir Robert Peel and Feargus O'Connor rolled into one – an explosive combination'.[3] The bombardment of Alexandria was thus a bluff, comparable with the successful bluffing of Turkey over Greece and Montenegro in the early days of the administration.

It is impossible adequately to explain Gladstone's motives, though almost certainly they were not dominated by sordid financial considerations as some of his bitterest contemporary critics asserted. What Gladstone in fact was doing was to stand firmly by a refusal to reverse trends in policy which were established by the time he took office in 1880. He maintained no such refusal over South Africa and Afghanistan, yet it might be argued that Egypt represented a different problem; events there were more closely and more obviously bound up with diplomacy generally and with relations with France in particular. It should also be remembered that the independent action of the Royal Navy off Alexandria occurred after the French fleet, poised for a joint action in defence of foreign property and nationals, had suddenly withdrawn. Yet, when all has been assessed, Gladstone's delight at the defeat of the Egyptians was scarcely in character, nor is his broad humanitarianism reflected in his brusque reply to Wilfrid Scawen Blunt, who asked for a message from Gladstone for the Egyptians: 'I think not... Let them read what we say in Parliament'.[4]

British domination in Egypt was consolidated by the appointment of Sir Evelyn Baring (later Lord Cromer) as consul-general in 1883. For the next twenty-four years he so influenced Egyptian affairs that he was, in effect, the ruler of the country. He was an administrator of exceptional talent, and his financial and governmental undertakings were of great benefit to the Egyptians as well as to British power in the vital areas of the Suez Canal and the Nile valley.

Africa had another blow in store for the Government, and for Gladstone in particular. In 1881 the Mahdi, a religious (or perhaps pseudo-religious) prophet led a nationalist revolt in the Sudan. Gladstone viewed the Sudan in a markedly different light from Egypt and described the Sudanese as 'struggling rightly to be free'. He did nothing, however, to hinder the Egyptian government in its attempts to subdue the Mahdi. On 5 November 1883 ten thousand Egyptian troops under the command of an Englishman – Hicks Pasha – were annihilated in the Sudan. In spite of strong pressure from the Queen, Gladstone resolved to evacuate the Egyptian garrisons from the Sudan. The decision was wise, though unpopular: the appointment as commander of the operation of General Gordon (whose eccentricities and aversion to discipline, though obscured in a fog of romantic mysticism, were notorious) proved disastrous.

Gordon was given no formal orders but the general burden of his responsibility was obvious: the garrisons were to be evacuated, and he was to decide the best way to do it. The Foreign Office rashly allowed him to be proclaimed Governor-General of the Sudan, and once in Khartoum Gordon set about formulating plans, not for withdrawal, but for the destruction of the Mahdi and the subjugation of the Sudan. Nothing was further from his mind than the evacuation for which he had been made responsible. By the Spring of 1884 Gordon was already in grave danger, but the Government thought it unnecessary to send troops to his assistance. Pressure of public opinion, however, compelled a change of mind, and Wolseley was sent with a relieving force from Egypt. He arrived at Khartoum two days after Gordon had been murdered.

The murder of the knight-errant, Bible in hand, by savages whom the Prime Minister had considered to be 'struggling rightly to be free' brought down a storm of hatred upon Gladstone. He was transformed from the 'G. O. M.' (Grand Old Man) to the 'M. O. G.' (Murderer of Gordon). The Queen was in the vanguard of the attack and attempted to humiliate Gladstone by sending him a telegram unciphered, so that anyone might read its condemnation: 'These news from Khartoum are frightful, and to think that all this might have been prevented and many precious lives saved by earlier action is too fearful'. Gladstone was certainly blameworthy for his delay in sending relief, but his greatest error was in allowing Gordon to be sent in the first place: the satisfaction of Gordon's thirst for martyrdom carried a heavy political price which Gladstone had to pay.

Meanwhile the programme of domestic reform for which Radical supporters of the Government had hoped materialised only slowly, although Joseph Chamberlain was active and constructive at the Board of Trade. Minor measures in 1880 – the Burials Act and the Ground Game Act – removed grievances of Nonconformists and tenant-farmers respectively, and in the same year Chamberlain followed Samuel Plimsoll's good work by passing a Seaman's Wages Act and the Grain Cargoes Act. In 1881 a measure finally abolished flogging in the Army and the Royal Navy. In 1882 the Married Women's Property Act emancipated women from the burden of handing over all their property to their husbands upon marriage, whilst the Settled Land Act facilitated the transfer of landed property. In 1883 Chamberlain was responsible for two important pieces of commercial legislation, the Bankruptcy Act and the Patents Act, and in the same year the Corrupt Practices Act was passed: together with the Ballot Act entered on the statute book eleven years earlier, it did much to do away with corruption at elections.

The outstanding achievement of the ministry in domestic legislation was a further reform of the franchise. Again the initiative came from Joseph Chamberlain, who was eagerly anticipating a conflict with the House of Lords – those who, in Chamberlain's words, 'toil not neither do they spin'. Chamberlain took up a proposal made in the previous decade by Trevelyan, that the county franchise should be equated with that in the towns, where all householders had had the vote since 1867. The Cabinet was far from unanimous, but the measure easily passed the House of Commons in 1884. The Conservatives sought to delay it by demanding that a redistribution of seats should precede the extension of the county franchise. Gladstone refused to be blocked, and public outcry grew. By late 1884 Gladstone and Salisbury agreed upon both the extension of the county franchise and a redistribution of seats, and both were passed without further opposition. In the redistribution of seats, towns (seventy-nine of them) with less than 15,000 inhabitants were disfranchised, and those with between 15,000 and 50,000 inhabitants were to have one M.P. instead of two. Towns with between 50,000 and 165,000 inhabitants retained two M.P.s. Elsewhere the country was divided into singular-member constituencies of roughly equal size according to population.

The reform of the franchise and redistribution of seats marked another significant step towards the creation of a democratic society, and incidentally fulfilled one of the demands of the old Chartists, that constituencies should be of equal sizes. The widespread creation of single-member constituencies, however, dealt a serious blow to the electoral prospects of the Liberal Party, which had been accustomed to reconcile its Radical and Whig elements by putting forward one Radical and one Whig candidate in the two-member constituencies. Given the increase in the electorate, the Whigs were bound to suffer heavily; looking further into the future, the emergence of a genuinely working-class political party was bound to undermine the strength of the old-fashioned Radicalism as well.

Ireland remained the most serious of the government's problems, and the one with which the Prime Minister was most deeply concerned. Whatever the inconsistencies and ambiguities of other aspects of his work during this period, the historian cannot but admire his dedication to his 'mission' regarding Ireland. The task was daunting, but the crusader was a man of prodigious courage and strength.

John Morley once declared that 'Ireland would not be a difficult country to govern – were it not that all the people were intractable and all the problems insoluble'. The natural intractability of the Irish had been intensified by generations of English misrule; it was to the solution of the insoluble that Gladstone was dedicated.

The basic ingredients of Irish misery and discontent in the nineteenth century were religion, land and government. The religious grievances of the Roman Catholic majority in a country ruled by a Protestant minority had been to a large extent mollified when the great Irish patriot Daniel O'Connell had forced Catholic Emancipation upon Wellington and Peel in 1829, and had thus enabled Roman Catholics to be elected to the House of Commons; Gladstone himself had freed Roman Catholics from the obligation of paying tithe to a Protestant Established Church when he disestablished the Irish Church in 1869. Religion ceased to be a predominant issue, although its capacity for promoting bitterness and violence was far from exhausted.

Gladstone had produced a Land Act in 1870 in an attempt to mitigate the hardships of insecurity felt by Irish tenants of Anglo-Irish, and often absentee, landlords. The Act had failed in its purpose because, although it stopped the eviction of tenants without cause, it failed to fix rents and thus left the way open to unscrupulous landlords who could adjust their rents to prohibitive levels and then evict their tenants for non-payment: so the problem of the Irish tenants remained to be dealt with in 1880. Above all, there was a feeling of genuine nationalism in Ireland, which saw the only real solution to

Ireland's problems in government from Dublin rather than Westminster. This growing demand for Home Rule found powerful representation among the increasing numbers of Irish Nationalist M.P.s who were elected to the House of Commons, especially after the Ballot Act had removed many inhibitions felt by the voters. Home Rule was destined to dominate the remainder of Gladstone's political life.

The sixty-five Irish Nationalists in the Commons were led by one of the most brilliant figures of nineteenth century politics, Charles Stewart Parnell. Aristocratic by background and temperament, and more typical in many ways of the Protestant Anglo-Irish landlord than of the Irish tenant for whom he fought, Parnell exercised a magnetic domination over the forces of Ireland, both in that country itself and in the House of Commons. In passion, ambition and political skill he could challenge Gladstone himself, until in the end Parnell was destroyed, not by his political enemies but by his own arrogance, recklessness and human weakness.

Gladstone was resolved to conciliate the Irish and to end the government of Ireland by coercion. He was faced, however, by the growing influence of the Land League under the presidency of Parnell, whose activities against the landlords were heavily subsidised by subscriptions from emigrant Irishmen in America and Australia. Gladstone's attempt to mitigate the effects of eviction by compensating evicted tenants was rejected by the House of Lords. Meanwhile, Irish violence – burnings, lootings, the maiming and slaughter of cattle – no longer stopped short of murder, and that of a most atrocious kind. In such a situation the unfortunate Captain Boycott added a new word to the language: he was the first victim of the social ostracism proclaimed by Parnell against the landlords and their agents who carried out evictions. Not only the landlords and their bailiffs, but any tenant who took over a holding from which the previous tenant had been evicted, were at once tainted with this new Irish social leprosy. The Land League was duly prosecuted for conspiracy, and the jury predictably failed to agree.

Gladstone reluctantly yielded to pressure from his Chief Secretary for Ireland, W. E. Forster (pleasantly and all too

aptly nicknamed 'Buckshot'), and in spite of the misgivings of
Chamberlain and Bright, as well as of Gladstone himself, a new
Coercion Bill was introduced at the beginning of 1881, followed
in March of the same year by a bill which suspended Habeas
Corpus. The measures ran into a fierce campaign of obstruction
which was brilliantly carried on in the House of Commons by
the Irish Nationalists under the direction of Parnell. Fili-
bustering speeches by the Irish members were counteracted only
by the extension of the disciplinary powers of the Speaker.

Gladstone was still intent upon winning over the Irish, and in
1881 he introduced his second Land Act, which produced the
attractive formula of the 'three f's': fair rents, fixity of tenures,
and the freedom to sell tenancies. The liberality of the measure
was somewhat soured by the fact that, as we have seen in his
dealings with the Boers, Gladstone again appears to be yielding
to the pressure of violence rather than of reason. In any case the
second Land Act was unacceptable to the Irish Nationalists,
whose ambitions were by now firmly fixed upon Home Rule:
Parnell seized upon the composition of the Land Courts as a
pretext for fierce rejection of the Land Act, and was duly
imprisoned in Kilmainham Gaol in October 1881. His imprisonment was far from rigorous and was, indeed, decidedly
convenient, since his mistress, Mrs O'Shea, was pregnant at the
time.

Forster's policy of coercion was utterly unsuccessful: it has
been estimated that during his period of office as Chief Secretary
for Ireland murders and shootings increased threefold and
agrarian outrages by sixty per cent. Gladstone opened negotiations with Parnell, through Chamberlain, who used the husband
of Parnell's mistress, as an intermediary: assistance would be
given to tenants who were in arrears with their rent in exchange
for the cessation of Irish violence. Lord Cowper, the Viceroy in
Dublin, resigned on grounds of ill-health, and Forster resigned
in protest: they were replaced by Lord Spencer and Lord
Frederick Cavendish, a young man to whom Gladstone was
particularly devoted. Within twenty-four hours of his arrival in
Dublin, Lord Frederick Cavendish was walking in Phoenix
Park with his permanent under-secretary, T. H. Burke, on 6

May 1882. Burke was attacked by a gang of 'Invincibles', and on trying to protect him Lord Frederick was also brutally murdered. Gladstone was shattered, and so were hopes of an end to coercion. A powerful and moving glimpse of Gladstone the human being emerges in Lady Frederick Cavendish's own account of the tragedy:

> Uncle William . . . his face . . . like a prophet's in its look of faith and strength . . . came up and almost took me in his arms, and his first words were, 'Father, forgive them, for they know not what they do'. Then he said to me, 'Be assured it will not be in vain', and across all my agony there fell a bright ray of hope, and I saw in a vision Ireland at peace, and my darling's life-blood accepted as a sacrifice for Christ's sake, to help to bring this to pass . . . I said to him as he was leaving me, 'Uncle William, you must never blame yourself for sending him'. He said, 'Oh no, there can be no question of that'.[5]

Even the extremist Fenian Brotherhood was horrified at the Phoenix Park murders, which were also roundly condemned by Parnell, Michael Davitt and other Irish leaders. The Arrears Act was modified and, inevitably, coercion was reintroduced, although the appointment of the Radical Trevelyan as Chief Secretary promised a certain amount of enlightenment. Bitterness and violence continued in Ireland, although the operation of the Land Act of 1881 brought some improvement in the situation of the Irish tenants.

It was the Irish M.P.s who brought about the fall of the government in June 1885 after Lord Randolph Churchill had approached Parnell, bargaining the end of coercion for Irish support for the Conservatives – a species of political jobbery which Gladstone disdained: 'It is right I should say that into any counter-bidding of any sort against Lord R. Churchill I, for one, cannot enter'.[6]

Salisbury took office with a minority Conservative government, and in the General Election held in November 1885 Parnell's instructions to his supporters in England to vote Conservative produced a deadlock: the Liberal majority over Conservatives was eighty-six, the precise number of Irish

Nationalists elected. Salisbury remained in office until January 1886, when Jesse Collings, one of Chamberlain's henchmen, brought down the government with his 'three acres and a cow' amendment, aimed at the absence from the Queen's Speech of any reference to measures to relieve agricultural distress.

Meanwhile Gladstone had undergone a conversion which some historians[7] have unhesitatingly assessed as the greatest act of political courage in the past century: he had become convinced of the necessity of a measure of Home Rule for Ireland.

Gladstone's decision was certainly made by the summer of 1885, and probably even by the preceding winter. Why did he conceal it until it was revealed in a moment of misguided zeal by his son Herbert, who told the Press on 15 December 1885? Almost certainly, Gladstone kept silent because he thought the measure could best be carried by the Conservatives with Liberal support. Such a point of view was both logical and cogent, bearing in mind the precedents of the Reform Act of 1867, the repeal of the Corn Law in 1846, and the granting of Catholic Emancipation in 1829. A most significant factor was bound to be the attitude of the House of Lords, where the overwhelming Conservative majority could obviously be more easily handled by a Conservative than a Liberal Prime Minister. Gladstone was also encouraged by Salisbury's appointment as Lord-Lieutenant in Ireland of Lord Carnarvon, one of the few Conservatives known to be sympathetic to Irish aspirations.

Herbert Gladstone's bombshell was devastating: the Conservative–Irish Nationalist alliance was shattered. Parnell was mortified at the way in which his electoral instructions had misfired (he had given anything from twenty-five to forty seats to the Conservatives!). Gladstone was placed in a most embarrassing situation with his colleagues, and was exposed to the unfounded but perhaps understandable assertion that he was prepared to capitulate to Parnell simply in order to regain office.

Gladstone formed his third ministry in February 1886 only after considerable difficulty. His failure to explain himself to his leading colleagues made them reluctant to join him, and only Harcourt came over wholeheartedly. Chamberlain, whose entirely sincere opposition to Home Rule was to prove decisive, joined the administration with the greatest reluctance and resigned at once when he saw the terms of the Bill, which were less moderate than he had expected. Gladstone introduced the Home Rule Bill in a magnificent speech of three and a half hours on 8 April 1886. Chamberlain and Hartington spoke strongly against the measure, which was defeated on its second reading on 8 June 1886, when Chamberlain led ninety-three Liberals into the lobbies against Gladstone.

The defeat, and more importantly the split which produced it, spelled disaster for the Liberal Party and condemned it, with only one brief respite, to nearly twenty years in opposition. Yet Gladstone's resources were not quite exhausted. In the general election of 1892, after he had hastily put together the so-called 'Newcastle Programme' of reform in 1891, 273 Liberals, 81 Irish Nationalists and 1 Independent Labour M.P. were elected, against 269 Conservatives and 46 Liberal Unionists – a majority for Home Rule of 40. 'Too small, too small', exclaimed Gladstone when the majority became known.

At the age of eighty-three, Gladstone introduced the second Home Rule Bill in February 1893: his conduct of the Bill through its various stages was little short of miraculous. The Bill had a majority of 43 on its second reading in the Commons and 34 on the third reading. In the House of Lords it was annihilated on the second reading by 419 votes to 41. Gladstone wanted to make an appeal to the country on the issue, but the Cabinet overruled him.

The imminence of Gladstone's resignation as Prime Minister was frequently rumoured in the months that followed, and his Cabinet colleagues waited in mounting frustration until at last, on 1 March 1894, he announced his retirement to the Cabinet. There was a good deal of weeping, though none of it, needless to say, by Gladstone himself, who used to refer to the occasion as 'that blubbering Cabinet'.

He died on 19 May 1898. At the news of his death the House of Commons adjourned at once. He is buried in Westminster Abbey and among those who bore him to his grave were two future Kings of England (the Prince of Wales and the Duke of York). His statue stands in the north transept of the Abbey, with those of Disraeli and Sir Robert Peel, a most remarkable trio of English political talent.

In the last analysis [writes Sir Philip Magnus] what Gladstone was is of vastly greater significance than what he did. Mortal men are condemned to see mortal events 'through a glass darkly' and the echo of dead political controversy sounds ever more faintly down the ages until it is barely distinguishable from that of the mythical war between the kites and the crows. Gladstone may be judged as a statesman; few would venture to judge him as a man. He dedicated his life to the task of teaching men and nations to govern themselves by schooling their passions, and thereby to realise on earth the spirit of the Christian ethic. By his radiant example, Gladstone did more than any statesman since the Reformation to give effect in politics to that ideal. In its service he started as the foe, became the agent, and ended as the prophet of the Liberal experiment.[8]

CHAPTER THREE

Interlude: Rosebery's
Wasted Talents

A most definite and inimitable personality, everything both to allure and compel. And yet here he is, the most tragic example in our time of a wasted and ineffectual life.

ARCHBISHOP RANDALL DAVIDSON

Politics is a struggle for power; Rosebery wanted the power, but shrank from the struggle.

ROBERT RHODES JAMES

HISTORY is essentially about people, and the failures in political life sometimes make as rewarding and interesting a study in human behaviour as do more successful statesmen. The career of Archibald Philip, fifth Earl of Rosebery, who succeeded Gladstone as Prime Minister in 1894, presents us with an enigma and draws the historian of politics irresistibly into the realm of personal biography, a region admirably explored for students of Rosebery by Mr Robert Rhodes James.[1] For the complexities and frustrations of the Rosebery administration and indeed the sorry spectacle of the Liberal Party in the decade which followed can be understood only in the light of the life and personality of a man whose intellect and talents promised much, but whose weaknesses and paradoxes of personality blighted not only his own career but also the future of his Party. He was an historian as well as a politician, and one of his enthusiasms was the career of William Pitt the Elder: if it is true, as one of his contemporaries asserted, that Rosebery wanted to rule like Pitt the Elder, the roots of Rosebery's failure are obvious, and

Rosebery was born over a century too late. Such an explanation is too facile, but it contains a vital germ of truth.

Rosebery was born in 1847, the son of Lord Dalmeny (heir to the fourth Earl of Rosebery) and Lady Wilhelmina Stanhope. He thus mingled in his veins the blood of a distinguished and influential Scottish family with that of the celebrated Stanhope line of statesmen and eccentrics. Lady Wilhelmina possessed no less than her share of Stanhope strength of personality, and never overcame her resentment at her failure truly to communicate with her elder son. In 1851 Lord Dalmeny died and his son succeeded to his title and became heir to the earldom. Three years later Dalmeny's widow married Sir Harry Vane, heir to the Duchy of Cleveland and a fortune of £97,000 a year.

Though Sir Harry was a generous stepfather, the young Lord Dalmeny's relationship with his mother remained strained and fruitless. The pattern of his later life was manifest: the child – introspective, sensitive, overwhelmingly shy, yet withal observant, 'canny' and occasionally charming – was indeed father of the man.

He was a scholarly boy: at the age of ten, whilst recuperating from burns received – for he was brave too – when rescuing the vicar's daughter from a fire at Chevening, he read Macaulay's *Essays*: '. . . to that book', he declared later in life, 'I owe whatever ambitions or aspirations I have ever indulged in'.[2] At thirteen he entered Eton as top of the new boys. He made few friends, but clung tenaciously to those he chose. He inspired that most dismal of judgements which beset schoolmasters in the writing of reports: that he possessed ability but was indolent. He did well only such work as was congenial to him. William Johnson, eccentric, emotional, but a great Eton schoolmaster, came to fear that his talents would be washed away in a drift towards 'Society' and the Turf.

In 1864 he visited the House of Commons and heard Gladstone's budget speech, and in the following year was a guest at Hawarden. But in 1865 also he met Disraeli and succumbed to the familiar charm. His response to Disraeli was far more excited than that provoked by Gladstone, and it is not difficult to understand his confession late in life that his greatest mistake was not to have followed Disraeli. But tradition – and some of the young man's Radical views at the time – militated against it, and he declined the offer to contest Darlington in the Conservative cause in 1867.

Meanwhile in 1866 he went up to Oxford, and in the all-too-congenial and idle atmosphere of Christ Church he set about cultivating the society of those who admired him. He was quite at home in the high living Bullingdon 'set' which also included Lord Randolph Churchill. A visit to the Derby in 1867 encouraged an already strong interest in the Turf, a pastime which, in spite of the benign patronage of the Prince of Wales, was fraught with hazards such as those which overcame the young Marquess of Hastings, who died bankrupt at the age of twenty-six.

In March 1868 the fourth Earl of Rosebery died, leaving his grandson his title and a gross income of some £30,000 a year. Financial independence added to his reluctance to do uncongenial work, and – though the vital importance of the fact was probably lost on him at the time – the title debarred him for ever from membership of the House of Commons.

At Easter 1869 Rosebery left Oxford rather than give up his ownership of the racehorse *Ladas*. His action was impetuous and the sacrifice unworthy: *Ladas* ran disastrously in the Derby. But something of the flippancy which Rosebery cultivated throughout his life may be judged from his laconic letter to his mother:

Dear Mother
    I have left Oxford. I have secured a house in Berkeley Square; and I have bought a horse to win the Derby.
Your affectionate Archie.[3]

Rosebery in London became 'the Prince Charming of the Age'.[4] He was handsome, affluent and gay, but there were limits: notably his refusal to turn his house into a brothel (albeit of the highest class!) to accommodate the Prince of Wales and his brother the Duke of Edinburgh and their euphemistically catalogued 'actress friends'.

He was by no means the empty-headed playboy. He was an acute and concerned observer of his contemporary society. His

judgement of the essentially middle-class appeal of the fashionable evangelical preacher Spurgeon – 'Spurgeon is the apostle
of the grocers' – was masterly; with it went an awareness of the
necessity to bridge class barriers, a theme which he powerfully
expounded in an address to the Edinburgh Metaphysical
Society in 1871. He cultivated the friendship of William
Rogers, rector of Bishopsgate, through whom he became aware
of the realities of life in the East End; he was also actively
interested in the development of Working Men's Clubs and
Institutes. He first attacked the House of Lords in 1874 in
Glasgow, and drew a reprimand from the Royal Family for his
pains. Though he frequently returned to that theme, he shrank
later in life from the wider implications of social legislation and
became a bitter opponent of what he dismissed as the 'paternalism' of the State: his social concern was always Whiggish
rather than Radical, and this was a fundamental reason why
the Liberalism of the early twentieth century left him stranded.

Rosebery was always a great traveller, and at this period of
his life he made three visits to America which profoundly
impressed him. The greatest event in his life occurred, however,
in England in 1878. He married Hannah Rothschild, in spite of
the opposition of his mother, who was anti-semitic, and of the
Jewish Press, which resented Gentile poaching on Jewish ex-
clusiveness. The wedding ceremony (conducted in both civil
and Christian forms) was highly fashionable: Lord Beaconsfield
gave the bride away, and the Prince of Wales proposed the
health of the couple. Marriage brought to Rosebery great
wealth – 'Rothschild', then as now, was synonymous with
'riches' – but much more important, it brought him content-
ment and personal happiness such as he had never known in the
strained relationship of his home life.

Rosebery had made his maiden speech in the House of
Lords in 1871, but his real interest in politics was aroused in the
late 1870s, when he supported Gladstone over the Bulgarian
atrocities and conducted the great man through the Midlothian
campaigns. Rosebery was very active on Gladstone's behalf
and used some of the techniques which he had observed and admired in the New York Democratic Convention earlier. The

Midlothian campaigns demonstrated not only Gladstone's remarkable powers and prestige, but also a personal following for
Rosebery in Edinburgh and Midlothian which perhaps surpassed and certainly rivalled even that of Chamberlain in
Birmingham.

Rosebery had been captivated and exhilarated by the excitement of the Midlothian campaigns and his tremendous personal
following there never deserted him, even to the end of his career.
Yet with a hyper-sensitiveness which became painfully characteristic, he declined office in the Government because of cheap
Conservative sneers that Rosebery had sponsored Gladstone
in Midlothian only to further his own career. Paradoxically,
however, Hannah came to be so ambitious on her husband's
behalf that the Gladstones took fright and became very cagey in
their dealings with their Scottish hosts.

In 1881 Rosebery became Under Secretary at the Home
Office with special responsibility for Scottish affairs. He
expected Scotland to loom larger in the business of the Government than it did, and his unsatisfactory personal relations with
the Home Secretary, the irascible Sir William Harcourt, added
to Rosebery's frustrations and bitterness and led to some stormy
exchanges with Gladstone. Rosebery's personal ambitions were
clearly interwoven with those of Scotland at this time, and the
Scots were jealous of the predominance given to Irish business.
Although he became a Privy Councillor in 1882, Rosebery was
bitterly disappointed at not being admitted to the Cabinet in
the reshuffle of the same year.

In June 1883 Rosebery resigned after criticisms in the House
of Commons. This was by no means the last occasion on which
he was to use resignation, or the threat of it. Like the tantrums
of a spoilt child, resignation can be a procedure particularly
subject to the law of diminishing returns, and Rosebery made
far too great a use of it. Already Sir Edward Hamilton – an Eton
contemporary and Gladstone's private secretary – clearly saw
Rosebery's weakness: 'I fear his over-sensitive, thinskinned
nature will stand sadly in the way of a really successful political
future'.

Rosebery took advantage of his respite from political office to travel to Australia, which made a great impression upon him. He was already an imperialist, and Australia strengthened his idealistic concept of Empire and led him to declare in Adelaide that 'the Empire is a Commonwealth of Nations' – a notion conspicuously more prescient than the Radical sage John Bright's dismissal of the notion of imperial federation as 'childish and absurd'.

In 1885 Rosebery was admitted to the Cabinet as Commissioner for Public Works; but in June 1885 the crumbling Cabinet at last collapsed and resigned. When Gladstone formed his third administration in 1886, Granville at the Foreign Office was aged and failing, and his obvious successor, Sir Charles Dilke was – in Gladstone's euphemistic phrase – 'not available' owing to his involvement in the Divorce Court. Rosebery became Foreign Secretary and during the six months which the Government lasted he impressed with his astute handling of the complex diplomacy concerned with the ambitions of Russia and Turkey in Bulgaria.

In 1889 Rosebery became first Chairman of the new London County Council. His ability in the chair, and his genuine concern with social problems, greatly enhanced his reputation, especially among the younger Liberals; but again his oversensitive personality let him down, and he would sulk if crossed or contradicted.

In 1890 the bitterest blow fell. Hannah died, and with her died much of Rosebery's political ambition. Her concern on his behalf had occasionally been enthusiastic to the point of tactlessness, but she had provided not only a driving force but most importantly a rock of affection and security such as he had never had before and could never find again.

He returned to the Foreign Office in 1892, with the amiable and much admired Edward Grey as his colleague in the House of Commons. Generally speaking, he maintained Salisbury's policy of non-involvement without complete detachment from European affairs. Relations with France were poor, as for example over Siam, but Africa was the focus of Rosebery's diplomacy. Uganda was the subject of a serious and acrimonious controversy in the Cabinet and Rosebery – the advocate of annexation and the passionate opponent of withdrawal – got his way only by devious and high-handed means. He clashed seriously again with Gladstone over Egypt, where a nationalist *coup d'état* threatened the British position. Rosebery in London and Cromer in Cairo were determined to maintain the British 'edifice' in Egypt, and Rosebery once more brandished his resignation before a British battalion was disembarked and the crisis passed.

Rosebery's speech in the Lords on Home Rule was notably lukewarm, and the final quarrel with Gladstone came when Rosebery passionately supported Spencer against him on the increased naval estimates which at length led to Gladstone's resignation and retirement. Meanwhile Rosebery had enhanced his national reputation by his successful mediation in the great coal miners' strike of 1893.

The leadership was the subject of a straight fight between Rosebery and Sir William Harcourt, although the issue was somewhat obscured by the double-dealing of John Morley, who had had the ambition of the Foreign Office or the Chancellorship of the Exchequer fed into his susceptible mind by Harcourt's oily and determined son Lewis – the picturesquely nicknamed 'Loulou' – who worked intrepidly behind the scenes to undermine Rosebery and to compensate for the ill effects of Harcourt's overbearing and contemptuous treatment of his colleagues. Rosebery enjoyed the almost unanimous support of the Liberal Press.

Rosebery took supreme office in most inauspicious circumstances. He was acutely conscious of his great predecessor and of his own role: '. . . acting as Mr Gladstone's political executor and winding up his political estate'. The Queen showed an unwelcome tendency to dictate to her new Prime Minister while maintaining the closest contacts with Salisbury.

The greatest and most fundamental difficulty, however, sprang from Rosebery's position as a Liberal Prime Minister sitting in the House of Lords. He was the last such. Almost drowned by the Conservative majority in the Lords, he needed the closest possible support in the Commons. He would not stoop to flattery to win such support from Harcourt, the Liberal

Leader of the House of Commons – and indeed Loulou was determined to wreck the Government if he could. The difficulties in the way of a Liberal Peer–Premier were enormuos; given the personality of Rosebery they were insurmountable.

The Prime Minister's opening speech in the House of Lords clearly implied that Home Rule was to be deferred – so much for the political estate of Mr Gladstone! – and Harcourt's budget proposals led to a serious quarrel between the two men. Rosebery commented on Harcourt's proposed Estate Duty in the context of Rosebery's pressing but illusory fear that the political parties might divide horizontally in society, with the Liberals forfeiting the support of the higher ranks. Harcourt was over-sensitive and brusque to the point of insolence in his response to Rosebery's criticisms, but there is substance in his taunts of Rosebery's 'high-toryism'.

Rosebery's talent was really for foreign policy; although he had entered into no formal contract to keep Harcourt and the Commons fully informed, he dealt less than fairly by the secretive manner in which he and his Foreign Secretary, Lord Kimberley, carried on their diplomacy. Harcourt, greatly strengthened by the success of his budget in the Commons, was outraged at the secrecy with which a treaty had been concluded with Belgium over the Sudan, and the treaty was cancelled. In 1895 Grey in the Commons pursued the forward policy in Africa by categorically and apparently spontaneously declaring the whole of the Nile valley to be a British sphere of influence. Spontaneous or not, Grey was certainly relaying his master's voice!

As Prime Minister, Rosebery acted with that mixture of frivolity and petulance, shyness and indecisiveness which characterised so much of his life. It is a melancholy fact that his Premiership is perhaps most memorable for his victories in the Derby in successive years, and even then such triumph was blighted: the Nonconformist Liberals not unnaturally showed little enthusiasm for such prowess, giving rise to some singularly petty and small-minded repartee from Rosebery.

The sordid business of Party management and machinery disgusted Rosebery: he preferred to know as little as possible about the support of Party funds by the purchase of peerages, for example. The overwhelming opposition of the House of Lords brought him back to the attack, notably in a vigorous speech at Bradford.

By February 1895 Rosebery had had enough, and once more resorted to resignation: on this occasion the bluff worked, and he remained in office with the promise of more reliable support in future. The Premiership was ruining his health, however, and he was the victim of appalling insomnia. His experience of 1895 conditioned his whole future attitude to public life: he could never forget the agonies of mind and health which he had suffered.

A further crisis in 1895 over the election of a new Speaker of the House of Commons was resolved with the choice of an amiable nonentity, William Gully. Rosebery was weary of office, and his opportunity for release came in June 1895 when the Government was defeated in the Commons on a motion condemning the inadequate supply of cordite to the Army.

'Rosebery wanted to be a Pitt, but ended up as a Goderich', commented Haldane. His shyness, his contempt for the business of politics, his ill-health, in particular the daunting difficulties confronting a Liberal who tried to be Prime Minister from the House of Lords, all overcame him. His greatest enemy was his own personality: 'he would not stoop; he did not conquer', said Winston Churchill. The historical significance of his Premiership is that his personal débâcle spelt disaster for his Party.

In the General Election of 1895 the Liberals collapsed: a majority of 43 in the old House of Commons was transformed into a Unionist majority of 152 in the newly elected House. The perverse satisfaction with which Rosebery viewed the results and blamed them upon the Radicals was scarcely shared by the disunited and contradictory remnants left by his indecisive leadership.

The later years of Rosebery's life – he survived his Premiership by nearly thirty-five years – present the inevitable tragedy of political influence inexorably slipping away from a man whom politics left behind, and who became – to borrow a phrase from the politics of the 1960s – an 'elegant anachronism'.

He resigned the leadership of the Liberal Party in October 1896, and was able to blame Gladstone, who had emerged once more from retirement to make a speech on the Turkish massacres of the Armenians which was far too crusading in tone to be acceptable to Rosebery. Rosebery's influence in Scotland remained unimpaired, but he withdrew further from public life, and spent weeks of each year at his villa in Naples.

He continued to preach Liberal Imperialism: he blamed Milner's inept negotiation for the outbreak of the Boer War, and was convinced of Chamberlain's complicity in the Jameson Raid; but war having started, he passionately advocated its energetic prosecution. He thus isolated himself from the centre of his Party, led by Campbell-Bannerman, and from the left, led by Lloyd George and Labouchere. Campbell-Bannerman's position as leader was weak, and there were passing thoughts that Rosebery might return; the rank-and-file members, though they admired Rosebery's talents, preferred to trust Campbell-Bannerman.

In 1902 the Liberal League was founded, dedicated to the unity of the Party and the cause of Liberal Imperialism. Rosebery became President, with Grey and Asquith among the Vice-Presidents. Alfred Harmsworth was a valuable supporter in the early days, and his popular papers ignored Campbell-Bannerman whilst giving the maximum publicity to Rosebery. In 1903, however, Joseph Chamberlain's speech on Imperial Preference exploded the tariff controversy in the Unionist Party and handed the initiative to the Liberals. The party unity thus stimulated increased in the next couple of years, and as unity increased, Rosebery's influence waned. Hamilton recognised in 1903 that '. . . one must reluctantly give up the idea of his ever being of any real use to his country. So all these splendid talents are to be thrown away. . . .'[5]

Rosebery prophesied that the Anglo-French agreement of 1904 'will lead you straight to war'. He warned Grey in 1905 that 'You are leaning upon an aspen [France] and the German emperor has 4 millions of soldiers and the second best Navy in the world'. In 1909 he gloomily described himself as 'the retired raven on the withered bough' and revealed how far he had

drifted from his Party and from the realities of politics by casti-
gating Lloyd George's 'People's Budget', and by an attack in
Glasgow upon 'paternalism'. This speech was foreshadowed by
his address as Chancellor of Glasgow University in 1908 in
terms both anachronistic and tasteless: 'The State invites us
every day to lean upon it. I seem to hear the wheedling and
alluring whisper: "Sound you may be; we bid you to be a
cripple. Do you see? Be blind. Do you hear? Be deaf. Do you
walk? Be not so venturesome. Here is a crutch for one arm;
when you get accustomed to it you will soon want another – the
sooner the better".[6] Rosebery had once been a great orator, and
could still occasionally rise to the heights: the Glasgow speech
illustrates how low he could sink. Such influence as remained to
him was dissipated by his inept and unpredictable behaviour
over the Parliament Bill in 1911: in the House of Lords he spoke
against it, declared that he would abstain – and voted for it!

He lapsed into prophecies of European doom which unhappily were abundantly justified. His last years were tragic:
his son Neil, on whom he doted, was killed in 1917, and in
November 1918 Rosebery was crippled by a stroke. His mind,
with its capacious intellect, remained active whilst his body
slowly deteriorated until he died in 1929. His latest and best
biographer, Mr Rhodes James, has remarked that 'His most
conspicuous failing was a complete inability to stand back, as it
were, from himself, and try to judge his actions from the point
of view of others'.[7] Once more, William Pitt the Elder comes to
mind.

CHAPTER FOUR

Lord Salisbury and Victorian Conservatism

We must learn this rule, that no men and no class of men ever rise to any permanent improvement in their condition of body or mind except by relying upon their own personal efforts. The wealth with which the rich man is surrounded is constantly tempting him to forget that truth, and you see, in family after family, men degenerate from the habits of their fathers because they lie sluggishly and eat and enjoy what has been placed before them without appealing to their own exertions. The poor man, especially in these days, may have a similar temptation offered to him by legislation, but the same inexorable rule will work. The only true lasting benefit which the statesman can give to the poor man is so to shape matters that the greatest possible liberty for the exercise of his own moral and intellectual qualities should be offered to him by law. . . .

LORD SALISBURY, speaking at Exeter, 2 February 1892[1]

ROBERT CECIL, third Marquess of Salisbury, was a member of that aristocratic family which, in spite of fluctuating fortunes, was already possessed of a name to conjure with in the history books because of the distinguished service of two of its generations to Queen Elizabeth I and James I. The third Marquess was a magnificent figure of a man and something of a Victorian oracle, whose high-domed head and flowing beard were taken to characterize the best of the solid intellectual and traditional virtues of the age. He emerges in the pages of the splendidly detailed and readable biography by his daughter, Lady Gwendolen Cecil[2] (whose work unfortunately stops short at 1892) as a serious, sensitive, deeply religious man steeped in tradition and conscientiously trying to practise Conservatism in the political context of his times.

His family and his home at Hatfield were the keystones of his life. He had been desperately unhappy at Eton and had derived at best a mixed sort of consolation from his relationship with a rather distant father. At Oxford, full of social pitfalls for aristocratic young men, he had emerged as a diligent student and a convinced Churchman, beset by nervousness and by indifferent health. His background made his attitude to politics.

He was opposed to democracy and regarded Disraeli's espousal of parliamentary reform in 1867 as a betrayal, but he played by the rules of the political game as they evolved in the second half of the nineteenth century. He was hesitant and uncertain in his assessments of public opinion, but he conducted his foreign policy, for example, on the clear understanding that the English people were the arbiters of English diplomacy: policy could be made only by those elected to govern. He was proud, yet enlightened: his imperialism was cautious to the point almost of indecision. He was certainly no 'Jingo' and was sternly opposed to the 'damned nigger' mentality which was part of the stock-in-trade of too many British imperialists and colonial administrators.

Salisbury came to the office of Prime Minister with an impressive political record and with the promise of outstanding ability in diplomacy. He had sat in the House of Commons before succeeding to the family title and was elected M.P. for Stamford in 1853 at the age of twenty-three. He was Secretary for India in Disraeli's second administration before becoming Foreign Secretary in 1878. He accompanied Disraeli to the Congress of Berlin in 1878, where Disraeli made such an impression upon Bismarck and whence the two statesmen brought back 'Peace with Honour' and the island of Cyprus as 'compensation' for their trouble.

Salisbury was the rather reluctant head of a minority Conservative government after the collapse of Gladstone's second administration in the middle of 1885: there could be no general election until the new electoral registers necessitated by the reform of the franchise could be completed in the autumn. The choice of Salisbury was inevitable, taking into account the conflict for the Party leadership in the Commons between the nominal leader, the pleasant but ineffective Sir Stafford

Northcote, and the flamboyant and ambitious Lord Randolph Churchill. Churchill and his so-called 'Fourth Party' represented almost as great an embarrassment to the Conservatives as to Gladstone, although Churchill's 'Party' lost a quarter of its membership with the defection of Salisbury's nephew Arthur James Balfour, who, with characteristic discretion, was tactfully ratting on Churchill in 1883. Yet Churchill was a force to be reckoned with: 'As for that, I could do very well with two departments; in fact, I have four, – the Prime Ministership, the Foreign Office, the Queen, and Randolph Churchill, – and the burden of them increases in that order' (Salisbury in 1886).[3]

Salisbury's position in the House of Lords was no great embarrassment, as it would have been to a Liberal, and was for example, to Rosebery. The overwhelming Conservative support in the Lords was naturally a source of great strength to Salisbury. In the Cabinet, the new Prime Minister held his colleagues on a notably loose rein: his colleague Sir Michael Hicks Beach (Lord St Aldwyn) wrote that

> Certainly, as Prime Minister he did not exercise the control over his colleagues, either in or out of the Cabinet, that Lord Beaconsfield did . . . Lord Beaconsfield kept a watchful eye on all his colleagues . . . Lord Salisbury left them very much to themselves unless they consulted him . . . I have known Lord Beaconsfield enforce his own view on the Cabinet after all its members but one had expressed a different opinion: Lord Salisbury frequently allowed important matters to be decided by a small majority of votes, even against his own opinion.[4]

Salisbury's first ministry was short and his opportunities were limited by the circumstances in which he took office. Salisbury himself held the Foreign Secretaryship: the dispute with Russia over Penjdeh in Afghanistan was settled, and French infiltration was checked by the annexation of Upper Burma. An attempt towards a settlement in Ireland was made in the form of a scheme to assist Irish land purchase – 'Lord Ashbourne's Act' – but more subtle and significant was the tentative approach made to Justin McCarthy on the possibilities of a form of Home Rule. Randolph Churchill's 'deal' with Parnell was immediately effective and led Parnell's voters into the Conservative camp, helping to produce stalemate in the general election of November 1885; the eighty-six Irish Nationalists exactly held the balance. Gladstone's conversion to Home Rule, with the Conservative change of front on the subject, threw everything into the melting-pot once more; the defeat of the Government on 27 January 1886 on Jesse Collings' 'three acres and a cow' amendment opened the door for Gladstone's first attempt to introduce Irish Home Rule.

The first Home Rule Bill changed the whole complexion of English politics by splitting the Liberal Party and by creating the group of Liberal Unionists who were eventually assimilated into the Conservative Party, which not infrequently came to be referred to as the Unionist Party. The general election of 1886 placed the casting vote squarely with the seventy-eight Liberal Unionists who were returned. Once more Salisbury took office with reluctance and only after earnestly entreating Lord Hartington – the leader, with Joseph Chamberlain, of the Liberal Unionists – to become Premier.

The conflict for the Leadership of the House of Commons was resolved by the elevation of Northcote to the peerage as Lord Iddesleigh and his promotion to the Foreign Office, though with Salisbury himself exercising close supervision of British diplomacy. Lord Randolph Churchill thus became the Leader of the Commons and Chancellor of the Exchequer. He was unquestionably the dominant figure in the Government, and at thirty-seven was the youngest Chancellor since Pitt. Then, at the very end of 1886, he committed political suicide. In his preparation of the budget for the following year, Lord Randolph advocated sweeping fiscal reforms: by extra taxation and saving, he planned to convert an estimated deficit of £400,000 into a surplus of no less than £12½ million, with which he intended to reduce income tax from 8d to 5d and to lower the duties on tea and tobacco, in addition to making grants totalling £5 million to local government. The proposals were masterly and characteristic of the imagination of the man, but he ran into trouble over the suggestion that some of the saving should be at the expense of the War Office. Salisbury declined to overrule the protests of W. H. Smith, the Secretary of State for War, and Churchill threatened resignation, a procedure by which he had already consolidated his hold over the Party machinery; since the budget proposals were still secret, no one could rally to his support this time, and Salisbury allowed Churchill to think that his resignation had been accepted. Lord Randolph, in a grandiloquent but foolish gesture, published his resignation in *The Times* and left himself without a leg to stand on. He had played into the hands of Salisbury and his henchman Balfour, neither of whom was as unsubtle as Lord Randolph perhaps thought. Lord Randolph was found not to be indispensable, and the right-wing Liberal Unionist G. J. Goschen was appointed to the Exchequer. 'I forgot Goschen!' exclaimed Lord Randolph.

At the Exchequer, Goschen proved himself an able successor to Churchill. He pursued a policy of cautious reform and carried out a good deal of Churchill's programme, though much more slowly and without the need to plunder the departmental coffers of his colleagues. He financed increased naval expenditure in 1889, for instance, by the imposition of a 1 per cent estate duty on estates over £10,000. In 1888 Goschen, with the assistance of the Governor of the Bank of England, Sir Mark Collet, undertook a highly successful conversion of the National Debt, which created new Consolidated Stock at $2\frac{3}{4}$ per cent for fifteen years, after which the interest was to fall to $2\frac{1}{2}$ per cent.

The concern of the Exchequer overlapped into local government, and in 1888 a most important piece of legislation was passed: the Local Government Act. Since the extension of the franchise in Gladstone's second ministry there had been increasing demands that the right to vote for local representatives, which already existed in 1835 in municipal corporations, should be extended to the counties. The Act of 1888 created sixty-two county councils, and made separate county borough councils for the larger towns (those over 50,000 in population). The greater London area was constituted under the London County Council. The county councils took over most of the traditional administrative functions of the Quarter Sessions. Voting was closely parallel to that in the boroughs: councillors were to be elected by householders, and unmarried women could vote, although they were disqualified from holding office. As the system of local government became established, the central government tended to be willing to delegate additional powers.

The second Salisbury administration is not conspicuous for its social legislation, and the most significant step in working-class life during the period was taken independently of the government: in 1889, under the leadership of the formidable Ben Tillett, the dockers struck for the celebrated 'tanner' – a standard rate of sixpence an hour – and won after a month. Their success gave encouragement to other workers and helped to create the 'new unionism' which will be examined in a later chapter.

In 1891 elementary school fees were abolished: the motives of the legislators were not entirely altruistic, for they feared that if the Radicals tackled the problem they might remove fees only in the State schools and thus leave the Church schools open to dangerous secular competition. In 1891 a further page was written in the story of legislation concerning factory conditions: a minimum working age of eleven was established, and a twelve hour day for women workers (with an hour and a half for meals). In the same year some protection was afforded to tenants by the Tithes Act, which made the owner of a property and not its occupier responsible for the payment of tithe. Finally in 1892 an attempt to relieve agricultural distress was made, but the Smallholdings Act was largely ineffective.

Ireland naturally remained a thorn in the flesh of the Government. Balfour became Chief Secretary for Ireland, and earned the nickname 'Bloody Balfour' by the coercive measures with which he attempted to combat an organised campaign of Irish violence. Parnell was unable to hold in check the extremism of people like John Dillon and William O'Brien, and his position was further compromised by the publication in *The Times* of a letter purporting to be written by Parnell approving of Irish violence and murder. The letter was linked to a series of articles on *Parnellism and Crime*. The publication coincided with the second reading of the harsh Crimes Act for the administration of Ireland, which was forced through the House of Commons by the use of the 'guillotine' to cut short debate.

Parnell's political honour was vindicated in lengthy proceedings which lasted into 1890 and in the course of which the celebrated letter published in *The Times* was shown to be a forgery by an Irish journalist, Richard Pigott, who was destroyed and driven to confession and suicide by a brilliant and merciless cross-examination conducted by Sir Charles Russell. Parnell's reprieve was short-lived. In the Victorian Era involvement in the Divorce Court was as socially fatal as the condoning of murder would have been. The scandal of Parnell's relationship with Mrs O'Shea broke in 1890 when O'Shea cited Parnell as co-respondent. Although Parnell might hope to hold the support of his Irish followers, that of the Nonconformist Liberals was gone for ever. Without that, the Irish might well ask, what could Parnell hope to achieve? The Irish Nationalists split, twenty-six remaining faithful to Parnell, and forty-four adopting the leadership of Justin McCarthy. Parnell's political power was shattered. He died on 6 October 1891. The second Salisbury administration's final gesture towards the Irish was made in the same year, when Balfour introduced a Land Purchase Act.

Lord Iddesleigh was induced to resign early in 1887. Salisbury (who returned to the Foreign Office) underwent a shocking experience shortly afterwards when Lord Iddesleigh fell dead in his presence. Salisbury's task in European diplomacy was complicated by the complex activities of Bismarck, who was trying to maintain contradictory – and secret – alliances with both Russia and Austria–Hungary. By 1890, the year in which Bismarck fell from power in Germany, good relations between Germany and Russia had broken down, and the basis of German diplomacy was the Triple Alliance of Germany, Austria–Hungary and Italy, whilst Russia moved towards an understanding with France, with whom she concluded the Dual Alliance in 1893.

Salisbury was not, as has often been supposed, an isolationist. Certainly he did not shrink from Europe, where he was regarded with great personal respect. He was a pragmatist, preferring to deal with situations as they arose, and averse to making formal alliances for what seemed very good constitutional reasons: he frequently reiterated his conviction that no British diplomatist could bind his country to go to war in general terms, for the participation of a country governed as Britain was would always be subject to the support of public opinion, and public opinion would inevitably depend upon the specific grounds over which a war was to be fought.

He was suspicious of France, which was perfectly understandable in view of the unstable nature of French politics, spiced as they were with militant chauvinism and with the alarming emergence of a leader such as Boulanger. Thus he was disposed in general to support the Triple Alliance, and he perfectly expressed his point of view when he candidly said that he wanted to 'lean upon' the Triple Alliance without being formally committed to it.[6] He did in fact go so far as to conclude a secret agreement with Italy in 1887 to maintain the *status quo* in the Mediterranean, an agreement to which Austria–Hungary later subscribed.

Foreign and imperial policy, of course, were so closely intertwined as occasionally to be indistinguishable. The Queen's Golden Jubilee in 1887 was made the occasion for a great colonial conference, but concern for Africa was predominant.

The exploration of Africa opened up not only that continent but a fruitful field for quarrels among the European powers. Belgium and France were active in the Congo, and after 1882 Bismarck too was ready to overcome his reluctance to be involved in colonial enterprises. So far as Britain was concerned, the Nile was the key to her predominance in East Africa, and Grey's declaration in 1895 that Britain regarded the whole of the Nile valley as her sphere of influence was consistent with the attitude of Salisbury's governments as well as Rosebery's.

Direct action by the Government was, however, very limited. Salisbury preferred to let the merchants do the work from which they reaped the profits. As in India in preceding generations, direct British governmental control evolved from commercial organisation and exploitation – and as in India serious complications sometimes followed. So, in the 1880s, British initiative in Africa rested largely with individual *entrepreneurs* and with the

c

great chartered companies: the Royal Niger Company (1886) the British East Africa Company (1888); and the British South Africa Company (1889). Of the great *entrepreneurs*, the out standing one, and the man whose activities and ambitions were fraught with most danger, was, of course, Cecil Rhodes - adventurer, diamond millionaire, and in 1890 Prime Ministe of the Cape.

The Government's possible rivalries with other Europear countries were shelved, if not settled, by a series of agreements In 1890, British interests on the upper Nile were safeguarded by an agreement with Germany by which Germany received the island of Heligoland in exchange for the recognition of British protectorate in Zanzibar. In the same year, Britain recognised French control in Madagascar in return for French acknowledgement of the British position in Zanzibar and in what is now northern Nigeria. Finally, in 1891, an agreemen with Portugal recognised the Zambesi as the boundary betweer British and Portuguese interests in East Africa, with free naviga tion of that river.

Salisbury's third ministry, which lasted from the Liberal electoral disaster of 1895 until his retirement in 1902, wa dominated by the Boer War and the events which led up to it which form the subject of a study in the following chapter.

In domestic policy, the high hopes and ambitions of th Government, and especially of Joseph Chamberlain, who was member of the Cabinet as Secretary for the Colonies, were soor blighted by the expense of the Boer War. A Workmen' Compensation Act was passed in 1897. Although its provision that employers should be liable to compensate workers fo injuries sustained at work did not apply to seamen, domesti servants or farm workers, it did set a healthy precedent. A mor serious shortcoming was that workers were allowed to 'contrac out' of its terms. Attempts to introduce a scheme of old ag pensions also came to nothing: over a hundred possible method were examined and rejected by a governmental committee and when at last an acceptable formula was found, it was to late – the Boer War was eating up all available funds. most important preliminary step was taken in 1899 with th establishment of the Board of Education, which bore fruit in the next administration.

Perhaps the most significant event in domestic politics occurred not in Parliament but in the Law Courts. In 1900 a strike took place on the Taff Vale Railway, in Wales, in the course of which the strike leaders organised picketing of a forceful kind, in clear breach of Trade Union Law, which permitted only 'peaceful' picketing. The Railway Company, instead of prosecuting the individuals concerned, sued the men's Union, on the grounds that the Union was responsible for the actions of its members. The Court upheld the Company's claim, and the Union was ordered to pay £23,000 in damages. The precedent thus established was, of course, potentially ruinous to the trade union movement.

Salisbury's conduct of foreign policy during his third ministry was complicated by the ambitions of Joseph Chamberlain, a colleague who was ready to take the fullest advantage of Salisbury's tendency to give the individual members of the Cabinet a free rein.

The essential factors in the European diplomatic problem in the 1890s were the development of the German Kaiser's ambitious *Weltpolitik*, and the trend of Russian expansion to the east. Rivalries were intensified by the existence of the two rival alliances, the Triple Alliance and the Dual Alliance. The glib assumption that the Far East was a preserve of European diplomacy was drastically upset by the emergence, after 1895, of Japan. In Europe, meanwhile, the fate of the Ottoman Empire remained to be settled: the 'Eastern Question' had still to be solved.

British predominance in the East, which had tended to be taken for granted, especially by the British, in the mid-nineteenth century had been rudely shaken by the 1890s. The Indian Mutiny of 1857 had destroyed the comforting illusion that the British ruled by consent in the sub-continent and the imperial title created by Disraeli in 1876 was a poor substitute, whilst the energies of Russian railway engineers and diplomatists continued to be pointed embarrassingly in the direction of Afghanistan. The alliance of France with Russia made matters worse and it is not surprising that Salisbury by now took a pessimistic view of the British situation in the East, but he stood firm for a time by his resolve that Constantinople must not fall into the hands of Russia.

Historians have for some time thought that Salisbury sought a solution in a plan to partition Turkey with German help; recent research, however, suggests that such a plan existed largely in the mind of Hatzfeldt, the German ambassador in London. The situation was seriously complicated by the Turkish massacres of their Armenian subjects, which began in 1894 and were renewed in 1896, after the failure of Britain, France and Russia to impose reforms on the appalling government of Abdul Hamid II. British policy was conditioned by the desire to relieve the Armenians if possible, but above all by the necessity to protect Britain's own interests from any Russian exploitation.

A feature of Salisbury's diplomacy was his refusal to resort to bluff, and his concern to save Constantinople was seriously compromised by the insistence of Goschen at the Admiralty that the Royal Navy had not the power to force the Dardanelles and thus to command Constantinople. Though not personally convinced, Salisbury allowed himself to be overruled, and when the Turks renewed their atrocities against the Armenians in 1896, he set about trying to restore the concert of Europe, a policy eloquently expressed in his famous Circular of 20 October 1896. A conference of ambassadors in Constantinople drew up a programme of reforms, but the work was interrupted by the foolish declaration of war on Turkey by Greece.

Salisbury's experience led to a realignment of British diplomacy. The insistence that the Royal Navy could not force the Dardanelles led Salisbury to abandon his emphasis upon the integrity of Constantinople, and to switch to the Nile as the centre of British influence in the Near-Eastern area. The Kaiser tended to become the protector of the Sultan, British relations with Austria-Hungary deteriorated, and the general direction of British diplomacy moved away from the Triple Alliance and towards the Dual Alliance.

Salisbury was thus led into a deeper involvement in Africa than he had anticipated. The administration of Africa by hartered companies was very congenial to Salisbury, but any xtension of British influence was bound to lead to conflict, specially with France. Relations with France were strained in pite of the efforts of Courcel, the ambassador in London, and f an amicable settlement of disputes over Siam in 1896.

The emphasis upon the Nile led to plans for the reconquest of he Sudan. Salisbury was at first half-hearted, but the situation vas made more urgent by the defeats of the Italians at the hands f King Menelek and his Ethiopian army. The Anglo-French risis which ensued on the Nile helped to speed up the settle- 1ent of differences on the Niger, over which a convention was 1ade in 1898.

Kitchener advanced into the Sudan with 8,200 British and 7,600 Egyptian and Sudanese troops, together with 66 field ieces and 60 river guns, and duly slaughtered the followers of he Khalifa (the Mahdi's successor) on the Nile at Omdurman n 2 September 1898. Kitchener's troops did not all behave well, nd the shooting of prisoners drew a characteristic reproof from Kitchener, who condemned the waste of ammunition. Kitchener imself behaved disgracefully in ordering the desecration of the Mahdi's tomb, and it was widely believed that he used the Mahdi's skull as an inkstand. Not all his troops shared his nthusiasm: the young Winston Churchill, who charged with he 21st Lancers, was a good deal more enlightened than his ommander:

This place had been for more than ten years the most sacred and holy thing that the people of the Sudan knew. Their miserable lives had perhaps been brightened, per- haps in some way ennobled by the contemplation of something which they did not quite understand, but which they believed asserted a protecting influence. It had gratified that instinctive desire for the mystic which all human creatures possess, and which is perhaps the strongest reason for believing in a progressive destiny and a future state. By Sir Herbert Kitchener's orders the Tomb had been profaned and razed to the ground. The corpse of the Mahdi was dug up. The head was separated from the body . . . The limbs and trunk were flung into the Nile. Such was the chivalry of the conquerors![8]

Kitchener moved on to Fashoda, where a French party had raised the French flag, at a point some four hundred miles south of Omdurman. The situation was potentially very ugly, and statesmen, with the conspicuous exception of Salisbury, made heated speeches. Yet the whole matter demonstrated French weakness: the French Government was in trouble over the Dreyfus affair, and when the British stood firm and placed the Royal Navy on a war footing, refusing to negotiate until the French flag was lowered at Fashoda, the French recalled their force on 2 November 1898. Egypt was in British hands, and the Sudan securely under British administration.

In the Far East, the need to maintain the 'open door' to trade with China was an overriding consideration. The Kaiser stirred up trouble in 1897 by seizing the bay of Kiaochow, and the Russians retaliated by sending their fleet to Port Arthur in the following year. Unable to persuade the Russians to budge, Britain protected her interests by leasing Weihaiwei. Salisbury was ready to make commercial, though not political, concessions to the Russians in Manchuria in return for the recognition of British predominance on the Yangtse. In 1900, however, a rather neglected factor in the situation made itself felt in the persons of the Chinese themselves. The Boxer Rising found an ageing and ailing Salisbury confused and hesitant: an attempt at an Anglo-German agreement on China produced a singularly ambiguous treaty in October 1900.

Meanwhile, in 1895, a dispute had arisen with the United States over the boundary between Venezuela and British Guiana. President Cleveland adopted a belligerent attitude and asserted the Monroe Doctrine. Salisbury in turn recognised the Monroe Doctrine, but not its validity in the dispute over Venezuela. The matter was settled, after wrangling over procedure, by arbitration, and the settlement was favourable to the British claims. Anglo-American relations generally were improved after the Venezuela dispute, and a final agreement in 1902 over Panama acknowledged American supremacy in the Caribbean area.

Salisbury gave up the Foreign Office in 1900 and it was his successor, Lord Lansdowne, who dealt with the crisis threatened in Manchuria when Russian military forces exploited the confusion which followed the suppression of the Boxer Rising. Lansdowne hoped in vain for an understanding with Germany in the Far East, and the treaty which he concluded with Japan in 1902 was in the nature of a second-best solution. It was also favourable to Japan: it promised neutrality if either power were attacked by one enemy, support if attacked by more than one, and opened the way for vast Japanese conquests.

Germany loomed large in British diplomacy, and not least because of Joseph Chamberlain's persistent efforts to bring about a great Anglo-Saxon alliance. Salisbury was hesitant, and was convinced that 'Germany will blackmail us heavily'. Chamberlain's grandiose (though far from nonsensical) scheme came to nothing, not least because of the German distrust of Chamberlain himself.

Salisbury's retirement from his greatest love, the Foreign Office, marked the first step in his retirement from political life, which came in 1902, when he made way for his nephew, Arthur James Balfour, who was destined to preside over the wreckage of the Party as Salisbury had understood it. Salisbury died in 1903, thus being spared the sight of the débâcle of 1905–6.

CHAPTER FIVE

The Boer War and its Impact at Home and Abroad

> The conflict which now opened in South Africa was not a conflict of interests. Between conflicting interests compromise is always attainable. It was the conflict of two nationalities, two faiths, two passions, two absolutes. Between absolutes, force is the sole arbiter.
>
> ÉLIE HALÉVY, *Imperialism and the Rise of Labour* p. 73

THE quarrels which exploded into the great Boer War in 1899 were rooted in nearly a century of suspicion and mistrust, in the course of which there had occurred spasmodic outbursts of hatred and violence. The British capture of Cape Colony from the Dutch in 1807 and its purchase at the Congress of Vienna in 1815 brought face to face in South Africa British and Dutch settlers, and the conflicting ideologies which they represented. Schooled in the hard doctrines of the Dutch Reformed Church, the Boers convinced themselves of the natural inferiority of the Kaffir, a view not shared by the more enlightened of the British settlers. The young Winston Churchill regarded their differences as the real cause of the Boer War:

> The true and original root of Dutch aversion to British rule is not Majuba Hill nor the Jameson Raid but the abiding fear and hatred of the movement that seeks to place the native on a level with the white man ... The servant is to be raised against the master; the Kaffir is to be declared the brother of the European, to be constituted his legal equal, to be armed with political rights. The dominant race is to be deprived of their superiority ... 'Educate a Kaffir?' said the Boer. 'Ah, that's you English all over ... they were put here by the God Almighty to work for us ... Insist on

their proper treatment, will you? Ah, that's what we're going to see about now. We'll settle whether you English are to interfere with us before this war is over.'[1]

Such a penetrating analysis reads somewhat ironically in the light of the pro-Boer sentiments expressed by many of the most progressive Englishmen of the time; it is a tragedy of history that what Churchill wrote at the outbreak of the Boer War might have served equally well as a commentary upon the South African withdrawal from the Commonwealth some half a century later.

The abolition of slavery throughout the British Empire in 1833 provoked (in spite of heavy bribery in the form of 'compensation') the Great Trek of 1836 and the creation of the independent Boer states of Natal, the Orange Free State, and the Transvaal. The Zulu menace had justified the British annexation of Natal in 1843 but successive governments had pursued inconsistent policies towards the other two Boer states until in 1881 Majuba Hill forced Gladstone into the confirmation of the independence of the Transvaal.

The situation in South Africa in the 1880s was complicated by the power and ambition of one man, the supreme embodiment of both the potentials and the perils of the British government's policy of opening up Africa by the efforts of chartered trading companies. Cecil Rhodes combined enormous wealth and prestige in Africa with a formidable influence in London, and was thus able to bring powerful pressures to bear upon the British government. Dictator of the great Chartered Company and 'King of Kimberley',[2] his visionary and grandiose project for a Cape to Cairo Railway led him to intrigue for a route through Bechuanaland, where the establishment of a British protectorate effectively blocked the Boer republic of the Transvaal on its western frontier.

The discovery of gold, and the exploitation from 1886 onwards of the Witwatersrand gold field, which produced the mushroom-like growth of Johannesburg – the society produced by the gold-rush was described by a contemporary as 'Monte Carlo superimposed upon Sodom and Gomorrah'[3] – threw into vivid relief the problems of the relationship between Boer and

Briton on Boer territory. The British immigrants who flocked to the Rand were treated by the proud Boers as social outcasts, and stigmatised as *Uitlanders* ('outsiders'). The *Uitlanders* enjoyed no vote and no political rights, although they were accorded the privilege of being punitively taxed, not only on their profits from the mines, but on all mining equipment which had to be brought into the Transvaal from outside.

Meanwhile, the arrogance and ambition of Paul Kruger expanded in direct proportion to the wealth of the Transvaal, and relations with the British government were not eased with the appointment to the Colonial Office of Joseph Chamberlain, whose suspicion and distrust of Kruger were more than reciprocated. In 1894 the Transvaal was further isolated by the assumption of British control in Tongaland, which cut off the Transvaal from the sea, leaving Delagoa Bay as its only inlet for seaborne trade.

Rebellious feeling which simmered among the *Uitlanders* in Johannesburg was reaching boiling-point and a full-scale rebellion was contemplated. Kruger found himself obliged to procrastinate. He was preparing to yield concessions to the Reformers' Committee in Johannesburg, when a piece of crass irresponsibility played into his hands and enabled him, once the immediate danger was over, to arrest all those *Uitlander* leaders whose identities had been revealed to him in the course of negotiations.

The Jameson Raid, which took place at the very end of 1895, thus helped to preserve Kruger's régime. Dr Leander Starr Jameson's wild scheme was to ride with a party of filibusters into the Transvaal and raise the disgruntled *Uitlanders* into open revolt. He had boasted that 'anyone could take the Transvaal with half a dozen revolvers', and he misled his followers by telling them that they had the support of the Imperial Government. The Raid, carried out with less than 500 men, rather than the 700 which Jameson's exaggeration has sometimes deceived historians into estimating, was an abysmal failure. Racked with dissension and indiscipline, shadowed and outmanœuvred by the Boers, the raiders, far from raising the *Uitlanders*, suffered a humiliating defeat and plunged *Uitlanders* and British government alike into an embarrassing predicament to which the German Kaiser characteristically added his contribution by sending a telegram of congratulation to Kruger.

An immediate controversy arose, which has persisted to the present day. To what extent were the British government and British influence responsible for the Raid? Of the complicity, not to say the inspiration of what Élie Halévy has called 'the headstrong arrogance of this megalomaniac',[4] Cecil Rhodes, there was no doubt whatever, and he was forced to resign as Prime Minister of Cape Colony and (though only temporarily) from the board of the Chartered Company. Joseph Chamberlain's involvement, however, was much less clearly defined. Clearly he knew about the plans for a rebellion in Johannesburg, and he never attempted to disguise the fact: '. . . my case is that while I knew all about the revolution I knew of nothing so mad as Jameson's Raid'.[5] Chamberlain claimed that his first knowledge of the Raid was as late as 29th December, when he tried desperately to stop it. Certainly he was acquitted by the official enquiry which was held, but the evidence was incomplete and in particular seven vital telegrams were missing. Chamberlain spoiled the effect of his acquittal by a blatant attempt to whitewash Cecil Rhodes in a speech in the House of Commons, which led critics at the time and since to suppose that Chamberlain was being blackmailed on the strength of material contained in the seven missing telegrams. Élie Halévy[6] was convinced of Chamberlain's complicity, although the most recent historian of the Raid is disposed to take an opposite view: 'Chamberlain's honour, on any fair assessment, was vindicated. Not so his judgement.'[7] Jameson and his fellow-raiders were the obvious and immediate scapegoats: handed over by their Boer captors, they were tried, convicted and sentenced in London.

The Jameson Raid sharply and violently focused the bitter animosities between the Boers and the British in South Africa, and such hatreds were not to be modified in the years which immediately followed.

In 1897 Sir Alfred Milner was appointed British High Commissioner in South Africa. The choice was an unhappy one, for although Milner was one of the typically brilliant products of

Victorian vintage Balliol and an able administrator, he was a poor and impatient diplomatist. Even worse, he was steeped in an unhappily militant imperialism: 'The more I see of it the more proud and convinced I become of the great service which jingoism has rendered to humanity in these regions'[8] was scarcely the spirit in which to conciliate the Boers after the provocation of the Jameson Raid. Milner based his claims to interfere in the internal affairs of the Transvaal upon the incessant wranglings over the interpretation of 'suzerainty' in the 1881–4 agreements.

Meanwhile Chamberlain sought to curb the tyranny imposed upon the *Uitlanders* by an increasingly aggressive Kruger: in 1897 Boer imports of war material through Delagoa Bay reached a value of £256,291 and Johannesburg became a virtual fortress. In February 1898 Kruger's position was consolidated by his sweeping victory in the Transvaal presidential election, and he became little short of a dictator. The intransigent and pessimistic Milner was already writing to Chamberlain in terms of 'reform or war'. Cecil Rhodes had returned to the board of the Chartered Company in 1898 and his influence was naturally deeply distrusted by the Boers.

The *Uitlanders* were in a situation which became daily less tolerable, so that an individual outrage drove them to desperate measures. The murder in Johannesburg of Tom Edgar by a Boer policeman, who was not merely acquitted but actually commended by the judge at his trial, provoked a massive petition directly to the Queen by over 20,000 Britishers on the Rand, and the petition was strongly backed up behind the scenes in a despatch from Milner, who wrote that:

> The spectacle of thousands of British subjects kept permanently in the position of helots, constantly chafing under undoubted grievances and calling vainly to Her Majesty's government for redress, does steadily undermine the influence and reputation of Great Britain and the respect for the British government within the Queen's Dominions.[9]

The members of the British Cabinet were reluctant to go to war with the Boers, and none was more reluctant than Joseph

Chamberlain – those who called the war 'Joe's War' when it came did him less than justice – but on the spot in South Africa Milner was, it seems, virtually committed in his own mind to war. He carried on the negotiations with the Boers with an ill-concealed lack of enthusiasm: a vital conference between Milner and Kruger at Bloemfontein opened on 31 May 1899 and dragged on until Milner lost patience and broke it off on 5 June; a telegram from Chamberlain to Milner arrived too late to prolong the talks.

Meanwhile not all the Boers were so militant as Kruger: the Cape Dutch, whose *Bond* party had been victorious in the Cape elections in 1898 were vainly trying to moderate the extremists in the Transvaal. On 13 August Jan Christiaan Smuts put forward liberal proposals to settle the grievances of the *Uitlanders*; Kruger then hedged them about with such qualification as to make them unacceptable in Britain. In September Chamberlain's last attempts at conciliation failed and on 9th October Kruger issued an ultimatum which made war certain. Reitz, the Transvaal Secretary of State, proclaimed the pride – not to say arrogance – of his government: 'As once Spain at the height of her power with her bloodthirsty Duke of Alva and her invincible armies was compelled to drink the bitter chalice of defeat, so today the same God shall deliver our enemies into our hands.'[10]

The strategical situation at the outbreak of war did something to confirm Reitz's optimism, and has been understandably compared with the problems which faced the British over a century earlier at the outbreak of the War of American Independence.

A glance at Map I on p. 19 illustrates the extent of the problem of communication between the home government and the army in the field, and of providing reinforcements. The Boers were splendid horsemen and natural guerilla soldiers: they deployed some 50,000 mounted infantry, and could arm as many as 80,000 men if the Cape Dutch could be persuaded to join them. The British had no more than 14,750 soldiers in South Africa, and could reinforce them only at the rate of 4,750 a month. Not for the first or the last time in British

II. South Africa (The Boer War)

history, the War Office let down the fighting troops. There existed a chaotic lack of co-ordination and there was no General Staff in South Africa. The mobilisation in England of 47,000 men – very soon to be urgently needed on the battlefield – proceeded in a dilatory and haphazard fashion. In fact, the strength of the Boers was underestimated by almost everybody: even had Lord Wolseley's plans been carried out – and they were regarded as absurdly over-cautious – they would certainly have proved inadequate.

The Boers, militant though they were, let their enemies off the hook. Had they concentrated their military effort in the Cape they must surely have dealt a mortal blow to British power in the area, but they were distracted by their fixation with the need to gain Durban (in Natal) as a seaport, and they made the fundamental military blunder of dividing their resources into units which were too small and too widely scattered.

Notwithstanding the shortcomings of their overall strategy,

the Boers dealt a series of humiliating tactical blows in the early months of the war. Between October and December 1899 they besieged the important centres of Kimberley, Ladysmith and Mafeking and invaded the whole of northern Cape Colony. In December 1899 the British forces – and British complacency at home – received a succession of shattering setbacks during what was quickly christened 'Black Week': Buller, trying to relieve Ladysmith, was trapped by Botha on the Tugela River and overcome at the battle of Colenso; Methuen attempted the relief of Kimberley and was trapped at Magersfontein; and Gatacre's efforts to stem the tide of invasion in Cape Colony were defeated at Stormberg.

During the first nine months of 1900 the British forces were heavily reinforced under the command of the already legendary Lord Roberts, the hero of Kandahar, who took out Kitchener as his Chief of Staff. Roberts knew his strategy and concentrated his forces. Victories followed. French raised the siege of Kimberley; Roberts himself entered the Orange Free State and defeated Cronje at the bloody battle of Paardeberg; Bloemfontein was occupied and the Orange Free State was annexed. Buller relieved Ladysmith and on 17 May 1900 Roberts invaded the Transvaal. Colonel Mahon relieved Mafeking, in whose defence Robert Baden-Powell had played a part which has brought joy to the hearts of adolescent Englishmen ever since, and on 5 June Roberts crowned his campaign by occupying Pretoria. Roberts then returned home to an assured place in the legends of his fellow-countrymen – and over their mantelpieces, adorned with his portrait on china plates and in more conventional frames. After a war which had until then been, in spite of its bitterness, singularly free from atrocity,[11] the task of mopping up the remnants of Boer resistance was entrusted to Kitchener, the victor of Omdurman.

For nearly two more years, the war dragged on. Beaten on the battlefield, the Boers took to the veld and waged a persistent and irritating guerrilla warfare. Kruger had fled to Holland, and the Boer horsemen found inspiring leaders in Botha, Smuts, de Wet and Hertzog. Kitchener's solution to the problems posed by the will-o'-the-wisp Boer guerrillas was characteristically thorough:

the fighting-men were deprived of supplies and support by the systematic burning of farms and the incarceration of the civil population in compounds called – with an ominous foreshadowing of things to come in European history – 'concentration camps'. The idea was borrowed from events a few years previously in Cuba, where the warfare had scarcely been such as to set a civilising example. Although conditions in the South African camps should not be supposed to have established a precedent for the brutality practised in their later namesakes, they were harrowing enough to cause pain, misery and death to the women and children and aged who were impounded in them. Kitchener's methods were sickening, but successful – and success was his aim, then as always.

By the spring of 1902 Boer resistance petered out and peace was concluded at Vereeniging. The Transvaal and the Orange Free State were once more annexed, but were promised self-government. Attempts to conciliate the Boers were made by providing for the retention of Dutch as the official language, and a British government grant of £3 million was made towards repairing the ravages of war. Self-government was promised and achieved: the Union of South Africa was created in 1909 and a year later the first united Parliament met. The Statute of Westminster (1931) finally confirmed the dominion status of the Union. The history of South Africa has been an unhappy one, however. In spite of the appearances of harmony with Britain, especially reflected in the career of Jan Smuts, who became one of the most respected of the Empire's elder statesmen, the differing attitudes of Briton and Boer have never been reconciled. The Liberal statesmen who helped South Africa to responsible government could hardly be expected to have foreseen the nature of the society which they were creating. The changing nature of the Commonwealth since the second world war produced a climate of opinion which the South Africans found increasingly uncomfortable. They proclaimed themselves a republic within the Commonwealth in 1961, and the South African association with Britain and the Commonwealth ended when the South African government's policy of *apartheid* forced her withdrawal from the Commonwealth.

The Boer War had aroused vigorous passions in England, where enthusiasm for imperialism was at its most aggressive in the years following the battle of Omdurman. Although the wilder manifestations of popular enthusiasm had little effect upon governmental policy, they were widely reported in South Africa: reports, for instance, of popular support in Britain for Jameson certainly helped to consolidate Boer patriotism and unity.

The British public, as is its wont, approached war in a spirit of complacent optimism – 'all over by Christmas' seems to be a macabre and recurring delusion in modern times – and received a rude awakening when the news of 'Black Week' broke. Élie Halévy retained vivid recollections of the transformation of public morale:

> I was in London. I remember seeing the troops on their way to the front marching through the streets to the cheers of the crowd. I remember a few days later watching in the halls of clubs and in hotels the tape unroll its tidings of defeat. I can still see the old gentleman – obviously a retired army officer of superior rank – who threw himself on me, while I was reading the news, to ask in anxious tones 'Have they come to blows?'. And in the porch of the old War Office in Pall Mall I remember the little group whose composition was continually renewed, standing in front of the official list of dead and wounded. One evening when I was there it divided to let a carriage pass, at the back of which we caught a glimpse of Balfour, wearing a look of profound dejection; he was coming, like everyone else, in search of news.[12]

Resolution in face of disaster is happily as characteristic of British public feeling as undue optimism at the outbreak of war. The news of Black Week stiffened the national sinews, and produced no less than 200,000 recruits for the Army in eight weeks. The Queen probably reflected popular feeling when she wrote to Balfour: 'Please understand that there is no one depressed in *this* house; we are not interested in the possibilities of defeat; they do not exist.'[13]

Those who opposed the war were at once branded as 'pro-Boers' and were treated with great hostility. Bodies such as the 'Stop the War' Committee, and the South African Conciliation Committee were denigrated in a public opinion which was embodied in an almost unanimous Press: only the *Manchester Guardian* and the *Westminster Gazette* stood out against the war, and the supposedly Liberal *Daily Chronicle* dismissed those of its staff who expressed opposition to the war.

When victories did come they were the occasions for manifestations of the worst sort of jingoistic excesses: the overflowing of crude emotion which greeted the news of the relief of Mafeking added a new – and mercifully short-lived – word to the language. It is regrettable that in the outbreak of 'mafficking' so little thought was spared for the real underlying causes of the war, which a few observers like Winston Churchill had perceived. In celebrating victory for victory's sake too little attention was given to the fact that the ideology which was being defeated was worth defeating. But if we interpret public reactions in 1900 in the light of what we now know of the South African régime in the twentieth century, we do less than justice to our predecessors. Not all of their contemporaries, though, shared in the general enthusiasm: 'How can I help feeling sad?' exclaimed the Radical John Burns amid a mafficking public, 'Don't you see England is falling to the level of France?'[14]

To the Liberal Party, the Boer War was yet another wedge driven into the crumbling edifice of unity. Leading figures in the Party found themselves deeply divided from their fellows. Rosebery's Liberal Imperialists were genuine idealists, and they prided themselves, probably justly, on being something more than a mere imitation of the jingoist Conservatives. Although they might regret the war, however, and condemn the faulty conduct of the negotiations which had preceded it, they rallied to the Government once hostilities had begun. Amongst Liberal leaders who supported the prosecution of the war were Asquith, Grey, Fowler and Haldane, to say nothing of the petulant and increasingly anachronistic figure of Rosebery himself. Of the Liberal old guard, only Harcourt and John Morley openly opposed the Government.

The war presented Campbell-Bannerman, who had cut

anything but an inspiring figure since assuming the leadership of the Party in 1898, with an important crisis of confidence. For a time he tried to follow a middle path, but the concentration camps and the burning of farms brought out his true instincts: 'When is a war not a war?' he demanded. 'When it is carried on by *methods of barbarism* in South Africa'.[15] Campbell-Bannerman was fiercely attacked within his own party for his speech, and political opponents accused him and those of his supporters who echoed his appeal to humanitarianism of prolonging the war by giving encouragement to the enemy! Campbell-Bannerman's leadership was certainly shaken, but he survived.

The fiercest Liberal criticism of the Government came, naturally, from the left wing of the Party, and especially from Labouchere and Lloyd George. It was the Boer War which thrust Lloyd George into the limelight, and in the fierce glare of unpopularity his radical sentiments and his splendid oratory flourished. In his condemnation of the war, he embodied the feelings of many Nonconformists, and particularly those of Wales, with the struggle of a small and essentially Protestant nation whom they tended to see in grievously oversimplified terms as a reflection of themselves.

Lloyd George turned in blistering personal condemnation upon the Chamberlain family, accusing Joseph and his brother and his son of profiteering from shares in armaments firms which held government contracts. He failed to move public opinion, but he ensured lasting place for himself in the history of the period.

The Government seized the opportunity offered by the victories of 1900 to consolidate their position in the House of Commons, and the 'Khaki Election' was held in September 1900. The results of the election give us the opportunity of assessing the effectiveness of criticisms of the Liberals as 'pro-Boers" since, needless to say, every possible use was made of the label during the campaign. Joseph Chamberlain himself set the standard: 'Every seat lost to the Government is a seat gained by the Boers'. The scurrilous talents of cartoonists and poster-painters were enlisted: Lady Asquith recalls that 'Posters presented pictures of eminent Liberals offering tribute to President Kruger, helping him to shoot British soldiers and haul down the Union Jack'.[16] The most surprising upshot of the campaign was that it was so ineffective: the scraping of the bottom of the barrel of electioneering chicanery produced only six extra seats for the Government. Ironically, the wholesale labelling of Liberals as 'pro-Boers' worked distinctly to the advantage of the Liberals when, in later years they came to have governmental dealings with the South Africans; and it certainly helped their relations with organised labour.

Abroad, the Boer War placed Britain in a position of anything but splendid isolation. Scorn and derision were poured upon the exponents of what was vilified as militant, bullying imperialism: the Kaiser's attitude was distinguished not so much for its extremism – for all Britain's critics on the continent adopted an extreme posture – as for the fact that he got his blow in first with the delivery of the Kruger telegram. The bitterest irony was reserved for Joseph Chamberlain's schemes for the great Anglo-Saxon alliance. Joseph Chamberlain was the lightning-conductor for all the fiercest European attacks upon Britain at this time, and it did not escape notice that the first war in which Britain became involved since Chamberlain had propounded his scheme had thrust Britain into conflict with the representatives in South Africa of Holland – a small, but proud and independent Teutonic nation.

CHAPTER SIX

Balfour, Chamberlain and Tariffs: Conservative Collapse

No political event in recent years has produced so startling an effect as the pronouncement on fiscal policy made by Mr Chamberlain . . . at Birmingham.

The Annual Register, 1903, pp. 130–1

THE administration headed by Arthur James Balfour from Salisbury's retirement in 1902 until Balfour's resignation in December 1905 presents the historian with a paradoxical balance-sheet: solid and worthwhile achievement stands in stark contrast to the wreckage of the party which seemed so firmly established in power in 1902. Two men dominated the political scene, and themselves constituted a striking contrast in method, background and personality.

Balfour was born in 1848, into the political purple: he was the nephew of Lord Salisbury, and his political career developed within the aegis of the Cecils and of their formidable influence over the Conservative Party. He is a fascinating, though scarcely – in spite of Mr Kenneth Young's best efforts[1] – an attractive, character. He was an intellectual, and he wrote learned philosophical treatises. He was fastidious and elegant almost to the point of effeminacy: one of his early nicknames was 'Pretty Fanny', and he could certainly demonstrate a feminine bitchiness towards defeated political enemies, as when he was at pains to ensure that C. T. Ritchie was rewarded for a lifetime of distinguished public service with a mere barony in 1905, rather than the viscountcy which he was entitled to expect. Balfour flourished in the rarified cultural and social atmosphere of the clique known as 'the Souls': he remained a bachelor, but his effeminacy was only superficial, and nobody thought it appropriate to apply to him the description with which contemporaries had baited the younger Pitt – 'the immaculate minister, who knew no woman'.

Balfour's elegant and gentlemanly glove concealed the iron hand of a shrewd and ruthless politician, and throughout his political career he displayed a very highly-developed instinct of self-preservation. Winston Churchill compares him at a later stage in his career with 'a powerful graceful cat walking delicately and unsoiled across a rather muddy street'.[2] Balfour most opportunely deserted Lord Randolph Churchill and the 'Fourth Party' in time to join his uncle Salisbury in assisting Lord Randolph's political suicide.

Meanwhile, Balfour climbed without undue exertion the rungs of the ladder of political advancement. He was President of the Local Government Board in 1885–6; Secretary for Scotland in 1886–7; and from 1887–91 Chief Secretary for Ireland, a hazardous office in which he won himself the unlovely soubriquet of 'Bloody Balfour'. From 1891–2 and 1895–1902 he led the Conservative Party in the House of Commons with a mixture of elegance, eloquence and insolence, and in 1902 he entered into his political inheritance. There was no real contest for the leadership: Hicks Beach, the Chancellor of the Exchequer, was a disillusioned man and a non-starter, whilst the one man who might have outmanœuvred Balfour was ill, and was in any case conscious of being 'a prisoner of the Cecils',[3] unable ever to do to Balfour what he had done to Gladstone.

Joseph Chamberlain might by ability and idealism have become leader of each of the great political parties; yet he was responsible for wrecking each of them in turn. Some thought him potentially more dangerous still: Rosebery observed that his 'epitaph may yet be "Having wrecked both parties in the State he set to work to wreck the Empire" '.[4] The wheel of Chamberlain's contribution to political life came almost full circle. Breaking up the Conservatives contributed, more than any other single factor, to restoring the fortunes of the Liberals whom he had so severely damaged over Home Rule that Gladstone, forgetting his Christian charity, declared in 1887 that 'Chamberlain is the greatest blackguard I have ever come across'.[5]

Chamberlain's whole background was worlds removed from Balfour's: he was the self-made man *par excellence*. Born in London in 1836 into the commercial middle class, he was the third son of the Master of the Cordwainer's Company, and a Liberal and a Nonconformist by inheritance. Joseph was educated in Canonbury and at University College School, London. In 1854 he moved to Birmingham to look after his father's interests in a screwmaking firm. Within twenty years he had taken over his rivals and retired with a fortune: his commercial prosperity was not matched by domestic happiness: two marriages were blighted by death, and it was not until his third marriage in 1888 that he knew lasting happiness and security within his home – a factor which should perhaps be borne in mind in considering his political actions, and particularly his lack of judgement which did not match his prodigious talents and overpowering idealism. It seems undeniable, too, that he was to some extent tarnished by his introduction to high society, but the orchid in the buttonhole, cards with the Prince of Wales, and so on, were perhaps necessary demonstrations of how far Chamberlain had come since he was first received by a suspicious House of Commons in 1876, when Disraeli had characteristically remarked that 'at least he wears his eyeglass like a gentleman'.[6]

Birmingham was to Chamberlain what Hatfield was to the Cecils, and, at least at the beginning of his career, his Nonconformity equalled in its conviction the pretensions of their High Churchmanship. It was in Birmingham that Chamberlain served his political apprenticeship and nurtured his radicalism, which was intense enough for him to be suspected as a republican; but his hold on Birmingham made him Mayor from 1873–5, and saw him returned unopposed, along with John Bright, as M.P. for the city in 1876. Birmingham never deserted him, and was represented by him in the House of Commons even in his last stricken and pathetic years. Chamberlain in return made some of his greatest speeches in the city, and in 1877 made it the centre of the Federation of Liberal Associations, the celebrated 'Caucus', which was such an important ingredient in the evolution of modern party political organisation.

Chamberlain has already been seen in action. He made his early reputation as a Radical and spokesman of Nonconformity. There seems little doubt that had he been prepared to compromise over Home Rule he could have become the leader of the Liberal Party, but even at this comparatively early stage his views were coloured by his concern for 'Imperial integrity' and he chose to wreck his party rather than to yield over Ireland. As Colonial Secretary under Salisbury he was regarded with a good deal of justifiable suspicion but his experience, particularly of the Colonial Conferences of 1897 and 1902 and of colonial aid against the Boers, strengthened his Imperialist convictions. Especially after the failures of his attempts to turn Salisbury's foreign policy towards a great Teutonic alliance, the concept of a truly unified Empire coupled with radical domestic reform came to obsess Chamberlain as the great solution to Britain's problems at the opening of the twentieth century. The great controversy over tariffs and the disintegration of the Conservatives sprang directly from Chamberlain's convictions.

Much work remains to be done by historians before anything like a full picture of Joseph Chamberlain emerges. He is done less than justice by the tedious and insufficiently critical work of his official biographer, J. L. Garvin, whose study is in any case incomplete. Mr Julian Amery has contributed rather more perceptive further volumes, but it is a pity that the Chamberlain papers should have been out of the hands of historians in general for so long. Fortunately, however, there is Dr Gollin's masterly exposition of that most significant episode in Chamberlain's career, the conflict over tariffs.[7]

Chamberlain was not alone in his concern for Britain's position in the world at the turn of the century. To agricultural depression – no less than a quarter of the nation's arable land went out of cultivation in the last quarter of the nineteenth century – was added the alarm of British industry in face of rising foreign competition, and the depressing effect of the mismanagement of the Boer War. Britain alone could obviously not compete with the new and rapidly expanding nation-states of the world – Germany, the United States, Japan, even Russia – but Chamberlain was convinced that the Empire as a whole could do so.

Social reform in Britain on the scale which Chamberlain knew to be essential was a practical impossibility without some far-reaching theoretical and practical reorganisation of governmental methods of raising money. Thus the fiscal element in Imperial development was particularly attractive to Chamberlain, but it was by no means divorced in his mind from the consideration of Imperial defence and the desirability of a genuine political federation. The Imperial leaders themselves, particularly the French-Canadian Prime Minister of Canada, Sir Wilfrid Laurier, suspected political federation as an attempt to maintain British domination over the emerging nations of the Empire; they fought shy of political and military commitments, placing the emphasis squarely upon the advantages to be gained from Imperial co-operation in trade. An early initiative towards Imperial Preference – the importation of Imperial products on fiscal terms more advantageous than those allowed to other countries – had come from Canada in 1896, but the first significant shots in what was to become a bloody political battle were fired in 1902.

In his budget in 1902 Sir Michael Hicks Beach revived the old registration duty of 3d per cwt on imported corn and 5d per cwt on meal, as a short-term expedient to cope with the budget deficit left by the Boer War. Laurier in Canada was not slow to pronounce upon the significance of such a proposal, and in May 1902 Chamberlain made an ominous speech at Birmingham. The Radicals at once leapt to the defence of Free Trade, an article of British political and economic faith since 1846, and castigated the idea of an 'Imperial Zollverein', whilst conjuring up the spectre of the 'small loaf'. In October 1902 Chamberlain openly proposed to the Cabinet an Imperial Preference upon imported corn. Balfour's caution was shared by the King: neither wanted a repetition of the political confusion and animosity which had followed Peel's repeal of duties on corn in 1846.

Chamberlain's impression that the Cabinet was agreed upon an Imperial Preference upon corn imports was rudely shaken in 1903. Hicks Beach had been succeeded as Chancellor of the Exchequer by C. T. Ritchie, a very able administrator – he had been responsible for the great reform of local government in 1888 – and an obdurate disciple of Cobden and Free Trade: in the budget of 1903 Ritchie repealed the corn duty of the previous year. Meanwhile, a tour of South Africa had hardened Chamberlain's Imperialist resolve.

On 15 May 1903 Chamberlain made his epoch-making speech in Birmingham. The ardour of his followers, notably that of L. S. Amery, was aroused, but so too was that of his opponents, with Lloyd George, who heartily despised Chamberlain for his 'betrayal' of the Liberals in 1886, in the vanguard. Lloyd George never lacked courage, and he went so far as to attempt to beard the lion in his den by speaking in Birmingham. He never made his speech and was lucky to escape with his life: one unfortunate citizen of Birmingham was indeed killed in the disorders which attended Lloyd George's visit to the city.

In the House of Commons, however, Lloyd George was conspicuously more successful in his efforts at once to humiliate Chamberlain and to embarrass Balfour. In a superb speech in May during a debate on Old Age Pensions, Lloyd George taunted Chamberlain (who had committed himself to support for Old Age Pensions as early as 1891) and cornered him: Chamberlain was compelled to link the financing of pensions with his proposals on tariffs. Even Balfour could not conceal his discomfiture. Later in the month Lloyd George succeeded in goading Chamberlain still further into a specific reference to taxes on food, which provoked open opposition from Winston Churchill and Lord Hugh Cecil on the government benches.

Balfour was meanwhile procrastinating with characteristic skill and soothing the Liberal Unionists, but by July it was clear that there were two distinct factions among the Government's supporters. Chamberlain was concentrating his attack outside the House of Commons, and his opponents within his own party did likewise. On 13 July they formed the Unionist Free Food League, to which Chamberlain responded within a week with the creation of the Tariff Reform League – the use of the word 'Reform' being a transparent attempt to curry popular favour. Since so much of the sniping took place outside Parliament, the influence of the rapidly developing resources of the popular Press became paramount: Chamberlain's closest support came from J. L. Garvin and the *Daily Telegraph*, along with the *Daily Express*. Harmsworth, the great apostle of mass-circulation newspapers, was intent above all on being on the winning side: he reflected the general public hostility to what were inelegantly called the 'stomach taxes', whilst favouring industrial protection.

Amid a turmoil of which the tariff controversy was only a part, Balfour maintained his habitual sang-froid. He had careful research conducted into the theories of tariffs and decided that the strongest case was for retaliatory tariffs against foreign competition from countries who protected their own industries by tariffs. After courting Chamberlain with the famous *Blue Paper* which provisionally accepted both industrial protection and taxes on food, he ran into trouble within the Cabinet and particularly with the Duke of Devonshire, the leader of the Liberal Unionists and – perhaps more significantly – a potential rival of Balfour himself. So Balfour abandoned specific proposals, including of course the *Blue Paper*, and took refuge behind the general principle of 'Fiscal Reform'. Principles in politics are notoriously less vulnerable than specific proposals.

By September 1903 the situation of the divided Government had become critical, and circumstances enabled Balfour to make an exquisitely unscrupulous demonstration of his grasp of political realities. On 9 September Chamberlain offered his resignation on the grounds that he wished to be free to carry his campaign to the country. Balfour struck a bargain with him: Chamberlain was to be allowed to go and proselytise the country, whilst Balfour would undertake measures of moderate fiscal reform; the connection between them should be maintained by the promotion of Chamberlain's son Austen as Chancellor of the Exchequer. Needless to say the bargain was grotesquely one-sided, and Chamberlain had been completely outsmarted: whilst he literally wore himself to death campaigning around the country, Balfour sat comfortably in office under no obligation to do anything at all, since the timing of any steps of 'moderate fiscal reform' was left entirely to him.

Moreover, Balfour had yet other harvests to reap. He kept Chamberlain's resignation secret and turned on the Free Traders within the Cabinet. He forced the resignation of the Chancellor of the Exchequer (Ritchie) and the Secretary for Scotland (Balfour of Burleigh), both of whom were opposing him on the assumption – which Balfour sedulously fostered – that Balfour was supporting Chamberlain. Lord George Hamilton, the Secretary of State for India, resigned under a similar misapprehension. The Duke of Devonshire, of course, was a bird of an altogether different feather: he was much more dangerous to Balfour out of the Cabinet than in, and he allowed himself to be reconciled – but only for a time: when Ritchie saw through the whole plot, Devonshire realised that he had been tricked and his old-fashioned whig conscience got the better of him, forcing his resignation in September 1903, much to his own relief and to Balfour's evident chagrin.

King Edward VII was determined to play his proper role in this political turmoil. He had hoped to bring about a reconciliation within the Cabinet by refusing permission for the immediate publication of the resignations of the Free Traders: this was no hindrance to Balfour, who simply ensured that the royal injunction reached him 'too late'. The King again attempted to put the brake on by opposing some of the new appointments, notably that of H. O. Arnold-Forster to the War Office. Once more he was over-ridden by Balfour, although the King had the no doubt mixed satisfaction of seeing Arnold-Forster make a very considerable hash of things at the War Office.

So the great campaign for tariff reform passed from the

Cabinet and the Commons into the wider forum of the nation at large, where the appeal of the reformers made a diminishing impact as industrial recession gave way to returning prosperity. Chamberlain's inspired and high-minded convictions had many of the attributes of missionary crusading zeal, but around the country he found his arguments pursued by the masterly and relentless logic of what Campbell-Bannerman was wont to describe as 'the Sledgehammer' – the rock-hard and crystal-clear oratory of Asquith.

Meanwhile the Unionist Free Fooders were gaining strength: the Duke of Devonshire became President of the Unionist Free Food League, which included some fifty Conservative M.P.s: their supporters were openly told not to vote for Conservatives who were tariff reformers, and there might well have been a definitive alliance between the Free Fooders and the Liberals, had the latter not been weakened by their luke-warm support for the leadership of Campbell-Bannerman.

Open battle was now joined between the two factions of the government party, some members of which were going over to the Liberals; their most significant recruit was Winston Churchill, who crossed the floor of the House of Commons in May 1904. The Liberals were unquestionably winning the battle for the minds of the electors. A succession of by-election defeats led Austen Chamberlain to press for a general election: he was convinced that the Government would lose, but confident that while the Liberals were making a mess of things the Conservatives could be reorganised and reunited. Balfour, however, was still procrastinating: he announced in Edinburgh in 1904 that if he won the next general election he would hold a conference of colonial and Indian leaders and would then submit their recommendations at yet another general election. By this time he seems to have become convinced of the desirability of retaliatory tariffs as a sound middle course, but he persistently refused demands that he should make his position plain. Early in 1905 in Manchester, and again in Sheffield and in Edinburgh, he was still hedging.

By this time, for a mixture of reasons both good and bad, Balfour was merely delaying the inevitable collapse of the

Government, occasionally resorting to the expedient – humiliating surely for any Prime Minister but Balfour – of leading his supporters out of the Chamber of the House of Commons rather than submit to defeat. In November 1905 there was an open rupture in the Cabinet precipitated by a dispute between Lord Londonderry (President of the Board of Education) and Austen Chamberlain. On 4 December 1905 Balfour at last resigned: the great tariff controversy had wrought its havoc.

Meanwhile, before the dam burst, and even whilst the flood waters of party ruin were lapping about them, Balfour's ministers had significant achievements to their credit, some of which go some way towards explaining and even justifying the tenacity with which Balfour clung to power.

Perhaps the greatest single piece of legislation, though one fraught with controversy, was the Education Act of 1902. The details of the Act owed much to the perception and skill of Sir Robert Morant, perhaps the greatest civil servant in the history of English education. School Boards were abolished and their work handed over to Education Committees of County and Borough Councils. Provision was made for the development of Secondary Schools throughout the country. The Act, indeed, established the machinery by which state-maintained education has functioned in this country ever since. But we fail to understand the bitter controversy which raged over educational development in this period until we take into account the great importance which was attached to it by sectarian interests in an age when the love of Christians for one another was prone even more than nowadays to be bounded by the walls of the local church or chapel. Nonconformists objected to the provision within the terms of the Act of 1902 for Anglican and Roman Catholic schools to be subsidised. Already there were more children in Church schools than in the Board Schools which had been introduced in 1870, and there were villages where only the Church school, with its Anglican doctrines, was available to Nonconformist children. Now, with the promised subsidy, the chance that the Church schools might gradually be replaced by non-sectarian Board or Local Authority schools seemed to disappear. The eminent Baptist, Dr Clifford, led a campaign against the Act. His followers, the 'passive resisters', refused to pay that part of their rates which was devoted to education and were prosecuted in droves, whilst Local Authorities in Wales had to be forced by the Government to implement the terms of the Act. Religion continued to lay a chill and uncharitable hand over educational proposals throughout the early decades of the century.

The Land Purchase Act of 1903 was a progressive measure which helped Irish tenants to buy the holdings which they rented from the the great landlords: Parliamentary grants of 12 per cent helped tenants to meet the prices asked by the landlords.

Controversy raged once more in 1904, over proposals in the Licensing Act – a good example of the powerful voice of the brewing interest, long since an established factor in English politics. The Act reversed a decision of the House of Lords, which had threatened the security of the brewers' profits by ruling that ale-house licences were valid for a year only at a time, and could be revoked by local magistrates. The Licensing Act now protected the brewers by decreeing that Quarter Sessions should become the licensing authority, and that where the renewal of a licence was refused compensation should be paid to the dispossessed licensee from a levy upon the whole trade. The whole temperance movement resented what was regarded as a concession to the brewers, and gave wholehearted support to anti-government candidates when the general election was held.

Foreign policy and Imperial defence provided the most cogent pretexts for Balfour's tenacity in clinging to office. The *entente* with France and the first Moroccan crisis, along with the final settlement of the alliance with Japan, also loomed large amongst Balfour's cares.

Much has been made of Balfour's concern that plans for a new 18-pounder gun for the army should be far advanced before a Liberal government had the chance to ruin them. His greatest enthusiasm in the realm of defence, however, was his share in the creation of the wholly reorganised Committee of

Imperial Defence, which realistically recognised the need for a supreme command and for the close co-ordination of the Army and the Admiralty. The idea was an excellent one, but one may doubt the effectiveness with which the idea was implemented, especially in the light of the conspicuous lack of co-operation between the Army and the Navy before 1914, and of Kitchener's alleged remark that the Cabinet deserved the V.C. for its courage in declaring war in 1914 without any adequate supplies of arms, ammunition and general military equipment. The fact that, nonetheless, the British army was better prepared for war than has usually been the case in the country's history, was largely due to the achievements of the Liberal Secretary for War, Haldane. Balfour made disappointingly little impression on the War Office.

At the Admiralty, however, Balfour was much more successful, and stimulated the great reforms introduced by Lord Cawdor and the formidable First Sea Lord, Admiral Fisher. The Cawdor–Fisher programme introduced new concepts in training, and placed a realistic emphasis upon engineering skill. Above all, it introduced a new element into naval strategy in the *Dreadnought*: 'You are the godfather of the *Dreadnought*', wrote Fisher to Balfour.

But Balfour's time was now running out. By the middle of November 1905 Chamberlain had won control of the National Union of Conservative Associations and was urging the case for a general tariff. Balfour resigned on 4 December 1905. In the New Year the Liberals were swept into power and Balfour suffered the indignity of losing his seat, having to look elsewhere for a safe passage back to the House of Commons, at the head of a parliamentary party now only 157 strong: since over a hundred of them were Tariff Reformers Balfour was forced to give way on the most controversial issue of his time, although in July 1906 Joseph Chamberlain himself was crippled by a stroke. Balfour remained leader of the Conservatives until 1911, and he continued to exercise a formidable influence over politics long after that.

Meanwhile, the Liberals were in power. Balfour's majority had in any case been an inflated one, produced in the artificial atmosphere of the 'Khaki election', and the Liberals had made significant inroads into it in by-elections. The greatest weakness in Balfour's position was, of course, the rift in his own party, but the Government had also encountered a formidable body of public opposition to some of their particular policies. For instance, Nonconformist opposition had been hardened both by the controversy over education and by the Government's Licensing Act. The hottest issue in the general election campaign was that of 'Chinese slavery' in South Africa. The radical and Nonconformist conscience was aroused by the appalling conditions of Chinese labourers in the Rand goldfields; 46,000 of them had been allowed into South Africa by Balfour's government after the peace settlement. Indentured into virtual slavery, these Chinese worked sixty hours a week for two shillings a day, lived in atrocious conditions, and were beaten by their employers. Dark rumours that the Balfour government would similarly import Chinese labour into the coal mines of South Wales were, needless to say, fostered rather than scotched by Lloyd George.

The long-term perspective of history has invested Joseph Chamberlain with more wisdom than he actually possessed when he prophesied that the Liberals would be 'hissed off the stage' – one of the better examples of how he would let his enthusiasm outrun his judgement. His experience of Asquith's opposition during the nationwide campaign over tariffs should have taught him more about the Liberals than he was willing to learn.

CHAPTER SEVEN

Working-Class Radicalism: The Growth of the Labour Party to 1906

> The last has not been heard of the Socialist movement either in the
> country or in this House . . . just as sure as Radicalism democratised
> the system of government politically in the last century so will Socialism
> democratise the country industrially during the century upon which we
> have just entered.
>
> KEIR HARDIE, in the House of Commons, April 1901[1]

RADICALISM as expounded by Joseph Chamberlain or even
Lord Randolph Churchill exercised a stimulating effect upon
the politics of its own time and established an irresistible
pattern for future political attitudes within the established
parties – at least within significant elements of them. But the
constructive and at times militant radicalism of the working
class, the political inheritance of the Chartists, found other
outlets. Such channels were not always deliberately sought,
for a persistent feature of the working-class movement in the
late nineteenth century was the controversy between those
who believed that most could be achieved by the permeation
of Radical policies through the Liberal Party and others who
maintained that genuine working-class radicalism could be
expressed only through a genuine working-class political party.
The extension of the franchise in 1867 and 1885 had not
simplified the issue, for it was, of course, still arguable that
more was to be achieved by making Liberal Party candidates
dependent upon working-class votes than by trying to con-
centrate the labour vote sufficiently to return labour candidates

The direct ancestor of the Labour Party was the Labour Representation Committee (L.R.C.), which was founded at an historic, though little-publicised meeting in the Memorial Hall, Farringdon Street, London, on 27 February 1900. The L.R.C. drew together the various working-class and socialist organisations in an attempt to establish what Keir Hardie described as:

> ... a distinct Labour group in Parliament, who shall have their own whips, and agree upon their policy, which must embrace a readiness to co-operate with any party which for the time being may be engaged in promoting legislation in the direct interests of labour, and be equally ready to associate themselves with any party in opposing measures having an opposite tendency. ...[2]

Hardie's formula, embodied in an amendment put at the Memorial Hall Meeting, was at once forthright and flexible. It committed the new party to no rigid dogma and to no detailed programme, and left the door wide open to the disciples of 'permeation' as well as to the advocates of concentrated working-class political action.

The delegates who attended the Memorial Hall meeting represented the most significant exponents of the political interests of the working class – the trade unions, the Fabian Society, the Social Democratic Federation and the Independent Labour Party.

The trade unions represented the most formidable body of organised labour in the country, but they were far from representing an organised expression of militant socialism. It was only recently, indeed, that the whole complexion of the trade union movement had been altered by the addition of the 'new unionism' to the entrenched interests of the proud, prejudiced and often reactionary skilled workers of the craft unions.

The trade unions that participated in the foundation of the Trades Union Congress (T.U.C.) in 1868 were essentially composed of skilled craftsmen – those to whom Marxists used to refer as the 'labour aristocracy'; the unskilled were unorganised and generally powerless. Indeed, even the strength of the skilled craft unions was liable to fluctuate according to prevailing economic conditions. When work was short, individual workers were not unnaturally more willing to compromise with the employers than when the activities of the unions were backed by the pressure of shortage of labour, which inevitably placed the employers on the defensive. Thus, the depression of the 1870s made deep inroads into the ranks of trade union membership. From something like 594,000 in 1874 the membership of trade unions had declined to about 381,000 by 1880. The same depression effectively, if temporarily, killed off attempts to organise the unskilled workers.

During the 1880s improved economic conditions encouraged a revival, which was stimulated in part by the Liberal Party's preoccupation after 1886 with Home Rule, which seemed to relegate social reform as a political programme: to most Radicals the so-called 'Newcastle Programme' hastily concocted by Gladstone in 1891 appeared to be merely a Liberal carrot dangled before the working-class voter.

The whole emphasis of trade unionism underwent drastic changes before the end of the nineteenth century, with the advent of the 'new unionism'. The unskilled workers achieved an organisation and political potential never previously attained. The pattern was set by a successful strike in 1888 of the girls employed in Bryant & May's match factory, and the unskilled were greatly encouraged (not to say astonished) when the London gas workers achieved the desired eight-hour day without even a struggle. Further incentive sprang from the success across the Atlantic of the American Knights of Labor who numbered half a million by 1887. Perhaps the most significant impetus of all was given to the movement, however, by the great London Dock Strike of August 1889: led by the redoubtable Ben Tillett, the dockers campaigned for their 'tanner' – a rate of sixpence an hour. There was a good deal of public sympathy for the dockers, stimulated no doubt by the publication of Charles Booth's penetrating analysis of poverty in the capital, *London Life and Labour*. Tillett, for all his powers, had no great organising experience, and signifi-

cantly there came to his assistance two socialist leaders, John
Burns and Tom Mann.

The new unions, in fact, gained much sympathy and practical help from socialist organisations, and the Socialists
reaped the benefit in prestige which was handed to them by
the apathy and occasionally the downright opposition of the
old craft unions to the 'new unionism'. By 1890, the new-style
unions, though still not constituting a majority, were undeniably a force to be reckoned with in the T.U.C. The difference between old and new was firmly stamped upon the
very appearance of their leaders, as John Burns noted in 1890:

> The 'old' delegates differed from the 'new' not only physi-
> cally but in dress. A great number of them looked like
> respectable city gentlemen; wore very good coats, large
> watchchains and high hats – and in many cases were of
> such splendid build and proportion that they presented
> an aldermanic, not to say a magisterial, form and dignity.
> Among the 'new' delegates not a single one wore a tall
> hat. They looked workmen. They were workmen. They
> were not such sticklers for formality or Court procedure,
> but were more guided by common sense.[3]

The new unions suffered once more from the depression
of the 1890s, but they were already a potent force in the north
of England, especially in Bradford, where in the early 1890s
there were even two parliamentary candidates on behalf of the
working class, Ben Tillett and the Manchester journalist
Robert Blatchford. Blatchford was particularly influential
in the north: 'I find his converts in every direction', wrote
H. M. Hyndman in 1892. The influence of the new unions
in Bradford stands in striking contrast to the situation in London,
where the old-established craft-unions continued completely
to dominate the London Trades Council.

In 1895 at the T.U.C. in Cardiff the influence of the new
unions and of the Socialists came into the open: Tom Mann
estimated that of the 370 delegates more than eighty were
members of the Independent Labour Party. Two steps marked
the downfall of the old-style domination of the trade union
movement: in future trades councils were to be excluded, by

the resolution that only active working-men could attend; and the institution of the card-vote created a method of voting which ensured that each union's vote should carry a weight directly proportional to the size of its membership.

It was not to be expected that the decisions of the T.U.C. at Cardiff in 1895 would transform the attitudes of the separate unions overnight. In 1897 the miners clearly demonstrated the power of traditional attitudes, when the Yorkshire miners supported the Liberal candidate in a by-election at Barnsley against no less formidable an I.L.P. candidate than Pete Curran. The miners' votes carried the Liberal to victory. The deeply rooted prejudices of the miners were particularly hard to break: living in closely-knit and homogeneous communities, they were accustomed to the exercise of political power by using their community spirit to bring pressure to bear upon Liberal candidates, and they preferred established methods rather than the risks attaching to an unknown and ill-defined labour movement.

The new unions, however, were particularly anxious that the Socialism from which they had derived such welcome support should find a concerted expression in a working-class political party, and all around them the hold of the skilled craftsmen was slackening. The transformation of the engineering industry, for instance, compelled the exclusive ranks of the Amalgamated Society of Engineers to slacken their own rigid qualifications for membership. An added stimulus towards more militant political action derived from a hardening of the attitudes of a significant number of employers, particularly after the encouragement of legal judgments such as that in the Taff Vale case,* which provided a vital focus for arguments for closer trade union organisation. There was a noticeable development of groups such as employers' federations, and there was a very genuine fear among many workmen that the worst features of the American system of Trusts might spread across the Atlantic.

A microcosm of what might be achieved on a national scale was already in evidence in Liverpool since 1894. There,

* See above, p. 67.

the local Trades Council entered into the fullest collaboration with branches of the Independent Labour Party, the Social Democratic Federation and the Fabian Society to form a local 'Labour Representation Committee'. A similar organisation developed in Glasgow. The decisive conversion of a majority of trade unionists was achieved on a card vote at the T.U.C. in 1899, when James Holmes of the Amalgamated Society of Railway Servants proposed a resolution which had been vigorously advocated by Keir Hardie before the T.U.C. had assembled. The terms of the resolution were momentous and unequivocal:

> That this Congress, having regard to its decisions in former years, and with a view to securing a better representation of the interests of labour in the House of Commons, hereby instructs the Parliamentary Committee to invite the co-operation of all the co-operative, socialistic, trade union, and other working organisations to jointly co-operate on lines mutually agreed upon, in convening a special congress of representatives from such of the above-named organis- ations as may be willing to take part to devise ways and means for securing the return of an increased number of labour members to the next Parliament.[4]

The resolution was carried by 546,000 votes to 434,000, and the trade union movement was ready to place its growing resources at the disposal of a labour party. By the turn of the century, those resources were considerable: in terms of money alone, the trade unions were worth some £3,700,000 in 1900.

As we have seen, the influence of dogmatic Socialism in the early history of the trade union movement was limited, and in the working-class movement as a whole the outright Socialists were in a minority. Indeed, the Labour Party, even when formally constituted, did not officially adopt an avowed Socialist policy until 1918.

During periods of comparative prosperity militant Socialist dogma tended to be submerged in the realities of life among a more or less contented working class. The forces of labour in such circumstances tended readily to accept the political leadership of the Liberal Party.

The other ingredients of the L.R.C. when it was founded in 1900, however, represented the various shades of such Socialist thought as existed in the country. The most extreme views were those of the Social Democratic Federation (S.D.F.) which had been founded in 1884 on the basis of the Democratic Federation which had been created three years earlier.

The views of the S.D.F. were far from embodying the attitudes of most working class politicians, and were rather a sort of distillation of many of the sporadic and diffuse expressions of early socialist thought in the country. Such manifestations were greeted with little widespread enthusiasm, for, as we have observed, prosperity tended to breed complacency in the working class as well as in other sections of society. Thus, the Socialists' recognition of the existence of such a thing as a 'labour interest' was bound to be largely theoretical in the early stages: it found its earliest expression in the protests of such men of letters as Ruskin and Carlyle against the harsh social conditions created by the rapid development of factory-systems.

The leader of the S.D.F. was H. M. Hyndman, a Cambridge graduate, journalist, businessman, and disillusioned Tory Democrat. Hyndman, who incidentally made a very poor impression upon Karl Marx, founded the Democratic Federation in 1881 and was converted to a thoroughgoing Socialist policy in 1883. Dogmatic movements attract dogmatic members whose harmony is rarely sustained for long. The S.D.F. was no exception. Hyndman proved to be an increasingly dictatorial leader, too often straying beyond the bounds of logic and intellectual honesty, and some of the most significant of his colleagues were driven to form fragmentary movements of their own, like William Morris's short-lived Socialist League.

Moreover, militant Socialist agitation made little real headway, even in the conducive conditions of economic depression. Chronic unemployment formed the background to Socialist demonstrations during 1886 and 1887. On 13 November 1887 the police broke up processions which were converging on Trafalgar Square in spite of an official ban upon a large-scale Socialist meeting there. John Burns, whose

inflammatory oratory had added even more zest to the movement in 1886 than he had intended, was arrested, convicted
and imprisoned, along with R. B. Cunninghame Graham, a
picturesque figure and a recent convert from Radicalism.

The failure of agitation, which soon became less attractive
anyway as industrial conditions improved with the passing of
the recession in trade, led to serious re-thinking of Socialist
methods. Violence became less fashionable than propaganda.
Progress to Socialism through constitutional channels became
a more attractive formula, particularly as the Socialists
shrewdly observed the effectiveness of a highly-organised
minority party in the shape of the Irish Nationalists.

Some effective action, and a taste of things to come, stemmed
from H. H. Champion – 'a Tory at heart and a Socialist by
conviction'[5] – who deserted Hyndman and from 1887 onwards
used the newly constituted Labour Electoral Association to
badger Liberal local constituency parties.

Meanwhile, the staunchest advocates of constitutional
action and 'permeation' of the established political set-up were
to be found amongst the members of the Fabian Society,
which had been founded in 1884. A leading figure was the
young George Bernard Shaw, one of the many British Socialists
who owed their political conversion to the work of the American
Henry George. Shaw bears eloquent testimony to the inspiring
effect upon him of George's advocacy in 1884:

> He struck me dumb and shunted me from barren agnostic
> controversy to economics. I read his *Progress and Poverty*,
> and went to a meeting of Hyndman's Marxist Democratic
> Federation, where I rose and protested against its drawing
> a red herring across the trail blazed by George. I was
> contemptuously dismissed as a novice who had not read
> the great first volume of Marx's *Capital*.
> I promptly read it, and returned to announce my complete
> conversion to it. Immediately contempt changed to awe,
> for Hyndman's disciples had not read the book themselves,
> it being then accessible only in Deville's French version
> in the British Museum reading room, my daily resort.[6]

Historians are far from unanimous about the extent of

Fabian influence in the formation of the Labour Party: Philip
Poirier, for example, in emphasising the role of the trade
unions, declares the Fabian contribution to have been minimal:
'The Fabian contribution remained peripheral and advisory
and was at no time decisive'.[7] Whilst it is true that the Fabian
intellectuals, in their prime concern for ideas, tended to neglect
the practical importance of the unions – the Webbs in particular
adopted a patronising attitude towards the working class and
their leaders which was not lost on a man as astute as John
Burns – they nevertheless exercised an undeniable impact
upon the opinion of Socialists and the public generally, at a
time when the emphasis in Socialist action was moving away
from agitation and towards propaganda. A further weakness
of the movement was its absorption in London, which involved
a neglect of the great Socialist potential in the industrial
provinces. Yet in London Fabian socialism did exercise
practical influence, especially in education: Sidney Webb at
the London School of Economics and Graham Wallas on the
London School Board may justly be regarded as pioneers.

In its early days the Fabian Society strongly urged the
strategy of 'permeation' and the Fabians, amongst others,
cherished over-optimistic hopes of Rosebery's 'progressivism'
on the London County Council. By 1893, however, such hope
had so far faded that Shaw heralded a significant change of
front with his vigorous pamphlet *To Your Tents, O Israel*, which
declared the necessity of independent action in the cause of
labour.

Thus, by the early 1890s the streams of working-class
opinion were beginning to flow together in the unambiguous
direction of independent action. And the most decisive development was undoubtedly the foundation of the Independent
Labour Party in 1893.

It was no accident that the meeting which founded the
I.L.P. met in the Labour Institute in Bradford, which by the
90s had become a centre of serious and energetic Labour
propaganda: by the end of 1892 there were no less than three
thousand members of a variety of working-class societies and
clubs in the city. It was in the North that propaganda had met

with most success: whilst Labour newspapers were failing with monotonous and depressing regularity in London, the *Clarion* and the *Workman's Times* were flourishing in the North. It was, indeed, from the *Workman's Times* and in particular from its editor, Joseph Burgess, that the initiative for the foundation of the I.L.P. stemmed. Further north, the Scottish Labour Party offered something of a model, and a further stimulus was derived from the results of independent candidatures in the general election of 1892.

In 1892 Ben Tillett won a great moral victory in Bradford where, although he failed to win the West Bradford seat, and indeed was bottom of the poll with 2,749 votes, the enthusiasm of the Bradford Labour Union carried him to within 600 votes of the successful Liberal.

Of more practical significance, however, was the fact that in the 1892 general election Keir Hardie was returned for West Ham South. Keir Hardie is a monumental figure in the history of the Labour movement, and indeed of the House of Commons. Dr G. P. Gooch has recalled the impression which Hardie made upon him in the House of Commons a few years later: he had the aspect of 'an Old Testament prophet. I never saw him smile'.

Hardie was born in 1856 in Lanarkshire, the illegitimate son of a farm-servant and a miner. His early years were spent in the appalling poverty which afflicted workmen like his stepfather, who was only occasionally employed. The boy was first sent to work at the age of eight, as an errand-boy, after which he was introduced to the mine as a 'trapper', one of those luckless boys whose task it was to open and close trap-doors to allow the underground trams to pass. He educated himself at nightschool, and the first outlets for his social missionary zeal were in the temperance movement and the Evangelical Union, with which he became associated in spite of a firmly agnostic home background. His energies naturally were channelled into the trade union movement, and he was dismissed for organising his own workmates. Like Shaw in a different environment, Hardie was very strongly influenced by the work of Henry George and he was, not surprisingly, attracted towards the extreme Socialism of the S.D.F. In London in 1887 he met Eleanor Marx and Engels, but he was repelled by Hyndman and the other dogmatists. He extended his influence in the trade union world through his monthly magazine, *The Miner*, which he founded in 1887, and in the same year he challenged the hierarchy of the T.U.C. In 1888 he contested the by-election in Mid-Lanark on behalf of the miners, a useful apprenticeship for his successful fight in West Ham in 1892.

Keir Hardie's influence in the foundation of the national I.L.P. was decisive, along with that of Burgess and W. H. Drew of the Bradford Labour Union. Of the 120 delegates who attended the foundation-meeting, the great majority came from Scotland and the North of England. Although there was a distinctively Socialist flavour to the meeting, obvious animosity towards Hyndman existed and the necessity for close co-operation with the trade unions was clearly recognised. Thus the aims of the new movement appeared to be economic rather than political, with particular prominence given to the demand for the eight-hour working day.

In its early days, the national I.L.P. was dogged by dissension and disappointment, and by the crucial organisational issue of whether the new movement should be a federation of the numerous local I.L.P.s or a genuinely centralised body. The S.D.F. was a particular thorn in the flesh, and the redoubtable John Burns was overtly hostile. The I.L.P. did much, however, to consolidate its position by repudiating Champion and his ambiguous 'Tory Socialism' and by winning the wholehearted allegiance of Keir Hardie.

Basic necessities like a central office and a secretary were acquired in 1895, and in the same year the obstructive tactics of the local Liberals in the election at Attercliffe presented the I.L.P. with a most important recruit in the person of James Ramsay MacDonald, who left the Liberals in protest. The general election of 1895 was on the whole frustrating and disappointing to the I.L.P. Keir Hardie lost his seat but was undismayed, and he clearly expounded the basic problem:'. . . But we must learn to fight elections'. In 1895, too, George Lansbury, S.D.F. candidate in Walworth, was displaying tendencies towards the acceptance of constitutional methods: the stern rebuke of Hyndman was symptomatic of the S.D.F. leader's increasing bigotry, and presaged the S.D.F.'s withdrawal from the L.R.C. as early as 1901.

The most marked tendency within the I.L.P. in the years leading to the foundation of the L.R.C. was the emergence of politicians of a new sort, bringing about a shift in emphasis away from the trade unions. The trend was marked by the withdrawal from the Council of the I.L.P. of Pete Curran, the great leader of the Gasworkers' Union, in 1898.

Two years earlier MacDonald had become a member of the Council. MacDonald is perhaps a classic example of the rise of a man from obscure origins, through self-education, to national prominence. He was born in 1866 in Lossiemouth, the illegitimate son of a farm-hand. Brought up by his mother and his grandmother, and soundly educated, he took the road of ambition to Bristol and thence to London, where poverty and intensive study combined to drive him to a breakdown. An apprenticeship as secretary to a Liberal politician led him into journalism. His membership of the S.D.F. was short-lived – like Hardie he was repelled by its dogmatism – but he joined, first the Fabians and then, in 1894, the I.L.P. MacDonald was destined to become a formidable figure in the Labour movement, though he never inspired the warm affection which was lavished upon Keir Hardie. Another of the 'new men' was Philip Snowden, whose powerful impact first upon Keighley and later in Blackburn belied his fragile appearance.

MacDonald became the first Secretary of the L.R.C. at its foundation in 1900, and he laid down in advance the broad lines of the new organisation, in which, although two-thirds of the member-unions of the T.U.C. were unrepresented, the militant Socialists were still in a minority. MacDonald had outlined the basic principles of the L.R.C. as follows:

1. That the candidates be run by Trade Union, Socialist and other labour bodies and have no connection with either Liberal or Tory parties.
2. That each party run its own candidates and find its own money.

3. That a joint committee of the organizations running candidates should be the political committee of the combined forces.[8]

The great issue which faced the L.R.C. from the outset was the extent to which, in spite of the first of the principles outlined by MacDonald, the Committee should seek some measure of working agreement with the Liberals. On the subject of the Boer War, the greatest political topic of the day, there was no formal contact, even with the anti-war Liberals. The Labour leaders tended to violent extremes in their condemnation of the war: many of them, Keir Hardie in the vanguard, quite misunderstood the nature of the Boer régime and Hardie went so far in his misconception as to declare that the British aim from the war was 'the enslavement of black labour and the pauperization of white labour'. John Burns was outspoken in support of the anti-war Liberals, and vigorously attacked Chamberlain: 'I protest against the incompetency displayed in the arrangements for the war, the hollowness of its object, the immorality of its aims, the stupidity with which the negotiations were conducted, and above all the want of taste, tact and temper too frequently shown by the Colonial Secretary. . . .'[9]

The cynics were to maintain that the energy which Burns expended on Chamberlain bought him his place in the Liberal Cabinet later.

In the 'Khaki Election', the first great electoral test of the growing Labour movement, the Government amassed on its side the entrenched forces of prejudice and a spurious patriotism. Hardie, unsuccessful at Preston, was elected for Merthyr: all the other I.L.P. candidates were at the bottom of the poll in their constituencies. Yet there was room for optimism, for over the country as a whole, the ten candidates put forward had averaged well over three and a half thousand votes each, the total poll in their support being 37,209. Of five other L.R.C. candidates, only Richard Bell of the Railway Servants was successful.

More immediately significant, however, were the results of the Taff Vale Judgment. In face of the threat of such a precedent, the ranks of labour closed: the affiliated membership of the L.R.C. more than doubled between 1901 and 1903, by which time it stood at 861,000. The Taff Vale Judgment was the factor which carried unions as hesitant as the Engineers and as reactionary as the Lancashire Textile Workers into the L.R.C.

Outstanding and encouraging by-election successes followed. In 1902, in face of Liberal confusion and procrastination, David Shackleton, the Secretary of the Darwen Weavers, was elected as M.P. for Clitheroe. In the following year, with considerable Liberal support, the well-known and respected Will Crooks converted a Conservative majority of 2,805 into a 'Labour and Progressive' majority of 3,299 in Woolwich, and *The Times* gave notice that the two major parties could no longer afford to ignore the 'Labour Movement'. Later in the year, in the context of the strong anti-Chamberlain feeling which surrounded the controversy over Tariff Reform, with its threats to ally Free Trade in food with Free Trade in labour, a by-election was held in the Barnard Castle constituency. Arthur Henderson defeated the Conservative candidate by 47 votes, but the real importance of his victory lay in the fact that the fight was a three-cornered one, with a Liberal actively opposing the L.R.C. candidate. The support of the Durham miners was probably the decisive factor in Henderson's favour, but the melancholy position of the Liberal at the bottom of the poll with 561 votes less than Henderson was perhaps the most ominous feature of the election.

The Barnard Castle by-election took place against a background of negotiation between Ramsay MacDonald and the Liberal Chief Whip, Herbert Gladstone. After protracted and veiled negotiations, during which both sides fought shy of any formal agreement, Liberal parties in constituencies in which L.R.C. candidates were proposed for the next general election were encouraged to give them a clear field. The broad agreement between L.R.C. and Liberals over Chamberlain's Tariff Reform policy and the clear demonstration in Barnard Castle that the Liberals could suffer at the hands of the L.R.C. underlined the desirability of such an attitude.

As the general election approached, the Labour movement

cleared its ground. A meeting at Caxton Hall, London, in February 1905, agreed that all sections of the movement would support L.R.C. candidates, and that the T.U.C. and the L.R.C. would not compete against each other in any constituency. Moreover, L.R.C. candidates were assured of further support which in some constituencies was to prove decisive: the Irish voters recognised that the Labour candidates were solidly in favour of Home Rule, and so gave their blessing to the L.R.C. The L.R.C.'s election manifesto placed the emphasis squarely on the issue of working-class representation and eschewed Socialist dogma.

The general election of 1906 was a triumph, and the agreement which Ramsay MacDonald had achieved with the Liberals was clearly vindicated: the movement had done what Keir Hardie had prescribed, and had learned how to win elections. In England and Wales only three L.R.C. candidates had been opposed by Liberals, and in at least one of those three constituencies, Wakefield, the behaviour of the local Liberal party had been widely regarded as a disgraceful betrayal. That year 29 L.R.C. candidates were returned, along with 24 'Lib.–Labs.' and miners, who still constituted a powerful independent body within the Labour movement. The outstanding success of the L.R.C. had been in Lancashire, where 13 of their 16 candidates were elected. The 29 L.R.C. members adopted the title of the Labour Party, and the miners affiliated with them in 1909. Keir Hardie became the first chairman of the Labour Party. The long prologue was over, and a new chapter in the history of British politics began.

CHAPTER EIGHT

The Turn of the Century: English Society 1900 – 1914

I was told that the Privileged and the People formed Two Nations.

DISRAELI, *Sybil*

AT half past six on the frosty evening of Monday, 21 January 1901, the longest reign in the history of the English monarchy came to an end in Osborne House on the Isle of Wight. Surrounded by her children and grandchildren – including the Kaiser Wilhelm of Germany, whose arm supported his grandmother during the last two and a half hours of her life – Queen Victoria died, more than sixty-three years after her accession. Outside, journalists stampeded to break the news to a waiting Empire, and soon preparations began for the military funeral which had been planned in great detail, and with no little enthusiasm, by the Queen herself. The funeral, decked in white rather than the traditional black which Victoria loathed on such occasions, and the entombment beside her beloved Albert at Windsor, seemed to mark the end of an epoch.

King Edward VII could not hope to match the remarkable prestige of his mother, although he was a popular figure at home and abroad. His devotion to the pleasures of life, such as high pheasants for breakfast, and the company of glamorous women from all ranks of society, may perhaps be accounted for by frustration as well as by natural inclination. He had waited a long time for the throne, and his mother – especially after Prince Albert's death – had scarcely concealed her lack of trust in her son. Although he developed a rather controversial stature as a leader of society, Edward was largely denied the experience of state affairs to which he felt entitled. By the time he came to the throne, such enthusiasm as he might once have possessed for the hard work of kingship – and there is the most meagre evidence that he was ever addicted to work – had evaporated. The new king made up for diminished royal importance in politics by the cultivation of his position as a colourful and popular social figurehead.

The role of the people generally in politics had been extended in 1884, although the franchise still had to be made genuinely universal. Labour, though, had embarked upon its political career, and in 1906 became a force to be reckoned with electorally.

Educational opportunities were further extended in 1902, but education remained a matter of grievous sectarian controversy, which in turn was reflected in political alignments. The growth of the educational system was one further factor in an expansion of the structure and power of local government. Civic universities developed during the decade, with the foundation of those at Liverpool, Manchester, Leeds, Sheffield and Bristol. The concern of the working-class movement for education was reflected in the creation of Ruskin College in 1899 and of the Workers' Educational Association in 1903, but they were not militant enough for the more radical Socialists, who created in 1909 the Labour College movement, which became a springboard for syndicalist ideas. Technical and scientific education still lagged behind the best continental universities, but in Cambridge J. J. Thomson was at work on research which was destined to burst open the boundaries of scientific knowledge and to transform human life.

The material resources of the nation in population continued to expand. The population of the United Kingdom in 1911 was 40·8 million, with a further 4·39 million in Ireland, compared with 91·7 million in the U.S.A., 64·9 million in Germany and 39·6 million in France. Over the decade since 1901, the population increased by over 4 million, in spite of the loss of some 2½ million by emigration. A declining birth-rate was more than matched by a death-rate the decline of which was particularly marked by a drastic fall in infant-mortality.

One of the features of the new century is the keeping of more accurate and scientific statistics – the raw material of the social and economic historian. The statistics indicate, for instance, that what had been regarded as a natural and permanent tendency of wealth to increase was the fruit of commercial optimism and self-satisfaction. In fact, after 1900, the increases in dividends and real wages slowed down and almost stopped. The development of productivity in such commodities as coal and steel was markedly slower than in the U.S.A. and Germany, and the alarm which Joseph Chamberlain felt about Britain's future as a world power is understandable. In spite of the advent of new techniques, their application was dilatory. Resources of power, in particular, were slowly exploited: a census of 1907, for example, indicates that for 6,984,976 employees (about half of the working population) only 10,955,009 h.p. was used.

Such decline and deficiency may be accounted for in part by the growth of foreign competitive industries guarded by stringent tariff barriers. More significant, however, was the over-confidence and plain lethargy of much British commercial practice. Productivity was hampered, too, by a defensive attitude on the part of trade unionists who believed that the amount of employment available was fixed as if by some economic law. It is interesting and somewhat alarming to notice that some of the ingredients of our contemporary economic problems existed over half a century ago.

After the disasters of late-Victorian years, agriculture enjoyed a limited revival, but its success depended upon having less land under cultivation, and there seemed no prospect that fields which had been abandoned would ever again come under the plough. Meanwhile, the drift of rural population into the towns continued.

The most remarkable social development during the first decade of the twentieth century was undoubtedly the revolution in transport. After a slow beginning, the electric tram now rapidly made its appearance in the most important British cities and towns – and for a time provincial centres like

Liverpool and Manchester outpaced London in the organisation of public transport. Apart from its technical interest, the tram is significant politically and socially. Municipal transport was usually financed by local government: as a public amenity publicly financed and administered, it was an important example of 'municipal Socialism'. Socially, improved transport provided a further stimulus to the development of suburban life: the people who rode in the trams were the ancestors of the 'commuters' of today. Suburban life came to absorb people other than the wealthy middle class, and gave rise to the creation of a 'lower middle class', living on the outskirts of towns, at some distance from their work.

Apart from public transport, the motor car was slowly making its impact upon everyday life. In 1909, Lloyd George instituted the Road Fund as a recognition of future needs. The future was foreshadowed also in the same year when Blériot flew across the Channel.

Other inventions of the period were destined to have far-reaching influences. The typewriter rapidly came into widespread use. The gramophone provided entertainment as well as preserving for future generations the voices of the past. The Italian Marconi pursued important experiments in wireless telegraphy in England, and vastly broadened the horizons of mankind. The resources of the wireless telegraph were dramatically demonstrated in 1910, when messages to a ship in the Atlantic led to the arrest of the escaping murderer Dr Crippen. Two years later, the 'unsinkable' liner *Titanic* struck an iceberg and foundered on her maiden voyage: 1,635 lives were lost, but many of the 732 who were saved owed their survival to distress signals transmitted by wireless telegraphy.

Amidst these exciting developments, the condition of the people of England still showed grievous shortcomings. The work of Charles Booth, who published his *Life and Labour of the People of London* in 1903, demonstrated prevailing poverty and misery amongst the labouring classes in London. In 1901, B. Seebohm Rowntree set a pattern for sociological enquiry with his *Poverty: a Study in Town Life*, which he followed in 1911 with *Unemployment*. Rowntree made a careful house-to-house survey of the city of York. Having researched into personal and family incomes, he proceeded to a computation of the minimum cost of the bare essentials of life. The results of his enquiries and calculations were startling: 27·84 per cent of the total population of York (and thus some 43·4 per cent of the wage-earners in the city) fell below what Rowntree calculated as the minimum subsistence level. On this basis, it has been estimated that over the country as a whole, 30 per cent of the population were existing below Rowntree's subsistence level, and, in Campbell-Bannerman's words, 'on the verge of hunger'.[1] The results of such conditions of life were daunting and depressing: 'Ignorance and apathy as much as ill-health were poverty's product; the slums were sloughs of wasted lives'.[2] One reflection of the physical effects of life in the slums may be found in recruiting for the Army: in 1899, 8,000 potential recruits out of 12,000 in Manchester were rejected as unfit, and in 1900 the Army reduced its minimum height for entry to five feet.

Here was a rich field for the sociologist and the reforming politician, and these were the basic problems which the great reforming administrations of Campbell-Bannerman and Asquith set out to solve. Notable among the social theorists was J. A. Hobson, a pioneer of sociology, who attacked unemployment in *The Social Problem* in 1901. H. G. Wells published *A Modern Utopia* in 1905, and in 1909 Beatrice Webb made a determined but unsuccessful attempt to provoke the reconstruction of the antiquated Poor Law. But the most practically significant of all the theorists was perhaps the greatest of English planners, William Beveridge: his study of *Unemployment* in 1909 was directly influential in the creation of Labour Exchanges.

Social comment was to be found in some of the literature of the period, particularly in the novels of Galsworthy and H. G. Wells. The appeal of the rather more rarefied atmosphere of the work of Henry James, George Moore and E. M. Forster was naturally more limited. In the theatre, the actor-manager tended to give place to the producer, the first great example of which was Harley Granville Barker. Galsworthy and Shaw (notably in *Major Barbara* in 1905) were the prominent social commentators amongst the playwrights. Elgar was now an established figure in musical composition; Ralph Vaughan Williams was at work, and was in no small measure responsible for the revival of interest in English folk-songs.

The most distinctive feature in the history of the Press during the decade was Harmsworth's purchase in 1908 of *The Times*, an event fraught with obvious dangers.

Apart from the prevailing poverty amongst the working class, the most interesting feature of the social history of the period was probably the extension of suburban middle-class life. There were two notable attempts at town-planning by industry, at Bournville and Port Sunlight. Along with the spread of suburbia went the extension of the English weekend and of a more leisurely attitude to life. Cycling increased as an enthusiasm, and scouting extolled the virtues of the open-air life. Dress became less formal: the lounge suit was now a recognised and even respectable mode of dress, whilst women achieved more freedom from the tyranny of the corset and the petticoat, and to cycling owed the comfortable innovation of bloomers.

Such was society in the first decade of the century: increasingly progressive, yet ripe for drastic reform. Soon it was to be thrown into the melting-pot of war.

CHAPTER NINE

The Zenith of Liberalism and the Beginnings of the Welfare State

The election of 1906 inaugurates a new era. . . . It will end, I think, in the break up of the Liberal Party.

BALFOUR to Francis Knollys[1]

THE general election of January 1906 returned 401 Liberals (including 24 Lib.–Labs.) 83 Irish Nationalists and 29 Labour members. Although Balfour's prediction was premature, for it was the World War which really broke up the Liberals, there was more than a grain of truth in his observation to Knollys. In the long-term context of politics, the 29 were destined to be of more significance than the 401. Meanwhile, the Conservatives were torn to shreds: they mustered only 132 seats, along with 25 Liberal Unionists. In general, therefore, the Government might expect to command a majority of 356. The composition of the House of Commons was, as Mr Colin Cross has shown in his excellent study,[2] overwhelmingly middle-class, whilst the total of 158 nonconformist M.P.s was unprecedented.

The administration which was swept into power in 1906 was an able one. Indeed, the least promising talent available to its leader, Sir Henry Campbell-Bannerman, appeared to be his own. He had been an undistinguished leader of the Liberals in opposition since 1899. He was sixty-nine when he became Prime Minister, and his political experience was merely routine: he had climbed the governmental ladder without reaching any height greater than the Secretaryship for War, which he had held under Gladstone and Rosebery. He was a millionaire, devoted to an ailing wife and to faith in the curative properties of the waters of Marienbad. Stolid, undramatic (save for occasional excursions into rhetoric like his attack on the use of 'methods of barbarism' during the Boer War), he was an appallingly bad speaker, tied to short-sighted reliance upon notes whose substance he did not always convey audibly to his audience.

So feeble was the impression made by Campbell-Bannerman in opposition that distinguished Liberals sought to insure against the liability of his leadership in office. Asquith, Grey and Haldane agreed in September 1905 in the 'Relugas Compact' (so called from the place in Scotland where Grey's fishing was interrupted by the negotiations) that none of them would take office unless Campbell-Bannerman went to the Lords, leaving Asquith as leader in the Commons. They realistically appreciated that a Government without them was inconceivable – the very factor which was their undoing when the Relugas Compact was put to the test by a Prime Minister considerably more astute than they had supposed.

For Campbell-Bannerman, far from withdrawing to the House of Lords to shelter from the strain of office, was transformed and invigorated by it, and survived the bitter blow of his wife's death as well as a heart attack of his own in 1906. In face of their leader's determination, first Asquith and then Grey and Haldane joined him rather than wreck the prospects of the new administration.

Some of the ground at least had been prepared for the new Prime Minister by his pleasant acquaintanceship at Marienbad during the summer of 1905 with Edward VII, whose judgement on this occasion turned out to be more astute than that of many of the professionals.

The House of Commons in 1906 was especially distinguished for parliamentary oratory. Among the new members were Philip Snowden and F. E. Smith, who were poles apart politically but both outstanding speakers, whilst Asquith, Lloyd George, Winston Churchill and, in his own style,

Balfour, were merely the most outstanding among many able orators. It was feared that Campbell-Bannerman might well be acted off the stage. But, in spite of his rather aristocratic style of living, he had always been a convinced and entirely genuine Radical. He gave expression to such convictions from the outset, and scornfully put the previous Government in its place: But they have lived for years on nothing but tactics, and now they have died of tactics'.[3] He astonished followers and foes alike by his caustic and brilliantly effective dismissal of Balfour: ... the Right Honourable Gentleman is like the Bourbons in the oft-quoted phrase – he has learned nothing and he has forgotten nothing – I say "Enough of this foolery". It might have answered very well in the last Parliament, but it is altogether out of place in this Parliament. The tone and temper of this Parliament will not permit it.'[4]

The Cabinet was mixed in complexion and remarkable in intellect. The Chancellor of the Exchequer was the brilliant Asquith, clearly destined for the Premiership, but quite prepared to wait patiently for it. The cultivated and sensitive Edward Grey became Foreign Secretary. He was fated to preside over the diplomatic journey to a holocaust as far removed as could be from the tranquillity of the natural beauty which he loved. He was much admired by his contemporaries: Asquith described him as 'sound, temperate and strong'.[5] Herbert Gladstone became Home Secretary and Chief Whip. Campbell-Bannerman was justifiably suspicious of Haldane, for 'Schopenhauer' was an arch-intriguer, so Haldane was denied the Woolsack which he coveted and was given the War Office. The aged Roman Catholic Lord Ripon led the Liberals in the House of Lords, whilst militant Radicalism was recruited in the persons of the dynamic Lloyd George and the working-class but increasingly reactionary John Burns (President of the Board of Trade and President of the Local Government Board respectively).

Campbell-Bannerman was prepared to give the talents of his ministers a free rein, and was disposed to listen to the promptings of his back-benchers and of the Labour M.P.s. He certainly reserved the right to intervene decisively in the House of

Commons in response to constructive proposals made during debates. The influence of the Labour M.P.s was reflected, for example, in the drastic reversal by the Trades Disputes Act (1906) of the Taff Vale Judgment, and in the inclusion of domestic servants within the terms of proposals for workmen's compensation in 1907.

Campbell-Bannerman lived to preside over significant measures of domestic reform. The efficiency of government through the House of Commons was stimulated by various procedural reforms initiated by Lewis Harcourt (First Commissioner of Works) and by the creation in 1907 of four standing committees. Two important steps in the development of the Law were taken with the creation of the Court of Criminal Appeal and the removal of the ancient piece of folklore which had prevented a widower from marrying his dead wife's sister. The progress of educational reform continued, in spite of renewed bitterness over sectarian issues and the wreckage by the House of Lords in 1906 of Birrell's bill which would have removed Nonconformist grievances. Progress was still channelled through Robert Morant, who remained as Secretary to the Board of Education: the expedient of 'pupil-teachers' was abandoned, and the last traces of 'payment by results' (a melancholy system for teacher and pupil alike) were swept away. Provision was made for the extension of places in secondary schools and for the development of State schools, and a notable piece of social legislation was the introduction of medical examinations in schools.

Most important reforms were also initiated by Haldane, who was a great success at the War Office. His reorganisation did much to prepare the Army in an imaginative fashion for the possibility of European war. A General Staff was created, and provision was made for a Regular Army, small but highly trained and ready for immediate service overseas. The British Expeditionary Force, as it was called, was 150,000 strong. Reserves were to be drawn from the creation of a volunteer Territorial Army, organised in counties and trained by Regular officers, whilst the Officer Training Corps was established in the Universities and in most Public Schools in the hope of providing 'officer material' in time of war – a hope which was duly fulfilled in 1914.

At the Admiralty, where Balfour had appointed Admiral Sir John Fisher as First Sea Lord in 1904, the traditional Liberal pacifism was thrown violently overboard. Able, passionately patriotic and wildly indiscreet, Fisher, who in 1907 produced a grandiose scheme to solve the problem of German naval competition by sinking the German Fleet without warning at Kiel, set about a large-scale programme of naval building. The first *Dreadnought* was ordered in 1905. Thereafter, old-style battleships were rendered obsolete by the new vessel, which was heavily armoured, heavily gunned, yet fast and manœuvrable. When the Germans responded to this challenge in 1908 by providing for the construction of four *Dreadnoughts* a year for the next three years, Fisher built up a public panic about the relative strengths of the two Fleets which found expression in the slogan 'We want eight and we won't wait!'

Another change of Liberal front was introduced when Campbell-Bannerman's administration began the delicate task of ushering the British Empire into the twentieth century. The task was a formidable one, for the familiar red shading in the atlases covered no less than a quarter of the map of the world, and the destinies of some 400 million people were at stake. The older children of the Empire were already feeling their feet and their coming-of-age was formally recognised in 1907 with the creation of 'Dominion Status' for Australia, New Zealand, Canada and Newfoundland. In South Africa the Government adopted the now familiar imperial practice of converting erstwhile foes into friends: after a Commission of Enquiry full internal self-government was granted to the Transvaal and Orange Free State and two years later, in 1909, the Union of South Africa (Transvaal, Orange Free State, Natal and Cape Colony) was created and accorded Dominion Status. Thus, in effect, the natives of South Africa were handed over to the tender mercies of the Boers, but given the aftermath of the Boer War and Liberal aversion to the repression of Imperial subjects, it is perhaps hard to condemn the Liberal government for its lack of foresight. Elsewhere in Africa, however, the

traditional expedient of the Chartered Company was still
employed.

The greatest problem, both in dimension and difficulty, was
India, where from 1900 to 1905 Lord Curzon had established
himself in the full panoply of vice-regal splendour. To him
India all too often meant simply the native princes. Shortly
before the great Liberal victory at the polls Lord Minto had
become Viceroy and had remained in office to deal as best he
could with the prickly personality of John Morley at the India
Office and the growing organisation of the Indian middle class
in the shape of the National Congress. Morley set out typically
with the rather paradoxical policy of compromising with the
Indian middle class whilst suppressing Indian nationalism! The
Secretary of State and Viceroy did, however, produce between
them a moderate yet significant measure of progress in the shape
of the Morley–Minto reforms, which alarmed the traditionalists
in the Indian Civil Service by providing for an Indian member
of the Cabinet to be nominated by the Viceroy, whilst the
Secretary of State was to choose two Indian members of the
Advisory Council. Both the Indian National and Provincial
Legislatures were expanded in scope, and elections on a limited
franchise were introduced, whilst communal representation was
granted to Moslems. The effect of the reforms was to remove a
great deal of the support for the extremists among the Indian
nationalists whilst strengthening the prestige of the moderates.
Strictly out of keeping, however, with the tenor of Liberal
reforms was the decision of King George V in 1911 to hold a
great Imperial durbar, which displayed many of the more
irritating symbols and pretensions of the old-style Imperial
régime in India. Perhaps the most important of the by-products
of the durbar was the removal of the Indian capital from Calcutta to the elegant New Delhi.

Yet in spite of the achievements of Campbell-Bannerman's
Government, many of its supporters were frustrated. Years
before, Rosebery had experienced the difficulties of a Liberal
House of Commons faced with a reactionary House of Lords,
whilst Joseph Chamberlain had inveighed against those 'who
toil not, neither do they spin'. Campbell-Bannerman, with an

overwhelming body of support in the Commons, was confronted
with an adverse majority of three to one in the Lords. Balfour
was blandly and utterly unscrupulous in his use of such a
splendid stumbling-block to reform, which in 1906 destroyed
two of the three major measures put forward, the Education
Bill and a Plural Voting Bill, designed to restrict to one vote
people qualified by property to vote in more than one constituency. In 1907 the Lords combatted the Radical battle-cry
of 'God gave the land for the people!' by rejecting outright a
Smallholdings Bill and a Scottish Land Bill. Campbell-
Bannerman declared that 'the British people must be master in
their own house' and proposed limiting the powers of the House
of Lords to a suspensory veto, by which they would be able to
delay for only two years a measure approved by the Commons.
The Prime Minister's proposal was embodied in a formal
Resolution of the Commons in July 1907. In November,
however, Campbell-Bannerman suffered a severe heart attack,
followed by another in February 1908, and the attack on the
Lords was not pressed home. But a pattern was established for
1911.

Campbell-Bannerman resigned on 1 April 1908 and died
three weeks later. His last meeting with Asquith, whom the
King had already designated as successor to the Premiership,
was poignant: 'You are the greatest gentleman I ever met. This
is not the last of me. We will meet again, Asquith.'[6]

Herbert Henry Asquith, the subject of an admirable recent
biography by Mr Roy Jenkins, had made his own way in the
world of politics to become the obvious heir of Campbell-
Bannerman. Born in Yorkshire into the middle class, he was
educated in London, where his headmaster perceptively commented 'simply place the ladder before him and up he went'.
Asquith likewise had a distinguished career at Balliol College,
Oxford, during the Mastership of the great Benjamin Jowett,
whose College was an institution where intellect and sense of
duty blended to produce national leaders in various walks of life.

For a decade Asquith made slow progress at the Bar and
supplemented his earnings by occasional political journalism.
He became Liberal M.P. for East Fife in 1886 and political

success greatly enhanced his legal career. His great promise was recognised by Gladstone, who made Asquith Home Secretary in 1892: Sir Philip Magnus[7] regards him as the best Home Secretary of the century. He returned to the Bar in 1895 and soon became fashionable and successful, establishing something of a precedent by pleading as a Privy Councillor before ordinary judges. His first wife, Helen Melland, died in 1891 and his career was further stimulated by his marriage in 1894 to Margot Tennant, a leading figure in the fashionable society of the time.

He was already the obvious successor to Campbell-Bannerman, but he was a patient man, and was the first of the makers of the Relugas Compact to recognise the need to compromise with the leader. As Campbell-Bannerman's Chancellor of the Exchequer he grappled with the problems of promoting social services without unduly increasing taxation – the perennial problem of twentieth-century Chancellors. He rounded off his work as Chancellor by presenting his own Budget after becoming Prime Minister in 1908.

Asquith found it necessary to travel to Biarritz to receive his appointment from King Edward VII and even had to dissuade the King from his fatuous and essentially impertinent notion that the new Cabinet might receive their seals of office in the Hotel Crillon in Paris.

Perhaps Asquith's greatest strength as Prime Minister was his willingness, once he had chosen his ministers, to delegate responsibility to them and to give them his full support. Thus full rein was given to reforming zeal, notably that of his two most interesting appointments, Lloyd George as Chancellor of the Exchequer and Winston Churchill as President of the Board of Trade. Lloyd George was already a highly controversial figure, in both public and private life: not merely for his appearance was he nicknamed the 'goat', and he is supposed to have remarked that it is preferable to be in the dark with a foolish virgin than in the light with a wise one! His attachment to Welsh Nonconformity was political rather than religious, and F. E. Smith's characteristically uncharitable taunt about 'whited sepulchres' was particularly apt.

Lloyd George and Churchill provided the great stimulus to social reform and the energy necessary to implement their own ambitious schemes; and they restored some of the Government's impetus when it was in danger of becoming becalmed by the end of 1908.

Already, however, Asquith's administration had achieved important social reforms. Asquith himself, in his Budget of 1908, had instituted Old Age Pensions, from which five million citizens benefited immediately. Single persons over seventy, provided their annual income did not exceed £26, received 5s a week; married couples received 7s 6d weekly so long as their joint income was not more than £39 a year. Persons convicted of a serious crime within the preceding five years were disqualified. The scheme was financed from taxation, in spite of which Asquith produced a Budget surplus of £5 million. Small though the pensions were, they may be said to have inaugurated a new era in social legislation.

Attempts during 1908 to settle the problems of denominational education were frustrated by the House of Lords, as was a Licensing Bill which, in the traditions of Liberal Nonconformity, would have closed one third of the public houses in the country within fourteen years. Three measures during the year were more successful: Churchill was responsible for creating the Port of London Authority; the eight hour day for miners was established by law, and the 'Children's Charter', largely the brainchild of Herbert Samuel (Under-Secretary at the Home Office) protected children from social abuses and created Juvenile Courts to deal with child offenders without the panoply or the open publicity of the adult courts.

Such achievements were hardly sufficient to outweigh the loss of popularity suffered by the Government when 1908 produced an unemployment rate of 10 per cent. The opposition was quick to blame Free Trade: the electors were quick to defeat the Government in six by-elections. The dynamic energies of Lloyd George and Churchill (himself the victim of the electors in a by-election in Manchester necessitated by his appointment as President of the Board of Trade but re-elected for Dundee) did much to revive the Government's fortunes.

Susceptible to the influence of Radical thinkers like Sidney and
Beatrice Webb, and social planners like William Beveridge
Churchill created the first Labour Exchanges, which not merely
fulfilled an important function in finding work, but were
essential to the administration of any scheme of unemployment
insurance, on which Churchill had set his heart.

It was Lloyd George, however, who fought the most decisive
social battle, and by using the Budget as his weapon, struck the
sparks which kindled into flame the constitutional crisis which
had been smouldering for a generation. Whether he deliberately
sought a showdown with the House of Lords is – and is likely to
remain – a matter of historical speculation, but once the fight
was on nobody enjoyed it more.

In presenting his first Budget in 1909, Lloyd George was confronted with the necessity of finding additional revenue to the
tune of some £16 million to pay for the *Dreadnought* programme
and for Old Age Pensions. Moreover, more money would be
needed for Lloyd George's own scheme for health insurance and
Churchill's plans for unemployment insurance. Nor was the
Chancellor blind to the advantages of presenting a large-scale
programme of social reform to an electorate whose support for
the Government was cooling rapidly.

It is ironical that the epoch-making Budget of 1909 was
presented in one of Lloyd George's worst parliamentary
speeches. The Chancellor was tired, and his presentation did
less than justice to his material, which left no doubt about
which section of the community was to pay the price of social
reform. Surtax was levied at the rate of sixpence in the pound
on the amount by which incomes over £5000 a year exceeded
£3000, and Death Duties were increased by one third. Income
Tax was increased from 1s to 1s 2d in the pound but was made
more equitable by the creation of relief on earned income and
allowances for dependent children. The duty on tobacco went
up by ½d an ounce, whilst that on whisky rocketed by 6d a
bottle. Duties imposed on motor cars and petrol were to be
devoted to the Road Fund, and a levy of 1s in the pound on
mineral royalties was to be devoted to miners' welfare. A failure
in the Budget was a low-rate capital gains tax on land, whose

W. E. Gladstone

Third Marquess of Salisbury

Lord Randolph Churchill

A. J. Balfour

The two nations at the turn of the century
above: *Poor children enjoying a Salvation Army picnic*
below: *A lady of leisure cultivates her mind*

Joseph Chamberlain, polling day 1906
James Keir Hardie waiting to address the crowd during the Tailors' Strike, 1912

Edwardian leisure

above: *La jeunesse dorée*   below: *Old women's outing*

Battle of Pilckem Ridge. Stretcher-bearers carrying a wounded man through the mud, 1 August 1917

The surrender of the German fleet to Admiral Beatty off the coast of Scotland, 1918. Destroyers entering the harbour.

H. H. Asquith

Lloyd George speaking at a dinner organized by the British Zionist Federation, 1931

General Joffre, President Poincaré, King George V, General Foch and Sir Douglas Haig: Beauquesne, 12 August 1918

*Ramsay MacDonald at
Paddington, 1923*

*Stanley Baldwin with his
wife and daughter
at Henley, 1924*

*The General Strike, 1926,
changing the guard at the
London Omnibus Depot*

*Man out of work in Wigan
in the Depression of the
1930s*

'He took water and washed his hands . . .'

'All behind you, Winston'

A Heinkel III over the Thames, 7 September 1940

Churchill touring Hitler's ruined Chancellery in Berlin after the surrender

Soldiers helping to clear debris after a bomb had fallen near Bank tube station, January 1941

A night out in London, 1941

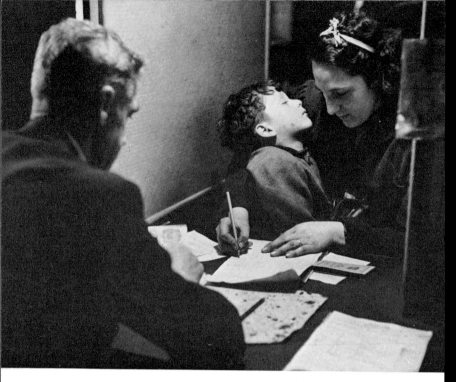

The state tried to help people made homeless by the bombing. The war hastened the emergence of the state as the greater provider – but there were more forms to be filled in now.

Bevin, Attlee and Morrison celebrate the victory of the Labour Party, 1945, at the Victoria Hall, Leicester Square

Housing: pre-1914 (above) *and between the wars*

Roehampton: a modern housing estate

Kitchens, old and new: a contrast in style

Aldermaston Mar 1965

The 'Mods' on the march, Brighton, 1965

revenue never covered the cost of its collection; it was abandoned in 1919, but it was an ominous measure, for the land had to be valued for the purposes of taxation: what further depredations might follow?

The Budget aroused surprisingly little popular excitement, but it was fiercely contested in Parliament. In no less than seventy days of debate the opposition concentrated upon the land taxes, and especially the threat to property implied in the need to register land. Lord Curzon led the Tory extremists, whilst Chamberlain urged the Lords to break a tradition established over two and a half centuries by rejecting the Budget.

At this stage, for the first time, Lloyd George spoke out on the constitutional issue, first in a speech in Limehouse, where he declared that 'A fully equipped Duke costs as much to keep as two *Dreadnoughts* . . . is just as great a terror and lasts longer'.[8] He warmed to his theme in a splendid speech in Newcastle, where he put the issue bluntly: 'It will be asked why five hundred ordinary men, chosen accidentally from among the unemployed, should override the judgement – the deliberate judgement – of millions of people.'

The representatives of those millions in the House of Commons passed the Budget on 4 November 1909. Conservative peers emerged from the ancestral gloom of their estates into the light of Westminster, supporting a motion to reject the Budget until it had been taken to the country in a general election: although moved by Lansdowne, the motion was drafted by Balfour, and it was carried by 350 votes to 75. The Lords were posturing as the defenders of the social order; yet they were taking a step contrary to 250 years of constitutional history, and by so doing were claiming a position of equality with the Commons, entitling them to reject a Commons vote of supply. Asquith was entirely right when he claimed that in such a position he was the true traditionalist, opposing the House of Lords in its 'usurpation of the rights of the Commons'.

The King agreed to a dissolution of Parliament, stipulating that the ensuing general election was on the issue of the Budget, and that another general election would be necessary before any

E

amendment of the constitutional powers of the House of Lords. The poll in the general election of December 1909 was the highest recorded to that date. It resulted in the loss of 104 government seats. The clear majority of Liberals over Conservatives declined dramatically to a mere two: the Government leaned upon 82 Irish Nationalists and 40 Labour members.

The new Parliament in 1910 was confronted with two major issues, the Budget itself and the reform of the House of Lords. The Conservatives were bitter: encouraged by the number of seats they had won, they were nevertheless frustrated that they had not won more. The price which the Irish were threatening to extort for their support of the Government was the virtual destruction of the powers of the Lords in order to make way for a Home Rule Bill: they agreed on an order of priorities by which a Resolution on the reform of the Lords was to precede the Finance Bill, which would then be followed by actual legislation to reform the powers of the Lords. In April 1910 Lloyd George's Budget duly became law.

Meanwhile, both the party leaders were playing a cool game. Balfour, fearful of inheriting fiscal chaos, avoided the defeat of the Government, whilst Asquith, pressed for details on what he would do to the Lords, produced a catch-phrase which stuck to him for the remainder of his career – 'Wait and see!'

Asquith's colleagues were by no means unanimous on what their attitude to the Lords should be: should the composition of the House be reformed (by the creation, for example, of life-peerages), or should the composition remain the same but the powers of the Upper House be modified? Asquith's patiently mild proposals were broadly similar to those put forward by Campbell-Bannerman some years previously: after a preamble on the reform of the composition of the House of Lords at some future date, it was proposed that the Lords should lose all power to delay money Bills; that their suspensive veto should apply for only two years; and that the maximum life of any Parliament should be reduced from seven to five years.

Edward VII was clearly perturbed by the implications of such proposals, but recent historians have doubted whether he could have greatly influenced affairs. However, his personal destiny did seriously disrupt constitutional history at this stage, for in May 1910 he died. Asquith received the news as he was homeward bound aboard the yacht *Enchantress* from Gibraltar: 'I remember well that the first sight that met my eyes in the twilight before dawn was Halley's comet blazing in the sky . . . I felt bewildered and indeed stunned'.[9]

Ministers were naturally reluctant to embarrass the new monarch, who was painstakingly conscientious in his constitutional attitude, though not over-perceptive in matters of political subtlety. A constitutional conference was accordingly held to seek a compromise. Lloyd George, who was essentially a pragmatist in politics (and it has been pertinently asked whether there is a difference between 'pragmatism' and 'opportunism' in politics) was seeking a coalition government, and was even prepared to negotiate on tariff reform. But the conference broke down on the likelihood that the House of Lords would reject Irish Home Rule, an issue pregnant with tragic significance for the near future.

Asquith was now determined on a decisive general election, which should be fought specifically upon the issue of reforming the powers of the House of Lords. King George V wanted two general elections, one on reform and then a second on any amendments which might arise. But Asquith stood firm, and the King's Secretary, Francis Knollys, performed a public service by deceiving the King about Balfour's attitude. Had George V known that Balfour was in fact prepared to form an alternative government, an ugly political situation might well have developed. Asquith threatened to resign and the King, knowing of no possible alternative, agreed to create if necessary enough Liberal peers to defeat the serried ranks of Conservatism in the House of Lords.

The general election took place in December 1910, to the embarrassment of the Labour Party, since the Osborne Judgment of the same year in the House of Lords had decreed that it was illegal for any part of trade union funds to be used for party political purposes. In spite of the removal of most of their campaign funds, however, Labour M.P.s returned marginally stronger in the new House of Commons. Numerous seats in fact changed hands, but in the overall result there was very little alteration in the balance of power, the Liberals having lost three seats and the Conservatives one. The reform of the House of Lords was naturally the most important factor in the campaign, but Home Rule and Tariffs were still very lively issues. Balfour, indeed, lost influential support within his party by proposing a referendum on tariffs.

The Parliament Bill, embodying the reforms earlier set out by Asquith, was subjected to numerous amendments by the Lords during June 1911, until Asquith informed Lansdowne and Balfour on 20 July that the King had agreed to create Liberal peers if necessary – and indeed Asquith had himself drawn up a list of several hundred potential Liberal peers which is still fascinating today. Faced with defeat, the extremist Conservatives in the Commons, led by F. E. Smith and Lord Hugh Cecil, created a disgraceful disturbance on 24 July and drowned Asquith's attempts to speak: the temperature within the House matched that of the hottest summer for seventy years.

In the closing stages of the struggle the Conservatives divided themselves into the 'hedgers', who were prepared to compromise rather than face what Curzon (who so greatly modified his earlier opposition as to vote for the Bill) regarded as the 'dilution' of the aristocracy; and the 'ditchers' (led by the octogenarian Lord Halsbury), prepared to fight to the last. The Bill passed the House of Lords by 131 votes to 114, 37 Conservative peers voting with the Government.

The conflict between the 'hedgers' and the 'ditchers' brought to a head dissatisfaction with Balfour's leadership. Characteristically, when faced with a 'Balfour must go!' campaign, Balfour resigned in November 1911, well knowing that no obvious successor existed. Balanced between the tariff reformers' claims for Austen Chamberlain and the traditionalist stand for Walter Long, the Conservatives compromised and chose Andrew Bonar Law, an able politician, but an iceberg of a man, lacking any redeeming vice and ruthlessly pursuing political power under the inspiration of the Canadian newspaper tycoon Max Aitken (Lord Beaverbrook). Lloyd George

has an anecdote which throws into relief the human charac-
teristics of Bonar Law (and of Lloyd George!):

> I remember before the War, while we were both staying at
> Cannes, driving with him on a sunny day along the road to
> the golf course at Cagnes. The sky was cloudless and the sea
> was blue as only the Mediterranean can be, while on our
> left was the white-topped amphitheatre of the Maritime
> Alps. I turned to Bonar and asked him if he did not think it
> beautiful. 'I don't care much for scenery', he replied in his
> rather toneless voice. The night before I had been to a per-
> formance of one of Mozart's operas – I think it was 'Il
> Seraglio'. It was the first time I had heard it and I was struck
> with its exquisite beauty. I mentioned the fact to Bonar
> Law, but his reaction to my enthusiasm was only to say 'I
> don't care much for music'. As we approached the golf
> course we saw some extremely pretty women also on the
> way to play golf. I called Bonar Law's attention to them.
> 'Women don't attract me' was his laconic answer. 'Will
> you tell me,' I said, exasperated at all this disdain for the
> attractions of life, 'what it is you do care for? Scenery –
> music – women – none of them has any meaning for you.
> What is it that you do like?' 'I like bridge', was the reply.[10]

The parliamentary reform of 1911 was rounded off by the
provision of payment of £400 a year for M.P.s, an important
step forward in progress towards democracy.

The resolution of the constitutional conflict, however, was
far from marking the end of the Government's troubles. Indeed,
even before the catastrophe of war broke upon it in 1914,
Asquith's administration was hovering on the brink of disaster.
Its principal worries concerned mounting industrial unrest, the
militant campaign for women's suffrage, and an increasingly
dangerous situation in Ireland which was callously exploited by
the Conservative opposition.

The root of industrial and social unrest was a persistent fall
in real wages, masked from the superficial viewer by the
contemporary boom in investment. As Miss Barbara Tuchman
has pointed out, the era before the Great War was only a
Golden Age to the few, and was in any case rosily tinted by
retrospective nostalgia after the war. In fact, in the decade or so
before the war, whilst the gross value of unearned income in

Britain rose by 55 per cent, retail prices rose by one-third and the actual value of wages fell by 13 per cent. Poverty struck hard at its victims: the Poor Law was harsh in the extreme, and the workhouse test was imposed on candidates for poor relief.

In 1910 and 1911 there was general unrest in industry and numerous strikes were marked by violence, the most grievous examples occurring in Liverpool, where two men were killed and some 200 injured. Trade union membership numbered over four million by 1914, and the creation of the Triple Alliance of Miners, Railwaymen and Transport Workers marked a significant trend in joint action. This was the great period of the syndicalist argument: militant trade union leaders like Tom Mann and A. J. Cook foresaw the achievement of the Socialist millenium by the kind of concerted industrial action calculated to paralyse the nation's economy and government and overthrow Parliament. Threats of this sort transformed Winston Churchill's attitude to social problems and led to his adoption of those reactionary postures towards strikers for which he later became notorious. The leaders of the Labour Party were far from unanimous in their attitude: idealists like Philip Snowden refused to compromise; Ramsay MacDonald was more of a realist and recognised the Labour movement's need of the Liberals to revoke the Osborne Judgment.

The legislative answers put forward by the Liberals to these problems undoubtedly laid the foundations of the Welfare State. Lloyd George and Churchill were responsible for two great pioneering schemes of social insurance.

In 1908 Lloyd George visited Germany, saw the Bismarckian social legislation in operation and was converted. The conversion of the Treasury was a more difficult matter, but in 1911 a scheme of health insurance was created to cover all workers earning less than £160 a year. The great civil servant Robert Morant was transferred from the Board of Education to implement the Government's plans. A total of 14 million people were covered at a cost to the employee of 4d a week, with 3d from the employer and 2d from the State. Free medical treatment was provided, with a maximum sickness benefit of 10s a week for up to six months.

In the Labour Exchanges, Churchill had already at his disposal the machinery for operating a measure of unemployment insurance which covered $2\frac{1}{4}$ million workers (without providing for their families). Employee, employer and State were each to contribute $2\frac{1}{2}d$ a week to provide an unemployment benefit of $7s$ a week for a maximum period of fifteen weeks in any year. To claim benefit, the worker had to 'sign on' at the Labour Exchange. Both schemes were subjected to a vigorous and varied campaign of opposition from vested interests ranging from the doctors to employers of domestic servants. Nevertheless, the methods of financing welfare on the basis of schemes of insurance rather than from direct taxation set an important precedent for future social legislation.

The two great measures of insurance, and other valuable reforms such as the Mines Act of 1911, the Shops Act of 1912 and the reversal of the Osborne Judgment by the Trade Union Act of 1913 (which decreed that trade unionists not wishing to contribute to the political levy should contract out) failed to stem the tide of industrial unrest, which continued right up to the outbreak of war. Moreover, a good deal of Lloyd George's vitality was sapped by his involvement in a scandal over shares in the Marconi Company – an involvement which Asquith rather disingenuously encouraged Lloyd George and others to attempt to conceal from the House of Commons. Churchill's energies, meanwhile, after a brief spell at the Home Office (1910–11) had been transferred to the congenial environment of the Admiralty, where he set to work with characteristic enthusiasm to create a Naval Staff and to meet the challenge of the German Fleet programme by measures which, after a struggle with Lloyd George, raised the Naval estimates by 1914 to the record level of £54 million. He defined the race in naval armaments between Britain and Germany in concise terms: 'It is expansion to them; it is existence to us'.

During this same period, the Government was harassed by the militant campaign for women's suffrage. The campaign was some forty years old and had been conducted in an eminently rational and respectable fashion by the National Union of Women's Suffrage Societies, whose members were usually called suffragists. In 1903, however, the Women's Social and Political Union (whose members were called suffragettes) was created, and the emphasis of at least this part of the campaign was transformed. Under the inspiration of the redoubtable Mrs Emmeline Pankhurst, who exhibited some of the more alarming tendencies of the natural dictator, the suffragettes undertook a programme of increasing violence which, though it certainly drew attention to the campaign, scarcely served to paint a convincing picture of the rational capabilities of potential women voters. Pillar-boxes were exploded, windows smashed, women chained themselves to railings and, at worst, set fire to buildings. In perhaps the most bizarre episode of all, Emily Davison threw herself in front of the King's horse at the Derby and was killed, providing the occasion for a funeral which combined the moving with the maudlin in confusing proportions.

It is doubtful to this day what useful service was rendered to the movement by the suffragettes, who certainly undid much of the good work so painstakingly achieved by the suffragists. Lloyd George, for example, was by no means unsympathetic to the cause of women's suffrage, but he was understandably put off by the excesses of the Pankhursts and their followers.

Asquith, liberal-minded in so many ways, was opposed to women's suffrage, and was duly rewarded with some of the most scathing attacks by the militants upon 'The Right Dishonourable Two-Faced Asquith'. The social implications of a proposal in 1909 for complete adult suffrage alarmed him, and so did the political implications of Conservative advantage in a proposal to enfranchise women householders. He stood firm in face of violent attacks both inside and outside the House of Commons, and stood by the actions of the Home Secretary, Reginald McKenna, who refused to be blackmailed by suffragette prisoners and ordered their forcible feeding when they went on hunger strike. Since the pacifist and sentimentalist George Lansbury castigated Asquith as 'the man who tortured innocent women', it is interesting to speculate concerning epithets which might have been applied to the Prime Minister had he let the hunger strikers die of starvation.

In fact, the enfranchisement of women in Britain was one of the positive results of the First World War, during which, in the best traditions of the suffragists, they seized their unprecedented opportunity for demonstrating their responsible contribution to national life to a degree which could no longer be gainsaid.

A Welsh grievance was met by the measure for the disestablishment of the Welsh Church, which was attacked by Conservatives. The operation of the reform was delayed by the outbreak of war. But Ireland was not to be so easily pacified, and provided extremist and unscrupulous elements within the Conservative Party with the opportunity of carrying their opposition to the very brink of civil war.

Liberal hopes for Ireland were centred in the work of the gentle, cultivated Augustine Birrell as Chief Secretary for Ireland from 1907 to 1916. Conservative opposition was focused on the understandable intransigence of Ulster, where religious bigotry was mobilised in the service of political opposition to any union with the Catholic south, union which the Ulstermen feared would be the concomitant of the Liberal policy of Home Rule for Ireland.

At the head of the Ulstermen was Edward Carson, a distinguished lawyer and a most dangerous political *prima donna*. He became Chairman of the Ulster Unionist Council in 1910 and in a theatrical gesture subscribed on his knees to the Ulster Covenant: nearly half a million Ulstermen followed him in swearing to use all means necessary to oppose Home Rule. A force of Ulster Volunteers, 100,000 strong, was created, ready to impose a 'provisional government.'

When the Government put forward its Home Rule Bill in 1912 the problem of Ulster was ignored, and concessions to Ulster were made too late to avert an ugly constitutional crisis. The House of Lords did not hesitate to use the suspensive veto which the 1911 Parliament Act had left in its hands, whilst some of the Conservatives were flirting dangerously with the idea of winning over the Monarch to a *coup d'état*. Conservative leaders did not hestitate openly to advocate unconstitutional action: Bonar Law wrote to the King's Secretary in terms of civil war; F. E. Smith said that from the moment Home Rule became law 'we hold ourselves absolved

E2

from all allegiance to this government'; and Carson had clearly cast himself in the role of dictator of Ulster.

On 9 March 1914 Asquith moved the third reading of the Home Rule Bill, which now included the provision that the voters of any Irish county could opt out of Home Rule for a period of six years. The provision failed to mollify Ulster, for in fact there were only four of the counties whose voters were likely to take advantage of it. Carson in any case objected to the time-limit on staying out. The Irish Nationalists naturally opposed any watering-down of the measure.

A crisis was foreshadowed when Lord Willoughby de Broke proposed that the House of Lords should refuse to renew the Army Act. The Government, fearing serious disorders in Ulster, took steps to reinforce the army units there, and precipitated a mutiny at the Curragh. There were demands that officers whose homes were in Ulster should not be sent to join the garrisons there. Such a demand was not unreasonable, but attempts to meet it were bungled by the Commander-in-Chief in Ireland, General Paget. An open announcement was made that officers whose homes were in Ulster could 'disappear' if ordered north; and other officers who were opposed to military action in Ulster were invited to resign. Brigadier Gough and fifty-seven out of seventy officers of the Third Cavalry Brigade were prepared to be dismissed if they were not given a written assurance that they would not be ordered into Ulster.

The mutiny at the Curragh was settled by negotiations in which the Secretary for War, J. E. B. Seely, went so far as to accede to Gough's demands. Thus the Government was unable to take military action in Ulster. Seely was dismissed, and Asquith personally took charge of the War Office. Some of the leaders of the mutiny, notably Sir Henry Wilson (Director of Military Operations), who had been actively intriguing behind the scenes, escaped punishment. With the Government effectively disarmed, the Ulster Volunteers were armed by gun-runners.

Such was the situation – Ulster armed (largely with German equipment) and Ireland taking up arms – when the tragic threat of civil war in Ireland was swallowed up in the greater tragedy of international war in Europe.

CHAPTER TEN

'Swimmers into Cleanness Leaping': The Idealism of War

Now, God be thanked Who has matched us with His hour,
And caught our youth, and wakened us from sleeping,
With hand made sure, clear eye, and sharpened power,
To turn, as swimmers into cleanness leaping,
Glad from a world grown old and cold and weary,
Leave the sick hearts that honour would not move,
And half-men, and their dirty songs and dreary,
And all the little emptiness of love.

RUPERT BROOKE, *Peace*

RUPERT BROOKE was the poet of the idealism of the early days of the war, before high sentiment was soured by bitter experience which killed one in every twenty-eight citizens of France, one in every thirty-two Germans, one in every fifty-seven Britons, and one Russian in every one hundred and seven. Brooke has been much criticised and even ridiculed by later generations; it should be remembered that he lived in an age when patriotism was not quite the rather ambiguous virtue which it is today, and that he died before the most appalling dividends of the war of attrition were paid. His feelings were mirrored in France, and certainly in Germany, where Thomas Mann could write of 'a purification, a liberation, an enormous hope. The victory of Germany will be the victory of soul over numbers'.[1]

Popular enthusiasm in Britain once the war had begun was manifested in a willingness to serve. In the week ending 5 September 1914, 175,000 men were enlisted, and by the end of September, a total of 750,000. Up to March 1916, a total of 2½ million came forward, all by voluntary recruitment, although the moral compulsion of Kitchener's pointing finger from the recruiting posters – 'Your Country Needs YOU' – was supplemented by the emotional blackmail of white feathers distributed by charming and eminently respectable ladies, and by the iniquitous oratory of Horatio Bottomley, whose purse waxed as fat as his person.

Popular enthusiasm and poetic idealism were scarcely reflected, however, in the attitude of the Government. The Cabinet was divided and hesitant, confused in part by the ambiguity of Grey's foreign policy, which reflected his whole personality: a colleague complained that Grey's 'avoidance of the point-blank amounted to method'. By August 1914, however, Grey, in what John Morley called his 'strenuous simplicity', was in favour of war, along with Churchill and his 'daemonic energy' (the phrase again is Morley's).[2] Lloyd George's attitude was crucial and characteristically ambivalent: it was thought that he might lead a peace party in an attempt to outbid Churchill for the succession to the Liberal leadership. Asquith himself, combining the War Office with the Premiership, was calm as ever but apparently indecisive.

The real issue in the early stages was how far Britain was committed to France. There was certainly no formal commitment, but informal negotiations had gone so far that to deny commitment was to raise once more in Europe the spectre of 'perfidious Albion'.

British foreign policy since the turn of the century had avoided involvement in the network of alliances which grew up in Europe. Germany and Austria were firmly allied, and Italy was prepared to join them so long as she did not have to fight Britain. France and Russia were also bound together. These alliances meant that even small-scale crises carried with them the threat of general war. Bismarck's forecast that one day the great European war would come 'over some damned silly thing in the Balkans' was all too amply fulfilled when at the end of June 1914 the Archduke Franz Ferdinand, heir to the Austro-Hungarian Empire, was murdered in Sarajevo by a Bosnian, Gavrilo Princip, trained in Serbia. Austria's determination to humiliate Serbia brought Russia to the defence of her fellow-Slavs and provoked the inexorable mobilisation of the great alliances.

Although Britain had not formally entered into any European alliance, she had settled her outstanding differences with both France and Russia. In 1904, Balfour's government brought about the Anglo-French Entente, which settled colonial rivalries between the two countries, especially in Egypt and Morocco. France recognised British predominance in Egypt, whilst Britain left the French a free hand in Morocco. In 1907, in spite of the unpopularity in Britain of the Tsarist régime, a convention was made with Russia. Disputes in Persia were settled by the recognition of a Russian 'sphere of influence' in the north and a British sphere in the south, with a neutral zone in between. Crises provoked by the Kaiser in North Africa showed where British interests lay. In 1905, the Kaiser made an inflammatory anti-French speech at Tangier. The resulting crisis was the subject of a conference at Algeciras in the following year, when Britain stood by France. In 1911, the German gunboat *Panther* provoked further international alarm at Agadir, and Lloyd George issued a stern warning to the Kaiser in an outspoken public speech.

Moral commitment derived from military and naval 'conversations' which began as early as 1907. Great impetus to joint military planning stemmed from the friendship which developed between General Henry Wilson and General Foch. Wilson was energetic, enthusiastic and efficient. In 1910, he became Director of Military Operations and by March 1911, he had formulated detailed plans for the mobilisation and embarkation of the British Expeditionary Force in the event of war. By July 1911, his consultations with the French amounted to a virtual commitment to the concentration of the entire B.E.F. at Maubeuge in the event of a German attack.

In 1912, the Royal Navy was no less morally committed by an agreement that the Royal Navy would guard the Channel and the North Sea, leaving the French to look after the Mediterranean. Grey, in discussion with Cambon, was still hedging over 'commitment', and the reader of Grey's winsome

Miles
0   50   100

Limit of German Advance 1914
Front Line July 1918
(after German offensive)

HOLLAND

Rhine

ANTWERP

BELGIUM

Schelde

Passchendaele

BRUSSELS   Louvain

Ypres

Calais   Lille   Liege

Messines   Meuse

Neuve

Chapelle   Mons

Bethune   Loos

Vimy   Sambre

Arras

Bapaume

GERMANY

Abbeville   Somme

Amiens   Le Cateau

Oise   Aisne   Verdun

Seine   Marne   Meuse

PARIS   Seine

F   R   A   N   C   E

III. The Western Front, 1914–18

memoirs, *Twenty-Five Years*, is at times hard put to appreciate the extent to which Britain was involved, as she certainly fully was in the eyes of the French.

Hesitation over commitment was largely swept away by the German violation of Belgian neutrality – an article of faith in British foreign policy – and procrastination remained only over the timing of a British ultimatum to Germany, which was at last delivered on 4 August. As the ministers waited in the twilight for the ultimatum to expire, Grey uttered his now-famous words of melancholy and moving prophecy: 'The lamps are going out all over Europe; we shall not see them lit again in our lifetime'.

The invasion of Belgium was essential to German strategy. France must be speedily removed from the war so that German troops could be massed against the Russian threat from the east. That the Germans would succeed in the west was taken for granted by the Kaiser, who told his departing troops: 'You will be home before the leaves have fallen from the trees'.

The blue-print of German strategy in the west was the Schlieffen Plan. Sweeping through Belgium, 'brushing the Channel' with its right wing, the German army was then to swing south and eastwards to envelop the French and take Paris. The schedule was planned with characteristic thoroughness. Von Moltke, Schlieffen's successor and military heir as Chief of the German General Staff, planned that Liège was to be open to the armies by the twelfth day from mobilisation, and Paris was to be in German hands by the thirty-ninth day.

The Germans 'justified' the invasion of Belgium by various fabricated pretexts, but they miscalculated the attitude of the Belgians themselves. Schlieffen had expected that the limit of Belgian resistance would be that the Belgian army of six notoriously undisciplined divisions might line the roads in silent protest as the German armies marched through. But King Albert, who had succeeded his unpopular uncle, Leopold II, in 1909, thought differently. After ensuring that no premature Belgian action compromised his country's neutrality, he organised resistance. His attitude captured the spirit of his subjects: 'If we are to be crushed let us be crushed gloriously', declared Bassompierre, Under-Secretary of the Belgian Foreign Office. The Belgian army was inefficient, and its heavy guns – ordered from Krupp of Essen – had understandably failed to arrive, but it prepared to defend its great frontier fortresses.

At Liège the Germans were held up for a fortnight before their enormous siege artillery succeeded in breaking the garrison's resistance. In fact Moltke's schedule had allowed for possible delay, and he was only two days late at Liège. However, as Mrs Tuchman cogently argues, 'What Belgium gave the Allies that mattered was neither two weeks nor two days but a cause and an example'.[3]

Violation of the treaty of perpetual neutrality – 'a scrap of paper' as the German Chancellor, Bethmann-Hollweg called it – was one thing; calculated atrocity was another. German troops, especially those of von Kluck's 1st Army, shot and pillaged their way through Belgium in a systematic attempt to terrorise the civil population into submission. Shooting of hostages and razing of villages became commonplace. Centuries of history went up in flames as they burned the university and the irreplaceable library of Louvain. European and American attitudes hardened as governments and peoples envisaged civilisation in peril from the Huns – the choice of word was, significantly, the Kaiser's own.

French strategy was incapable of meeting the Schlieffen Plan in its original form. For years the prevailing dictum in the French military academies had been 'the attack'. French troops were concentrated for a thrust through Alsace-Lorraine and the Ardennes. News of concentration of German troops on the German right wing delighted the French planners. 'So much the better', they reiterated, since the German centre must be inevitably weakened. In fact, the French seriously underestimated German numbers, because they never conceived that the Germans might use reserve units in their front line, with the same names as their regular units.

Predictably, too, the French were in trouble with the political and ecclesiastical affiliations of some of their generals. Fortunately, such attachments were no part of the stock-in-trade of their generalissimo, 'Papa' Joffre. Joffre had many short-comings as a commander, and he slaughtered scape-goats among his field-commanders literally by the dozen, but he was imperturbable. His coolness and lack of nerves rescued France from a disaster for which Joffre himself undeniably shared the responsibility. Awaiting his turn for greatness was General Foch, the great French military theorist, whilst the most impressive general among the French in the early stages was General Galliéni, recalled from retirement to command the defence of Paris.

Meanwhile, at the other end of Europe, the Russian steam-roller was preparing to exercise its mesmeric influence over the broad European battleground. Totally mobilised, the Russian army would number no less than a terrifying $6\frac{1}{2}$ million men. But numbers were not everything: supplies and logistics were chaotic, thanks to the indolence of the Minister of War, Sukhomlinov, a man resolutely opposed to 'vicious innovation'. Doubts on the quality of the Russian army (though the sheer courage of its individual members was not in question) had already been cast during the Russo-Japanese War. The British observer, Ian Hamilton, reported from Manchuria on the Russian army's 'poor intelligence; disregard of cover; disregard of secrecy and swiftness; lack of dash; lack of initiative and lack of good generalship'.[4]

Russian offensive strategy was complicated by geography: any attack into East Prussia must divide around the Masurian Lakes. In fact, Russian troops were committed to battle too soon, although by their actions the Russians helped the French. Moltke withdrew two corps from the Western Front to bolster his forces in East Prussia, whilst replacing the unreliable commander Prittwitz by the formidable combination of Luden-dorff, who had distinguished himself already in the west, and Hindenburg, who was called out of retirement.

A confused battle situation developed, the outcome of which during the last days of August 1914 was the decisive German victory at Tannenberg. The doctrine of envelopment was triumphantly put into action: 92,000 Russian prisoners were taken, and they lost over 30,000 dead and missing. Only the unsurpassed incompetence of their Austrian allies prevented the Germans from following up their victory. In a disastrous campaign in Galicia which culminated in the battle of Lemberg, the Austrians lost 250,000 casualties and 100,000 prisoners.

British involvement in the war continued to be marked by hesitation. Doubts over whether Britain should participate at all had been resolved by the violation of Belgian neutrality and the rejection by Germany of the British ultimatum, but hesitation ensued over whether the whole of the B.E.F. – or indeed any part of it – should be sent across the Channel. There was in some minds an apparently genuine fear that Britain might be invaded. The hesitation of Kitchener, who had been appointed to the War Office, was more soundly based. Unconvinced by Wilson's plans, Kitchener strove to preserve the B.E.F. as the nucleus of an army which he intended should number no less then seventy divisions after three years. His contemporaries, blinded by the vision of a war 'all over by Christmas', were incredulous, but Kitchener was in good company, for Joffre and even Moltke himself also foresaw a long war.

Kitchener's anxiety led him to press for Amiens rather than Maubeuge as the point of concentration for the B.E.F., but he had to give way, and the British troops duly concentrated at Maubeuge, ready for action on the left of the French line. If the soldiers were ready, their commander was somewhat less than willing. Sir John French – to whom Kitchener was later to apply the epithet 'calamitous' – was proud, unwilling to co-operate with the allies whose language defeated him, and unwilling to commit his troops to battle. His own post-war account of events, *1914*, casts a confusing cloud of evasion and half-truth over events. Perhaps the most remarkable feature of French's career is that he kept his command for so long, especially since the commander of his 1st Corps, Douglas Haig, cavalryman, posturer and friend of kings, was already casting doubts on his commander's capacity, whilst implying a much higher regard for his own.

British troops first went into action on 22 August, in a cavalry clash with German *Uhlans* at Soignies, on the road to Mons. The fate of Captain Hornby, in command of the British detachment, is sadly a prototype for the tragedy of so many heroes during the next four years. Awarded the D.S.O. for his victory, he was killed within weeks. The clash at Soignies served as a curtain-raiser to the battle of Mons.

Across the sixty-foot-wide canal at Mons on 23 August 70,000 men of the B.E.F. confronted the 160,000 men and 600 guns of von Kluck's 1st Army. The B.E.F. was better prepared than British forces usually are at the beginning of wars, but was weak in equipment for sieges or trench-warfare. A new element in warfare was demonstrated by the 63 aircraft of the Royal Flying Corps, but there existed a serious deficiency in another new ingredient. There were only 24 machine-guns per division (a proportion which Haig pronounced adequate). There were only 80 motor vehicles in the entire British army.

At Mons the Germans encountered the quality of the B.E.F., whose musketry was so good that the enemy thought they were being fired on by machine-guns – a psychological compensation for the lack of the real thing. The strategic withdrawal which followed Mons and preserved the B.E.F. covered 200 miles in 13 days. Sir John French was conspicuous by the efficiency with which his General Headquarters were always withdrawn well behind the front line – sometimes as far as 40 miles. In spite of the pleas of Lanrezac, French was of little assistance to the French 5th Army on his right, but the B.E.F. was a vital factor in preventing the envelopment which the Germans so desired and the French commanders so feared. The action of the retreating B.E.F.'s 2nd Corps at Le Cateau, for example, certainly helped to stave off a possible envelopment.

At first sight, the Schlieffen Plan appeared to be working well: the French, though fighting stubborn rearguard actions, were in retreat, and their great counter-thrust through the Ardennes failed. In the early days of September, as the ominous anniversary of the French débâcle at Sedan in 1870 approached, both sides were aware of its portent. Yet all was not entirely well with the German strategy. The melancholy Moltke[5] had not the nerve to maintain the tremendous concentration on his right wing. He withdrew two corps to the east, and

Belgian resistance necessitated the detachment of two of von Kluck's reserve corps to invest Antwerp. Von Kluck himself more than made up for Moltke's lack of confidence, and as a result he very considerably overestimated the deterioration of French morale.

Joffre remained unruffled in face of disaster. He planned to retreat to the Seine, if necessary sacrificing Paris, from which the government had already withdrawn to Bordeaux. Von Kluck now glimpsed an opportunity to envelope the entire left of the French armies. Departing from the set text of the Schlieffen Plan, he turned leftwards, brushing Paris on the east instead of taking the city, and crossed the river Marne. Galliéni in Paris saw his chance: 'They offer us their flank', cried his delighted staff officers. Moltke realised the danger in time. He called von Kluck back behind the Marne and halted the German advance exactly one month after the invasion of Belgium.

Joffre decided to fight on the Marne. Staggering the Germans by their resilience, the French troops – reinforced by soldiers conveyed in commandeered Parisian taxi-cabs – drove the Germans back to the River Aisne.

Then, as the front became stabilised and began to solidify into the dismal lines of parallel trenches, the race was on for the Channel ports. Flanders became the scene of the B.E.F.'s efforts. Though some historians have questioned the importance of the battle of Mons, none doubts that a decisive factor in the struggle for the Channel coast was the creation of a British salient at Ypres. The battle to hold that salient was absolutely vital to the security of the Channel ports. The battle known as 'First Ypres' lasted from 12 October until 11 November, and virtually destroyed the original B.E.F. But the Ypres salient held.

The war of attrition began. From Switzerland to the Channel, the lines of trenches put a premium on defence. Victory now would go to the side which first wore down the other. Paris was saved; the Channel ports were saved; but Germany was in possession of territory whose mineral and industrial potential was a crucial contribution to her resources for a prolonged conflict. Paradoxically, the near-success of the Schlieffen Plan had provided the resources to meet the long drawn-out war which the Schlieffen Plan had been designed to avert.

At sea, the Royal Navy was experiencing mixed fortunes. Before war broke out Churchill at the Admiralty had with his customary foresight and enthusiasm moved the Fleet, which was on manœuvres, to its battle-stations. The newly appointed commander, Admiral Jellicoe,[6] was nervous, understandably so in view of the lack of defences at Scapa Flow. But the Germans lacked any positive naval plan. German merchantmen were soon withdrawn from the high seas, and a bigger immediate problem for Britain was the danger of a serious dispute with the U.S.A. if the Royal Navy pressed too far its imposition of a blockade on German ports. However, the realisation that the war would be a lengthy one presented American merchants with the attractive prospect of Allied dependence upon American supplies – and the increased trade with the Allies more than compensated for lost trade with Germany.

An early naval opportunity was lost when the German battle-cruiser *Goeben* was allowed to enter the Black Sea and blackmail the Turks into an alliance with Germany. The task of the British vessels in the Mediterranean at the time was complicated by the Government's delay in sending their ultimatum to Germany, and by an understandable assumption that the *Goeben* would sail westwards against the French troop convoys from North Africa, rather than into the Dardanelles. All the same, had the *Goeben* been pursued into the Straits, the hand of the Turks might not have been forced. When Turkey entered the war in November 1914, a new and complicating dimension was added to the conflict.

Further north there was more success. On 28 August, in a confused action in the Heligoland Bight, three German cruisers were sunk. In the Indian Ocean, the German surface-raider *Emden* was hunted and destroyed.

Then, on 3 November 1914, came a setback when Admiral von Spee's Pacific Squadron sank two British cruisers at Coronel (off the coast of Chile). This reverse was avenged in the following month, when von Spee's ships steamed into the arms of Admiral Sturdee's force, which was coaling in the Falkland Islands. Four German cruisers were sunk, although the Royal Navy's guns were an ominously long time in administering the *coup de grâce*.

Perhaps the most striking event in the early stages of the war at sea occurred in May 1915, when a German U-boat sank the Cunard liner *Lusitania*. Among the 1,198 people drowned were 128 Americans. President Wilson's protest was strongly enough worded to lead to the curtailing of U-boat activity until in desperation unrestricted U-boat warfare was undertaken in 1917.

The futility of frontal attack against entrenched positions was amply demonstrated on the Western Front in the Spring of 1915. In March, the German line was broken at Neuve Chapelle, but it proved impossible to gain any real advantage In the prolonged battle of Second Ypres (22 April–25 May) gas was used for the first time. Three weeks of fighting at Aubers Ridge proved fruitless.

The need to reintroduce movement into a war which threatened to degenerate into stalemate prompted one of the most imaginative concepts of the war, which unhappily was wrecked in its execution. Churchill became the strong advocate of a campaign to force the Dardanelles and drive Turkey out of the war. An attempt in March 1915 to carry out the plan using the Fleet alone failed when it was discovered that the Turkish minefields had not been completely cleared. A naval engagement was transformed into a combined operation for which totally inadequate plans had been made. British and Australian troops attacked Gallipoli on 25 April: the Turks held them down to their beachhead. It became clear that, without substantial reinforcements, no progress would be made. Winston Churchill became the scapegoat for the failure of the enterprise.

Lack of progress in the conduct of the war gave rise to increasing criticism of a lack of governmental initiative. Two particular issues focused discontent and led to political upheaval. The lack of any overall direction of war supplies ed to a shortage of shells, which the Press – especially that part of the Press controlled by Northcliffe – whipped up into a national scandal. There was also a serious dispute at the Admiralty, which was probably an event of more significance to the future of the Government.[7] On 15 May, the First Sea Lord, the irascible Sir John Fisher, resigned: meanwhile Churchill was under severe attack as the supposed architect of the disaster in the Dardanelles. Under such pressure, the Government broke. On 17 May 1915, a coalition was formed. Lloyd George was created Minister of Munitions; McKenna was Chancellor of the Exchequer; Bonar Law came into the cabinet, taking over at the Colonial Office; Churchill was relegated from the Admiralty to the Duchy of Lancaster, and was succeeded as First Lord by Balfour; Labour came into the Government in the person of Arthur Henderson, who became President of the Board of Education.

CHAPTER ELEVEN

The Fall of Asquith and the Wizardry of Lloyd George

We are out; it can only be a question of time now when we shall have to leave Downing Street.

MARGOT ASQUITH, on the news of Lloyd George's appointment to the War Office, June 1916[1]

COALITIONS are notoriously restless affairs, and the Government formed in 1915 was no exception. It was hardly to be expected that those conflicting principles, such as Free Trade and Protection, which had been so divisive in peacetime could be easily reconciled, even under the pressures of war. The Cabinet met more frequently; but Asquith was never a natural dictator, and his lack of direction became increasingly obvious, especially when contrasted with the dynamism of Lloyd George at the Ministry of Munitions, where he turned the serious shortage of machine-guns, for example, into a grand total of 240,000 by the end of the war.

With such increased efficiency, there developed increasing governmental interference. Powers of requisition were introduced and extended. There was naturally some resentment at the manipulation of industrial labour, but the Government's initiative carried compensation in some improvement of factory conditions. Factory canteens were introduced, and a development full of social and political importance for the future was a remarkable increase in the employment of women. The worst aspect of the great increase in production was that its urgency outstripped control over exorbitant profits: some industrialists undeniably waxed fat on the carnage of war.

The economic consequences of war were already reflected in governmental policy. McKenna introduced a budget in September 1915 which raised the level of income tax to 3s 6d in the pound. Even more significantly, there began the erosion of the sacred Liberal principle of Free Trade: the 'McKenna Duties' imposed a 33⅓ per cent duty on such luxuries as cars, clocks and watches. However little intention McKenna may have had of introducing Protection, the effect of the duties was certainly protectionist: above all, a precedent had been set.

No matter what expedients might be introduced, by the end of the war the bill was enormous: the national debt rose from £625 million in 1914 to £7809 million in 1918, and by 1919 the purchasing power of the pound was only about one third of its pre-war level.

Meanwhile, the most pressing moral and political issue which confronted Asquith and his colleagues was the inadequacy of voluntary recruiting, which became ominous as the appalling cost in lives of the war of attrition made itself felt. The strategic necessity of an attack on the Western Front produced the battle of Loos, which began on 25 September. Within a week, the British army had suffered some 60,000 casualties. Conscription found strong and vociferous advocates, including Lloyd George: it was strenuously opposed by many Liberals, by their Irish Nationalist supporters, and by the Labour Party and the trade unions.

The hopes of breaking the deadlock on the Western Front were meanwhile dying a miserable death on the beaches of the Dardanelles. On 6 August a promising landing at Suvla Bay was turned into a fiasco by the indolence of General Stopford: the landing was unopposed, but Stopford remained at ease on a battleship and refused to advance until artillery was landed. The troops enjoyed sea bathing in the meantime. When at length the advance was ordered, the sand-dunes and hills were found bristling with Turkish machine-gunners, who had taken full advantage of the opportunity to move into positions which had been totally undefended on 6 August. Only small beachheads were left as a memorial to a campaign which had promised so much: their future provided a continuing and fruitful source of political and military disagreement. Increasingly it came to be realised that the geography of the Dardanelles was winning: as Mr A. J. P. Taylor remarks, 'The campaign could have succeeded only if it had been fought somewhere else'.[2]

In November 1915 Kitchener went out to Gallipoli to see for himself, and the politicians took advantage of his absence to reorganise the direction of the war. On 11 November, a new War Council was created, consisting of Asquith, Balfour, Lloyd George, Bonar Law and McKenna. Kitchener and Churchill were both left out, and Churchill characteristically resigned and went off to command a battalion on the Western Front. French was at last sacked from his command and replaced by Haig. The General Staff, which Kitchener had suspended, was re-created, and General Robertson became Chief of the Imperial General Staff. 'Wullie' Robertson had risen from the ranks, and was wont to silence criticism or suggestion from civilians with a terse 'I've 'eard different'. He laid down terms for his appointment which curtailed Kitchener's powers. All this had happened in Kitchener's absence, and had evaded the painful necessity of a direct confrontation with the great legend, of whom many of the leading politicians obviously stood in awe: 'We avoid by this method of procedure', Asquith pointed out to Lloyd George, 'the immediate supersession of K. as War Minister, while attaining the same result.'[3]

There was some relief at the end of 1915, though it was little enough. The Gallipoli campaign was finally brought to an end on the nights of 18–19 and 20–21 December by a brilliantly executed withdrawal of troops from Suvla Bay and Anzac Beach. Forces remained in direct contact with the Turks in the Middle East and in Salonika. In the Middle East, Lawrence of Arabia was soon to pursue his extraordinary career. More orthodox methods, however, were conspicuously unsuccessful at this stage: a campaign in Mesopotamia failed in the early months of 1916, and General Townshend surrendered at Kut with 10,000 men.

By early 1916, the problem of conscription could no longer

be shelved. A great offensive was planned for the spring which would undoubtedly consume large numbers of men. Various half-measures failed, such as the 'Derby Scheme' – that there should be voluntary attestation, with married volunteers being called upon only if there were insufficient single volunteers. There followed a plan to conscript only unmarried men. Finally, the Military Service Bill was introduced in January 1916. Asquith was faced with threats of resignation and with the opposition of the National Executive of the Labour Party, whom he appeased only with great difficulty. All compromise measures having failed, general compulsion was introduced on 3 May. And amidst all these difficulties, the Government was grappling with the problem of Ireland.*

On 31 May 1916 the first and last great set-piece naval battle of the war was fought. The battle of Jutland brought the two great fleets into contact. It exposed serious weaknesses in the construction of the British battle-cruisers, and demonstrated the skill of German naval gunnery. The outcome of the battle is still a matter of controversy. The Germans claim Jutland as a victory because they sank more ships than they lost. On the other hand, the German High Seas Fleet was never in action again: Jutland was sufficient to drive German naval strategy under water, and from then on they relied upon their U-boats.

Within a week Kitchener was dead, drowned when the cruiser *Hampshire*, which was taking him to Russia, was sunk. A great figurehead was removed. Horatio Bottomley celebrated the event with the most nauseating of his many maudlin effusions: Kitchener, he proclaimed, was not dead, just 'lent to God'. Kitchener, though he was certainly more than just the 'great poster' of Margot Asquith's contemptuous phrase, had become something of an embarrassment to the Government. But Asquith was no less embarrassed by the task of finding a successor, and it was three weeks before Lloyd George moved from Munitions to the War Office, with Lord Derby as his Under-Secretary. Asquith may perhaps not have realised that he was digging his own political grave; his wife was sure of it.

* See Chapter Fifteen.

The great offensive of the spring of 1916 was compromised before it started by the German onslaught on 21 February on Verdun. The great fortress was the key in the east to Paris, and was defended with great tenacity and appalling loss of life on both sides by the French under General Pétain. 'Ils ne passeront pas', he proclaimed, and his boast was justified: the corpses of his soldiers, by the hundred thousand, are their own most eloquent memorial.

On 1 July the British attack was launched on the Somme. Plans for a joint offensive were thwarted by the need to call French troops to Verdun. The Somme was to be Haig's ideal of the massive set-piece attack: heavy artillery bombardment was to precede an infantry breakthrough, making a gap through which the cavalry were to pour into open country beyond. Haig resolved to call off the attack if it became bogged down, but his conviction of 'divine help' (he fancied himself in intimate contact with the Almighty as well as with the Royal Family) got the better of him. Within 24 hours, 20,000 British troops were dead and twice as many wounded. By the time the offensive finally petered out, the British army had sustained 400,000 casualties. Recent historians have sought to find some justification for Haig's generalship, but his handling of the Somme offensive is difficult to excuse. The Somme dealt the death-blow to idealistic and romantic attitudes to war as far as Britain was concerned.

Even when the opportunity arose for a more imaginative tactic on the battlefield, it was wasted. By August 1916 the first tanks were ready – the fruits of Churchill's activity and contempt for protocol at the Admiralty. The old-style cavalrymen like Haig regarded tanks as not quite gentlemanly, and certainly not deserving of the honour of a special campaign. So, on 15 September 1916, as Churchill sadly records, 'This priceless conception was revealed to the Germans for the mere petty purpose of taking a few ruined villages.'

Meanwhile, Asquith added to his own and his Government's difficulties by agreeing to Commissions of Inquiry into the failures in Gallipoli and Mesopotamia. Attacks on the Prime Minister, in the Northcliffe Press and elsewhere, were becoming less and less inhibited, sometimes to the point of cruelty and libel, whilst members of the Government were increasingly distrustful of each other. On 13 November Lord Lansdowne produced a memorandum (later to be widely published) which argued with ruthless logic for negotiated peace.

Amongst other suggestions was one, eagerly seized upon by Lloyd George, that the conduct of the war should be put into the hands of a small War Committee, independent of the Cabinet and not necessarily including the Prime Minister. Negotiations took place (with Max Aitken hard at work behind the scenes) between Lloyd George, Bonar Law and Carson. Carson had once more come into prominence as a leader of the most violent attacks on Asquith and even as a potential rival to Bonar Law.

By late November, Press criticisms of Asquith had grown yet more intense, and there was an open lobby in support of Lloyd George. Bonar Law was hesitant, but under Aitken's influence he supported Lloyd George, partly at least in order to preserve himself from the threat of Carson.

Many Unionists were trying to force Lloyd George into the open in the confident hope that he would be defeated. They therefore urged Asquith to resign so that Lloyd George would fail to form a government and Asquith would be reinstated in a stronger position. When Bonar Law saw Asquith he did not put the issue so fully, and merely left the Prime Minister with the impression that the Unionists were demanding his resignation. So Asquith decided to come to terms with Lloyd George, but Northcliffe saw Lloyd George on the same night.

On the following day, Monday 4 December, *The Times* published an insulting leader, based upon an inspired leak, which made it appear that all power had been handed over to Lloyd George. Asquith understandably assumed that Lloyd George was the source, but it seems that Geoffrey Dawson, the editor, had acted independently of Northcliffe. Dawson's source seems to have been Carson; presumably Carson's source was Lloyd George.

Asquith at this stage revoked his agreement with Lloyd George, although the Prime Minister's position was now far from strong. Christopher Addison had informed Lloyd George that he already had the support of forty-nine Liberal M.P.s and would get at least eighty more if he formed a government. It is clear that even Asquith's most loyal supporter, Grey, was far from pressing him to stay on. Weary himself, he may well have felt a public desire for a change of leadership.[4]

Asquith obtained the King's leave to re-form his Government, and refused to create the War Committee on the lines which Lloyd George had laid down. Moreover, he firmly refused to replace Balfour at the Admiralty by Carson. The issue was now clearly a conflict for power between Asquith and Lloyd George.

At this stage, one of Asquith's most important supporters ratted on him. Balfour backed Lloyd George's demand that Balfour himself should be replaced by Carson! This was the decisive change of front. Not for the first time, Balfour's instinct of self-preservation coincided with an important decision on policy; he could hardly expect to be left out in the cold when Lloyd George formed a government.

Asquith, faced now with the prospect of trying to carry on without Lloyd George or Bonar Law – and hence without the support of the Unionists – resigned at 7 pm on 5 December 1916. The King, as he was bound to do, sent for Bonar Law. Asquith's attitude was now decisive: he refused to serve under Bonar Law. At a conference at Buckingham Palace at which Balfour's views were very influential, a formula was agreed upon: if Asquith could not be persuaded to serve under Bonar Law, Lloyd George was to form a government. Asquith persisted in his refusal. Asquith was understandably bitter about the part played by the Press in bringing about his downfall. It is clear to the historian that, although the Press hounded Asquith unmercifully, it was Balfour's betrayal which was decisive. Asquith was warmly treated by his followers, and was confirmed as Leader of the Liberal Party. Although this was a personal encouragement to Asquith, it created a virtually impossible political situation.

Lloyd George's government was strongly Unionist in its complexion. His War Cabinet consisted of himself, with

Curzon, Milner, Bonar Law and Henderson. Carson indeed went to the Admiralty, where he thoroughly bungled the job, and Balfour, with a pistol to his head, as he charmingly but inconvincingly phrased it, became Foreign Secretary. No Liberal member of Asquith's Cabinet survived in that of Lloyd George except Lloyd George himself.

CHAPTER TWELVE

The Weariness of War

What passing bells for these who die as cattle?
Only the monstrous anger of the guns . . .

WILFRED OWEN, *Anthem for Doomed Youth*

JUST as Rupert Brooke epitomised the idealism of the early days of the war, so Wilfred Owen, the greatest of all the war poets, expressed the increasing feeling of doom and bitterness in verse which half a century after the event still has the power to stab the reader to the heart. Some of his greatest poems have now been used with heart-rending effect in Benjamin Britten's masterpiece, the *War Requiem*.

The war dragged on, and distant thoughts of 'all over by Christmas' had faded like an empty dream. Now men looked reluctantly into the future and glimpsed no real hope of peace: in 1918 Smuts could see no prospect of peace before 1920. Trench warfare, the war of attrition, eroded men's spirits and slew 'half the seed of Europe, one by one'. Those sensitive men who survived have painted all too harrowing a picture of life on the Western Front. Robert Graves's *Good-bye To All That*, for example, shatters the illusions of any reader who still thinks of war as a glamorous pastime.

Pressures for a negotiated peace increased from the left wing as well as from Lord Lansdowne, who late in 1917 published in the *Daily Telegraph* the arguments which he had earlier set before the Cabinet. *The Times*, zealously patriotic, refused to publish Lansdowne's letter. Such sympathy as there was for Lansdowne and his point of view was muted: in public he was harshly criticised and bitterly attacked.

Living conditions at home, and social cohesion generally, deteriorated as the war went on. Working-class discontent found expression in demands for wage increases, and the first manifestation of revolution in Russia in March 1917 naturally had a stimulating effect upon the left wing in British politics. Early in 1918 there was a largely unjustified panic over food supplies which led to such stockpiling by housewives that the Government had to introduce rationing. Organised labour, resentful by 1918 of the excessive profits made by some manufacturers, slipped from Lloyd George's grasp; there were serious strikes, which Churchill (who became Minister of Munitions in July 1917) characteristically countered by threatening to conscript the strikers into the army.

Pressures for reform culminated in the extension of the franchise in June 1918. The reform of the electoral law broadly speaking created masculine democracy by introducing the principle that every adult male – except for peers, aliens, lunatics and recently convicted criminals – had the right to vote. A small number of citizens qualified for two votes. Those, for example, who were university graduates (with a vote in their own and in their university constituency) or were in business in another constituency from that of their private dwelling house, were allowed the double vote. Women were given the vote for the first time, but not yet on an equal footing with men. Women had the vote so long as they were over thirty, and were householders or the wives of householders.

Meanwhile the war had still to be fought. At least it could be said that governmental direction of the war had been transformed and revivified by the appointment of Lloyd George as Prime Minister in December 1916. 'It was', writes Mr A. J. P. Taylor, 'a revolution, British-style'.[1]

Lloyd George, as has already been seen, fits into no accepted British political pattern. He was uninterested in party, and fundamentally concerned with power, and its application. The basis of his own power was his popularity and the coercive effect which it exercised over his fellow-politicians. He is in every sense an untypical Prime Minister: he established round himself an imposing private staff, and he ran his War

F

Cabinet, which met almost every day, as an instrument of his will. This is not to say that he was a dictator: whilst he found his way comparatively clear in domestic politics, even he could not ride roughshod over the bulwarks of vested interest and traditionalist prejudice in the Admiralty and the War Office. It is one of the interesting points of contrast between the two great wars that whereas in the second, Churchill – an old soldier – could and would dismiss generals with an abandon that sometimes went beyond the bounds of justice, Lloyd George a quarter of a century earlier was saddled for far too long with the dead weight of Robertson and Haig.

Lloyd George galvanised the Government into action. He created new departments of state for such things as shipping and food as temporary additions to the normal peacetime basis of administration. Usually he chose professional men as the heads of these departments: many were great successes, but perhaps the most conspicuous failure was that of Neville Chamberlain as Director of National Service. The Government grappled with the wartime problem of rising prices. They were not entirely successful, but at least they established a principle: that of assessing prices on a basis of 'cost plus' a reasonable return.

Hamstrung in his direct relations with his generals, Lloyd George sought to by-pass them and present them with a strategical *fait accompli* by direct negotiations with the Allies. In 1917, in conference at Rome, he failed to persuade his Allies to launch a general offensive in Italy. On the Western Front, however, Joffre had been dismissed. His successor, Nivelle, had the inevitable 'plan' – this time for the attractive proposition of a victory to be won in forty-eight hours. Lloyd George, along with other optimists, hoped for great things from Nivelle, and on 26 February 1917 all British troops in France were placed under his supreme command.

Nivelle's plan was wrecked by delays: by the time he was ready to attack, the Germans had anticipated Nivelle's advance and had withdrawn behind the entrenched and heavily fortified Hindenburg Line. Before Nivelle's offensive collapsed, Canadian troops had added a lustrous, though appallingly

costly, page to their annals by the capture of Vimy Ridge
(9–14 April). Nivelle's failure brought his troops to the brink
of mutiny. Nivelle himself was dismissed in May 1917 and
replaced by Pétain, the hero of Verdun, but something of a
natural pessimist into the bargain – a trait which was to prove
even more decisive for his country's destinies in 1940.

Meanwhile, Lloyd George was attempting to consolidate
the role of the Empire, whose members were already committed
in the various theatres of war. In March 1917 there was a
meeting of the Imperial War Cabinet, to membership of which
India was now admitted, albeit in a rather half-hearted fashion.
There is, as many historians have noted, no little irony in
Lloyd George's following in the footsteps of Joseph Chamberlain.
He failed, however, in his attempt to achieve a united executive action; but the meeting did lead to the permanent admis-
sion to the British War Cabinet of Jan Christiaan Smuts,
one-time Boer enemy, and henceforth staunch member of the
Imperial family.

Perhaps the turning-point of the whole war came in April
1917, when the U.S.A. declared war, as a direct consequence
of the German resumption of unrestricted U-boat warfare in
January. The German action, however, threatened to prove
decisive as the Germans strove to starve Britain into submission before the United States could intervene. By April,
no less than a quarter of British merchantmen were sunk, and
the nation's stocks of grain provided supplies for only six
weeks. Lloyd George acted typically and went behind the
backs of his official Admiralty advisers to obtain expert opinion
that was less prejudiced, for the Admiralty maintained that
hopes of introducing a convoy system were doomed to failure
because the merchant skippers would not be able to keep
station! Lloyd George overruled the admirals, and the convoy
system was introduced, with spectacular success. In July 1917,
Carson, who had proved more of a liability than an asset as
First Lord of the Admiralty, was 'promoted' to the War
Cabinet, where he was equally ineffective and from which he
resigned in December 1917 in sympathy with Jellicoe, who was
dismissed. Eric Geddes became First Lord of the Admiralty

in July 1917. Thus Lloyd George had dealt ruthlessly with obstruction at the Admiralty; he was less successful in his desire to be rid of Haig.

The collapse of Nivelle's offensive had freed Haig from his reluctant dependence upon French command, and he was able to make plans for another offensive of his own. His apologists have maintained that his offensive in Flanders was the result of a desperate appeal from Pétain for action to bolster the tottering edifice of French morale, but this is questionable. In any case, the politicians were at first sceptical of Haig's confident plan for a great attack in Flanders: breaking out from the Ypres salient, the British, Haig claimed, would reach the Channel coast and roll up the Germans. Haig's confidence at last proved too much for the doubters, and they allowed themselves to be convinced.

The third battle of Ypres, usually known as the battle of Passchendaele, began on 31 July 1917. Once more Haig had persuaded himself and others that he would call off his offensive if it were held; once again he failed to do so. The battle, fought in a sea of mud which rendered stretcher-bearers, let alone tanks, immobile, lasted for three months. The total advance covered four miles and the ground gained was all evacuated in face of the German offensive of March 1918. The cost is disputed but certainly at least 200,000 men died and possibly as many as 324,000. This was the most pointless British battle of the war to date. Haig used the poppies of Flanders to commemorate the dead after the war. They were employed with a poignant simplicity by one of the poets of the war:

> In Flanders fields the poppies blow
> Between the crosses, row on row,
> That mark our place; and in the sky
> The larks, still bravely singing, fly
> Scarce heard amid the guns below.[2]

On 20 November 1917, tanks demonstrated what they might do: 381 of them broke the German line at Cambrai. But such was the imagination of the General Staff that no plans had been made to follow up a breakthrough, and the ground won was lost within ten days. By this time, in any case, the situation elsewhere was complex and threatening: in October, the Italians had been severely defeated at Caporetto, and in November the Bolshevik seizure of power in Russia led to the collapse of the Entente.

Only in the Middle East was there better news. Baghdad was captured, and in December 1917, Allenby's cavalry took Jerusalem. British success in the area had led Balfour to make on 8 November his historic declaration that Britain envisaged Palestine as a national home for the Jewish people.

In February 1918, Lloyd George had at least part of his way and Robertson was sacked and replaced as Chief of the Imperial General Staff by Sir Henry Wilson. Lloyd George naturally assumed that Haig would go too, but self-preservation got the better of his sense of loyalty, and he ratted on Robertson and clung to his command.

In the spring of 1918 Ludendorff staked all on a surprise attack to achieve a decisive breakthrough before the American troops became established in Europe. Haig ignored his intelligence reports of what to expect, and on 21 March the Germans struck at the join between the British and French armies and threw them back forty miles, though without decisively breaking the line. Lloyd George took over the War Office in person and rushed reinforcements to France, whilst personally appealing to President Wilson for the immediate use of American troops. On 14 April Foch was given supreme command of the allied troops and was urging a counter-offensive, but by May the Germans were over the Marne and only forty miles from Paris. Yet still the Allied line was unbroken and the Germans were in potentially perilous situations in exposed salients. By now half a million British reinforcements had arrived, and by the end of July there were twenty-seven American divisions on the continent.

The struggle against the U-boats was carried into their lairs with combined operations under Sir Roger Keyes against Ostend and Zeebrugge, though only with partial success.

In Parliament, Asquith's opposition made an abortive and

ill-advised attack upon Lloyd George, based upon dis
closures by Sir Frederick Maurice, embittered after his dismissa
as Director of Military Operations. The attack failed, and the
Liberals were irreparably split.

On 15 July the last German attacks on the Western Fron
petered out and five days later Ludendorff's offensive wa
called off. Early in August, tank attacks forced the German
back, but by September the Western Front was stabilised again
Stalemate had returned. But the 'side-shows' at last began to
pay off. Whilst Ludendorff's line was stabilised in the west
German support elsewhere crumbled. In September, Allenby':
defeat of the Turks at Megiddo led to the fall of Damascus and
in the same month the Allied armies moved forward in Salonika
Ludendorff dared not detach troops from the Western Front
and he knew that he was beaten.

On 4 October the Germans appealed separately to Presiden
Wilson for a peace, hoping, not without reason, to detach him
from the other Allies. After three weeks, on 23 October, the
Germans accepted the Fourteen Points which Wilson had pu
forward on 8 January 1917.[3] Would they prove acceptable to the
other Allies? Whilst they considered, events moved swiftly to
the armistice which was concluded at the eleventh hour of the
eleventh day of the eleventh month of 1918. German troop.
were still almost everywhere on foreign soil, but their resources
were exhausted. German morale was in ruins. On 30 October
the Turks surrendered, and on 3 November the Austro-
Hungarians gave in to the Italians. From the east, the spectre o
Bolshevism was abroad in the land, whilst in Europe and
beyond Nature took a hand with a deadly epidemic of influenza

The guns ceased firing. After an interval of awesome silence,
over the Western Front, the birds began to sing again. The
nations turned to the problems of making peace.

CHAPTER THIRTEEN

Britain and the Peace of Europe

The nations turned from the War wounded in body, in economic order,
and still more deeply wounded in soul.
LLOYD GEORGE, War Memoirs, p. 1986

BRITISH diplomacy between the end of the war and the fall of
the coalition government in 1922 was largely the personal work
of Lloyd George. His reputation was immense in Europe as well
as in England, where he appeared firmly established as 'the man
who won the war'.

In January 1918 Lloyd George had expressed his war aims in
a speech to British trade unionists. He denied that the war was
one of aggression against Germany. Belgium must receive
reparation and the restoration of her independence, whilst
Britain would stand firmly beside France. In the east, Poland
must be independent, and democratic self-government must be
assured for the peoples of the Austro-Hungarian Empire.
Future security lay in international organisation. This last point
was strongly emphasised during the last year of the war by the
activities of the Ministry of Information, which, under Lord
Beaverbrook's direction, did much to commit Britain to the
ideals of a League of Nations which were so strongly implicit in
President Wilson's Fourteen Points.

The Peace Conference was opened in Paris on 18 January
1919, and its affairs were dominated by the settlement with
Germany, although there was a multiplicity of peripheral
issues also to be settled. The war had changed Europe for ever.
The great issues of nationality could no longer be ignored at

Versailles in 1919 as they had been at Vienna a century before.

The British Foreign Office had done a lot of work in preparation for the Conference, but had failed to produce a clear-cut plan of action. Lloyd George, in fact, by contrast with the great traditional diplomatists, wrote no instructions for himself. He was determined to play British diplomacy by ear, and by improvisation. Essentially, and unlike the French, who were only too clear as to their objectives, Lloyd George believed in the necessity to preserve and conciliate Germany, even though he had allowed himself to indulge in some wild excesses about hanging the Kaiser and making Germany pay, in order to keep in harmony with popular enthusiasms during the post-war election.

As it happened, Lloyd George was able to moderate some of the more extreme demands of the French, although the peace settlement was still literally dictated to the Germans: they took no part in discussion, and when all the work had been done the terms were simply presented to them with a demand for their signature. The work of the Conference was originally entrusted to a Council of Ten (two representatives each from Britain, France, the U.S.A., Italy and Japan) but it was soon dominated by the 'Big Three' (Lloyd George, Clemenceau and Wilson).

President Wilson was, of course, the great inspiration of the League of Nations, whose Covenant was written into the peace settlement, but much of the practical work of drafting was done by Lord Robert Cecil and General Smuts. To Wilson, the League represented the practical expression of his idealism; to Lloyd George, it was an example of the international organisation of which he had spoken; to the French it was merely an additional safeguard against Germany.

In dealing with Germany, the problem of colonies presented least difficulty, although there was potential embarrassment in the fixed determination of Australia and South Africa to hold on to the spoils which they had won in New Guinea and South-West Africa respectively. The German colonies were dealt with by the creation of mandates, which Wilson summarised as an expression of 'the sacred trust of civilisation'. States granted mandates over former German possessions were entrusted with the care of those colonial peoples in accordance with Wilson's high principles. Needless to say, the mandates over New Guinea and South-West Africa were given to Australia and South Africa.

But it was the treatment of Germany herself which was the fundamental issue. The French were prepared to go to the limit and to advocate the dismemberment of Germany. Lloyd George exercised a restraining influence, and was able to conjure up the spectre of Bolshevism both inside Germany and to the east if the German state were too seriously weakened. Thus, Poland was not allowed to become as powerful as the French had wished: Danzig, for example, was made a free city, with neither Polish nor German nationality – a refinement which ironically sowed the seeds of dangerous controversy before the second World War.

No one disputed that France's frontiers must be protected against German resurgence. The German army was limited to 100,000 volunteers, and the Rhineland was made into a de-militarised zone. Provision was made for an allied army of occupation on the left bank of the Rhine and France gained control of the industrial resources of the Saar for 15 years, after which a plebiscite was to be taken.

The Kaiser – no doubt to the relief of Lloyd George – remained safe from hanging. He had taken refuge in Holland, and the Dutch refused to give him up.

The security at which the peace settlement aimed above all was to be guaranteed by a treaty between the U.S.A., Britain and France. This came to nothing when the Senate in the United States refused the two-thirds majority necessary to ratify any treaty. Thus, the United States never participated, and Britain and France failed to make an agreement between themselves.

The political aspects of the peace, however, were straight-forward by comparison with the economic question of reparations. The British electorate were not alone in their concern to 'make Germany pay', and certainly French official opinion was well in tune with the Conservative candidate who talked of getting as much from Germany as one can squeeze from a lemon – and then a little more. The problem of how reparations were to be assessed was rather more complex than it appeared to those in Britain, for example, who thought all that was necessary was to work out what the war had cost Britain and simply present the bill to Germany. The whole question of assessment was too difficult for the peacemakers, who deferred it for consideration by a later reparations commission.

The dangers inherent in reparations were plain at least to one distinguished economist, J. M. Keynes, who was convinced that a sound German economy was vital to the economic health of Europe as a whole, and set out his arguments strongly in *The Economic Consequences of the Peace* in 1919. Labour in Britain, too, was opposed to the economic milking of Germany by reparations. Yet Lloyd George found himself vigorously attacked at home, especially by Northcliffe in the columns of *The Times* and the *Daily Mail*, for his excessive leniency. He dismissed Northcliffe with contempt, but Northcliffe was by no means alone.

On 7 May 1919 the settlement was presented to the German representatives for signature. They at once protested at its severity. Lloyd George feared that the confusion which would follow any German refusal to sign might well get out of hand, and sought further modifications. For instance, he secured that a plebiscite should be held in Upper Silesia, rather than handing the area as a direct gift to Poland. On 28 June 1919, the Germans signed. The hard core of the settlement was thus achieved, although the Conference remained in being to settle other issues until 21 January 1921.

The most hopeful outcome of the Conference was the creation of the League of Nations, whose first Assembly was held in November 1920, but at the outset the League was seriously weakened by the absence of Germany, Soviet Russia, and above all the United States, whose Senate seemed obstinately set on a return to isolationism.

Diplomacy by conference continued. Lloyd George, who soon became the last national leader from the war still to be in office, delighted in conferences (which he was to exploit at home as a means of playing for time) and instigated no less than twenty-three international conferences between 1920 and 1922.

His diplomacy continued to be marked by improvisation and by the desire to be conciliatory, not only towards Germany, who must somehow be satisfied that the peace settlement was just, but also towards Russia, who must be won back into the family of European nations. His policy involved the risk of alienating France, already affronted by the collapse of the proposed three-power treaty to guarantee the settlement, and with whom Britain was obviously at cross-purposes over Germany.

So far as Russia was concerned, conciliation obviously implied the end of intervention against the revolutionary régime, intervention to which Winston Churchill was characteristically committed. There were three main areas of counter-revolutionary activity: in Siberia; around Murmansk and Archangel; and in the Caucasus. British resources to the tune of £100 million's worth of surplus supplies were sent to the White Russian rebels. Moreover, the Poles had invaded Russia and captured Kiev, and were receiving active French help. Labour was determined to thwart any similar British intervention on behalf of the Poles. By 1920 intervention in Russia had faded away, and the tide had turned against the Poles, who came to terms with the Russians in the Treaty of Riga.

The spate of conferences which Lloyd George inspired achieved little. The controversy over reparations remained the most dangerous issue (in both the short and long terms). German calculations of their bill were about one-seventh of the sum demanded by the Allies, and the Germans defaulted over the first payment of £1000 million: on 8 March 1921, sanctions were applied against Germany. On 27 April 1921, the reparations commission fixed the total liability at £6600 million and devised a method of long-term payment: each year £100 million were to be paid, together with 26 per cent of the annual value of German exports. These terms were met by Germany until the end of the year, when she threatened another default. The ominous question arose: how would Germany be able to meet her debt if her economy and her currency collapsed?

In January 1922 Lloyd George tried to bring about a *rapport* with France at a conference at Cannes. He found himself dealing with Briand, who was perhaps the most conciliatory of the French statesmen. Briand, however, was attacked and ridiculed by the French Press over an absurd game of golf into which he was persuaded by Lloyd George (whose handicap was distinctly superior to Briand's) and driven from office on 12 January. He was replaced by Poincaré: conciliation was definitely not Poincaré's favourite pastime, and he stood firm over France's demands against Germany. The Cannes Conference, promising at the outset, came to nothing.

At Genoa a conference on the grand scale again promised well, but achieved nothing when France threatened to pursue her policy alone. Lloyd George's hopes were disappointed, and his prestige was damaged.

A more fruitful conference was held in Washington from November 1921 to February 1922, although its success was centred in the Pacific rather than in Europe. General disarmament was raised as an issue, but practical results concerned navies. Britain surrendered her claim to naval supremacy and agreed to accept a parity with the U.S. Navy. There was still friction between France and Britain, but a four-power treaty was signed by which the United States, Britain, France and Japan agreed to guarantee the existing situation in the Pacific.

A problem which greatly exercised Lloyd George, and in the end provided the Conservatives with the pretext to drive him from office, was concerned with that traditional source of British diplomatic anxiety, the Turkish Empire. Parts of the Empire had been distributed among the Allies during the war, and the distribution had been confirmed by the Peace of Sèvres in August 1920. France was given a mandate over Syria, and Britain a similar responsibility in Palestine and Mesopotamia (Iraq). Constantinople had been promised to Russia, but in their high idealism the Bolsheviks repudiated the agreement, and in any case the situation had been complicated by the transformation threatened in Turkey by the rise of Kemal, who was likely not only to reform, but also to strengthen Turkey. British policy had been to encourage the demands of the Greeks against the Turks, and to encourage the Greek occupation of

Smyrna in May 1919. The support of Greece by Britain had been maintained at Sèvres with the stipulation that Greece should be strengthened in eastern Thrace.

The confusion wrought by the emergence of Kemal was worse confounded by the fall from power in Greece of Venizelos, on whom British diplomacy had set great store. France continued her support, but a renewed Greek offensive towards Ankara in 1921 was compromised by an alliance in March between Turkey and Russia. In October 1921 France came to terms with Turkey.

In 1922 it became clear that there was significant support for Turkey in India (where there was, of course, an important Moslem element in the population). The open declaration of this support, with the approval of the Viceroy, was vigorously opposed by the Foreign Secretary, Lord Curzon, who now attempted to mediate between the Greeks and the Turks. The Greeks, in fact, were in increasing difficulty. The Allied powers would not let Greek troops land along the Sea of Marmara. Kemal attacked, and the Greeks were defeated, losing Smyrna in September 1922. There now seemed to be a danger that Kemal would attack the Allied forces still in occupation of the coast from the Black Sea to the Dardanelles.

Especially vulnerable in such a situation was a British force at Chanak. The British officials botched the action which was taken, and the wrath of the Conservatives fell upon Lloyd George. A warning was sent to Kemal, and the governments of the Dominions were indignant when a published communiqué reached them before the ciphered telegrams. Poincaré added to the British embarrassment by ordering the withdrawal of French troops from Chanak: a hasty agreement had to be patched up with the French. A very tense situation developed during the last week of September, and there was support for the idea of a direct ultimatum to Turkey demanding the removal of her troops. The British commander on the spot, General Harington, procrastinated with a skill which would have done credit to Lloyd George himself, and so saved the situation. A convention was signed at Mudania on 11 October 1922. The Turks promised to respect the neutral zone and agreed not to reoccupy eastern Thrace so long as Greece withdrew from the area.

The situation had been saved, but the improvisation at which Lloyd George was so adept had revealed itself rather too obviously. In any case, its attractions were wearing thin, especially to those Conservatives who were itching to drive Lloyd George from office. 'The man who won the war' had made strenuous efforts to win the peace, but politically, his time had run out.

CHAPTER FOURTEEN

'A Fit Country for Heroes to Live in': Post-War Problems in Society and Politics 1918 – 1922

What is our task? To make Britain a fit country for heroes to live in.

LLOYD GEORGE in Wolverhampton, 24 November 1918

LLOYD GEORGE decided to hold a general election immediately after the conclusion of the armistice, and various cogent pretexts for such hasty action were put forward. It was certainly true, for instance, that the prolonging of the existing Parliament during the war, and the creation of a newly widened electorate in 1918, had rendered an election overdue. But no doubt the most compelling reason in Lloyd George's mind was the certainty that at such a moment the coalition government had victory in its pocket. That the coalition should be maintained was mutually beneficial to Lloyd George and the Conservatives. The Labour Party in any case withdrew from the coalition, but the Liberals were in a confusing situation. Local agents and organisers had to know which candidates had the backing of the leaders of the coalition. The solution was to provide such candidates with a statement of support signed by both Lloyd George and Bonar Law – a document contemptuously dismissed by Asquith as 'the coupon'.

On what basis was the coupon allocated? Lloyd George claimed that loyalty during the Maurice debate[1] was the crucial test; close examination, such as that carried out by Mr Trevor Wilson in his admirable study *The Downfall of the Liberal Party*,[2] reveals that this was an over-simplification. In fact, Lloyd George made a deal with the Conservatives and needed a formula which roughly fitted the number of Liberals who were to be accommodated: 159 Liberals and 364 Conservatives received the coupon, an arrangement which seems to represent a triumph for Sir George Younger, the Conservative manager. Lloyd George has naturally been accused of selling out the Liberals, but it may be that he was simply driving the best bargain that he could in the circumstances. Certainly most of the couponed Liberals were not opposed in their constituencies by Conservatives. The election anyway was certain to be marked by a pronounced swing to the right, so perhaps Lloyd George was, after all, salvaging as much as he could from an inevitable wreckage.

Certainly Lloyd George's early manœuvres promised well for the Liberals. On 12 November 1918 he made a markedly progressive and enlightened speech to his fellow-Liberals. Later developments were to indicate that this was perhaps a smoke-screen to mislead doubters amongst his followers like Churchill and H. A. L. Fisher. As the election campaign proceeded, Lloyd George allowed himself to be swept along by popular reactionary fervour until he seemed to be engaged in something like an outright war upon traditional Liberal principles.

At least Lloyd George now had a party of his own – the coalition Liberals. But his agreement with Bonar Law had bound him very closely to the Conservatives. Now his behaviour during the election campaign seriously compromised his radical reputation. If the Conservatives deserted him, he would be uncomfortably isolated, and nothing was more certain than that the Conservatives would desert him when he had outlived his usefulness to them, as he had by 1922.

The result of the coupon election was the predictable landslide for the coalition, which won a total of 478 seats: 333 were couponed Conservatives, 136 couponed Liberals, with 9 members of the National Democratic Party. Labour, fighting entirely independently and on a national scale, won 59 seats:

two leaders of the Labour Party, Ramsay MacDonald and Philip Snowden, lost their seats. Forty-eight non-couponed Conservatives were elected. There were 9 Independents, 7 Irish Nationalists, and 73 *Sinn Feiners* (including the first woman ever elected, Countess Markievicz) – all 73 of whom never took their seats. The Liberals without the coupon returned a mere 29 members, a diverse handful to whom the prospect of office ceased to be even a remote possibility. Asquith himself lost his seat. The most ominous sign for the future was the large number of Liberal candidates who were relegated to third place behind Conservative and Labour.

Early efforts to reconcile the Liberals with the Liberal supporters of the coalition failed. Open warfare seemed, indeed, to be declared when, at the end of 1919, Lloyd George put up one of his own 'Liberals' against the Liberal Sir John Simon in a by-election in Spen Valley: Labour won the seat! Lloyd George's attempts to conjure up the bogy of Bolshevism in Britain were unconvincing to Liberals. As Violet Bonham Carter characteristically remarked: 'When I think of Mr Clynes and Mr Henderson my flesh positively refuses to creep'.

The annual meeting of the National Liberal Federation at Leamington in May 1920 was a disaster marked by unruly scenes between Liberals and coalition Liberals. During 1920 Lloyd George set up his own Liberal organisation, and in 1922 the National Liberal Party was created. The Liberals were further weakened by the marked hostility from 1919 onwards of the Labour Party, and by the feebleness of Asquith's leadership, even after his return to the House of Commons following a triumph in a by-election in Paisley. The great man was a mere shadow of his former self, and the failure of the Asquithian Liberals (or 'Squiffites') encouraged the leaders of the coalition Liberals to prolong their agreement with the Conservatives. Although attempts to form a genuine 'Centre Party' failed, the 'fusion' which the attempts envisaged was virtually achieved so long as the coalition lasted.

Meanwhile, Lloyd George was more than fully occupied with the negotiation of peace abroad and with the task at home of making Britain 'a fit country for heroes to live in'. The House of Commons through which he was to work was noteworthy for the comparatively advanced age of its membership. Only about 100 M.P.s belonged to the generation which had actually fought the war, although perhaps Stanley Baldwin was unjust when he remarked on the predominance of hard-faced men who looked as if they had done well out of the war. It may be an exaggeration to think in terms of a 'lost generation' after the war, but much of that generation was certainly lost to political life.

The leading members of the Government reflected the alliance which had brought it about. Lloyd George was at the height of his prestige: his talents for political manipulation and his energy in getting things done were widely respected if not always admired. His tendency to work through his own group of personal advisers, independently of his colleagues, caused some resentment: his staff (temporarily housed in the grounds of 10 Downing Street) was ironically nicknamed 'The Garden Suburb'. Bonar Law probably reached the extreme of his influence during this period: his friendship with Lloyd George was still firm and, through the offices of Lord Privy Seal and Leader of the House of Commons, he was able to play a moderating part as well as exercise his control over the Conservatives. The energies and prodigious, if indisciplined, talents of F. E. Smith were rewarded with his appointment as Lord Chancellor with the title of Lord Birkenhead. Austen Chamberlain, very reminiscent at this stage in his life of his famous father, became Chancellor of the Exchequer; Balfour remained Foreign Secretary and Churchill held the War Office.

The necessities of war had helped to bring about a notable reorganisation of the machinery of government. Old hidebound ministerial traditions and protocol had been broken down. The Cabinet Secretariat under Sir Maurice Hankey had already established its great significance. Above all, of course, the war had broken down old nineteenth-century objections to direct governmental interference and had led to a remarkable increase in the size of the Civil Service: from a total in 1914 of 57,706 members, the Civil Service expanded by 1923 to 116,241, and by 1930 to 120,418.[3]

Acceptance of more direct governmental action helped to

stimulate, amongst other things, demands for the nationalisation of key industries. In the forefront with such claims were, naturally, the forces of organised labour, more closely-knit now than ever before. Their wartime divisions had been largely healed when Henderson left the coalition in 1917, and in 1918 a national Labour Party was constituted, with a programme of temperate social reform drawn up by Sidney Webb. The trade unions also felt their power and developed their organisation: in 1920 the General Council of the T.U.C. was created, whilst in 1921 the most formidable workers' organisation to date, the Transport and General Workers' Union, was brought into being by the genius of Ernest Bevin. The inception of the National Council of Labour was intended to provide a link between the Labour Party and the T.U.C. On the extreme left of the working-class movement, various bodies came together in 1921 to form the British Communist Party, which was firmly and consistently refused affiliation by the Labour Party. All these developments in the organisation of labour are obviously very important in the context of industrial unrest after 1918.*

The harvest of war which had to be gathered was formidable. The British Empire had contributed nearly a million lives to the Allied cause, some three quarters of a million from Britain herself. The casualty rate had been especially high amongst those junior officers who might have been expected to play a leading role in post-war life. Although no more than 1500 civilians had lost their lives during the war, about a million and a half men now returned to civilian life suffering from serious wounds, or from gassing, or who were psychologically wrecked from the effects of shellshock.

The Britain to which they returned was cold: there was a serious coal shortage immediately after the war. The weakening effects of wartime diet coupled with the difficulty of keeping warm in the post-war winter no doubt contributed to the virulence of the influenza epidemic which swept the country and ravaged the large towns: 7·9 per cent of the entire population of Manchester died, and at the height of the epidemic over the country as a whole, 7560 people died in a week early in

* See Chapter Seventeen.

November. To such social misery discontent was added, particularly over the demobilisation of servicemen. A scheme by which those who were most needed at home were to be released first met such opposition that it was hastily replaced by the principle of 'first in, first out'.

The redeployment of labour returning from the front was assisted by the efficient discharge of women workers from the factories, and was in any case made easier by the industrial boom which immediately followed the war. But there were difficulties ahead: as early as January 1919, a strike in Glasgow for the forty-hour week was marked by violence and threatened to grow into a general strike: among strike leaders imprisoned was a future pillar of the Labour Party, Emmanuel Shinwell.

In financial terms alone, the cost of the war was daunting. Britain owed some £850 millions to the U.S.A. She was in fact owed twice as much by her Allies, but mostly from Russia, from whom she was unlikely to be able to collect. The National Debt stood at fourteen times its pre-war amount. The situation was serious enough to warrant the consideration of a capital levy, but Bonar Law rejected such a solution.

At first the nation's industry and commerce were riding high on the tide of wartime prosperity, and there was every stimulus to investment, so much so that *The Economist* wrote of 'a craze for speculation'. No less than 11,000 new companies had been created by 1920. Investment brought a vast inflation of shares, notably in the Lancashire cotton industry, but also in most other major industries. Yet the truth was that many industries, especially shipbuilding, had greatly over-expanded during the war. Afterwards they could not maintain themselves, so that much of the immediate post-war investment in them was wasted. The Government's policy, with its increase in the floating debt, added to the inflationary trend.

The boom was short-lived. There were ominous signs of an impending slump in 1920, and by 1921 *The Economist* was writing of 'One of the worst years of industrial depression since the industrial revolution'. The collapse of wage-rates and the growth of unemployment helped effectively to kill Lloyd George's reputation with the working-class. The Government's response to the signs of depression was to hasten the decontrol of industries for which it had assumed responsibility during the war, and to introduce a deflationary policy. In April 1920, for example, Bank Rate was raised to 7 per cent, stemming the tide of investment. The Budget increased the excess profits duty.

The slump brought an immediate decline in wages and prices and a rise in unemployment. Wages in any case had failed to match prices: as far as the purchase of food was concerned, the 1914 pound was worth only 8s 8d in January 1919, 7s 9d in July 1920, and although it had improved to 9s 2d in July 1921, unemployment was by that time already severe. The trade unions concentrated their efforts upon wage demands, and there was serious and widespread industrial unrest in 1919, 1920 and 1921. Even the Metropolitan Police took strike action. But growing unemployment once more dampened – as in the early days of the Labour movement – the effectiveness of industrial action.

Lloyd George played for time by establishing a variety of commissions, and by calling a National Industrial Conference. He succeeded in frustrating demands for nationalisation. There were some practical steps. Whitley Councils, for example, which provided the machinery of consultation in particular industries, numbered fifty-six by 1920. The idea of arbitration in industrial disputes gained ground – and Ernest Bevin on behalf of the dockers showed what it could achieve – but the Industrial Courts Act of 1919 failed to make arbitration compulsory.

Before the serious effects of the slump stultified the Government's policies, at least two efforts at genuine social reform had been made. The Housing and Town Planning Act of 1919 signified an attempt to deal with the problem of providing the three quarters of a million new homes which were needed after the war. The initiative was given to local authorities, assisted by governmental subsidy of any need in excess of one penny on the local rate. Christopher Addison as Minister of Health was responsible for the plan as a whole; it succeeded in producing 213,000 houses but there was a good deal of unnecessary extravagance. In 1922, the economic situation put a stop to the Government's housing grants, and Lloyd George sacrificed

Addison as a scapegoat when the shortcomings of the scheme were attacked.

The Unemployment Insurance Act of 1920 extended insurance in case of unemployment to some 11 million people, and provided weekly contributory benefits of 15s for men and 12s for women. But the benefits were circumscribed by time limits. In any case, the galloping pace of unemployment during the slump swamped the whole scheme.

The slump was marked by a disastrous decline in overseas trade: in 1921, exports were 47·9 per cent less and imports 43·7 per cent less than in the previous year. The steel industry in particular suffered a disastrous decline in production. Wages generally fell, and unemployment rose rapidly: in December 1920, the total was 691,103; in March 1921, 1,355,206; in June 1921, 2,171,288; in December 1921, 1,934,030; in June 1922, 1,502,955. Certain industries were particularly hard-hit: in December 1921, 36·7 per cent were unemployed in iron and steel; 36·1 per cent in shipbuilding; 27·2 per cent in engineering; and 20·5 per cent in the building trade. Some areas of the country were harder hit than others: in December 1921, there was a 25 per cent level of unemployment in Northern Ireland; 21 per cent in Scotland; and 18 per cent both in the midlands and the north-east. Individual towns remained devastated by unemployment even after the worst effects of the slump had passed: in August 1922, the level of unemployment was still 60 per cent in Hartlepool; 49 per cent in Stockton and Barrow; 47 per cent in Brynmawr; 44 per cent in Handsworth; and 43 per cent in Jarrow.[4]

Working-class discontent manifested itself in demonstrations, often organised by the Communist-led National Unemployed Workers' Movement, which was formed in October 1920. The first of the 'hunger marches' which were to be an all too familiar feature of the country's life in the inter-war years took place in 1922.

The Act of 1920 was quite inadequate to alleviate such distress, and the Government embarked upon a series of acts which culminated in the Unemployment Insurance Act of 1922. The period of benefit was extended, rates of benefit were amended, and the level of contributions was increased. The provision that £30 millions could be borrowed from the Treasury instituted the concept of 'the dole'. Labour Exchanges were kept hard at work by the stipulation that recipients of benefit must be 'genuinely seeking' work.

An important principle had been conceded by the Unemployed Workers' Dependants Act of 1921, which provided for weekly payments from the Unemployment Fund of 5s for a wife, and 1s for a child. The rates were contemptibly low, even lower than those available from the old poor rate, but the principle of family allowances had been conceded – a significant stepping-stone to future social legislation.

In the wider economic context, the Government maintained a deflationary policy and instituted departmental economies. Under pressure from the Conservatives, Lloyd George set up a Committee under the chairmanship of Sir Eric Geddes in August 1921. Its first report, in February 1922, made recommendations which were dubbed 'the Geddes Axe': governmental savings of £75 million were prescribed. The Army estimates were to lose £20 million, the Navy £21 million. Education was to be cut back by £18 million (partly by a cut of 10 per cent in teachers' salaries); pensions were to be reduced by £3⅓ million. The recommendations were too stringent even for the Government, but cuts totalling £64 million were implemented.

Such policies naturally caused flutterings in the dovecotes of party politics. Particularly disruptive was the Safeguarding of Industries Act of 1921 which extended the dilution of free trade already signified by the retention of the McKenna duties from the war. The Act profoundly disturbed the Liberals, whilst it did not go far enough to satisfy the Conservatives.

Growing disputes over Free Trade versus Protection were merely symptomatic of the impending breakdown of the coalition. The Government was unpopular on counts other than its handling of the economic situation. Ireland and India also helped to focus discontent. The war had stirred Indian nationalism, which had been far from satisfied by the Government of India Act of 1919 which had left power firmly in the

hands of the Viceroy and the Executive Council and had maintained arbitrary police powers. In 1919, demonstrators at
Amritsar had been attacked, with the loss of 379 Indian lives:
1208 demonstrators were wounded. There was a growing
pressure in India for independence, led by the remarkable
figure of Mahatma Gandhi.

Lloyd George himself was very unpopular with many Conservatives, who resented the influence of his 'Garden Suburb'
and distrusted his manipulation of the honours system. The
scandal of the 'sale of honours' led to the establishment of a
Royal Commission which recommended that henceforth candidates for honours should be approved by three Privy Councillors
who were not members of the government of the day. The
political situation was further confused in 1921 by the temporary
retirement through ill-health of Bonar Law. He was succeeded
as leader of the Conservatives by Austen Chamberlain, who was
consistently loyal to Lloyd George. Bonar Law returned to
health and politics in February 1922.

Mr Trevor Wilson has argued that the real explanation of the
downfall of the coalition is to be found in none of these short-
term causes, but in the original nature of the alliance which
Lloyd George had made.[5] He was never really trusted by the
rank and file of the Conservative Party, who had been prepared
to cash in on Lloyd George's reputation as 'the man who won
the war' but who by 1922 were confident that they could
manage without him.

Early in 1922, Lloyd George wanted to seize the chance of
prolonging the coalition by holding a general election. He was
resisted by the Conservatives, who extended attacks which they
were already making on Liberal coalition ministers into an
assault on the coalition as a whole. Austen Chamberlain stood
by Lloyd George, but his appeal to his Conservative followers
for an early election on the basis of the coalition was met with
demands by the party manager, Sir George Younger, for
Conservative separation from the coalition. Lloyd George was
indignant at the political machinations of 'a second-rate
brewer', but in spite of the support of Chamberlain and Balfour,
he was powerless against the growing Conservative rebellion.

It was Chanak which forced the issue in October 1922.*
Chamberlain failed to rally Conservative support and resigned
the party leadership: his loyalty to Lloyd George probably cost
him the Premiership, and when Lloyd George resigned Bonar
Law became Prime Minister.

Lloyd George never held office again. The coalition Liberals
were his party, and they were now isolated. Lloyd George
would not even try for a reconciliation with the Liberals; he
preferred to play for time in the hope of the renewal of his
alliance with the Conservatives. 'Mr Lloyd George', wrote the
Manchester Guardian on 4 November 1922, 'is still Coalition,
whether the Conservatives will have him or not.'[6]

* See pp. 173–4 above.

CHAPTER FIFTEEN

The Agony of a Nation: Ireland

'But where can we draw water'
Said Pearse to Connolly,
'When all the wells are parched away?
O plain as plain can be
There's nothing but our own red blood
Can make a right Rose Tree'.

WILLIAM BUTLER YEATS, *The Rose Tree*

THE history of Ireland was a tragedy which generations of English misrule had done too little to alleviate. During the nineteenth century, however, those grievances which centred on religious discrimination and the actual ownership of the land had been largely removed. There remained the question of the government of Ireland. Pitt's Act of Union, conceived in goodwill but delivered in corruption, had become the focal point of Irish discontent and Gladstone's career had foundered in frustration with the defeat of his two Home Rule Bills.

The role of the House of Lords in the defeat of the second Home Rule Bill had been a clear warning of trouble to come. The Parliament Act of 1911 had seriously diminished the obstacle presented by the Lords, but the campaign of Carson and other extremists had introduced an element of bitterness perhaps unparalleled even in the annals of Irish history.

The outbreak of war had deferred the application of Home Rule, but in Ireland the situation remained perilously inflammable. In face of the outspoken threat posed by the existence of the aggressive Ulster Volunteers, the Irish Volunteers in the south maintained their open drilling. The most extreme of Irishmen sought German help. Sir Roger Casement, veteran of a distinguished and enlightened career in the Consular service, canvassed Irish captives in German prison camps. His lack of success was more than matched by the futility of his landing in Ireland, where he blundered straight into the arms of his British enemies. He was destined to be condemned after the humiliation of a vicious prosecution at the hands of F. E. Smith. He was hanged on 3 August 1916 'for the wearing of the green', as the patriotic Irish song had it; his remains were restored to Ireland only after nearly half a century had passed.

The failure of the expected German support was evident even before the fiasco of Casement's landing, and an Irish rising, planned for Easter 1916 was cancelled by John MacNeill, chief of staff of the Irish Volunteers. His order was deliberately disobeyed by Volunteer contingents in Dublin. The rising which occurred was thus the work of officers in calculated mutiny against their own command: at least one of them, Patric Pearse, the leader of the rising, was consciously courting martyrdom.

On Easter Monday 1916, the men under the command of Patric Pearse, Eamon de Valera and others seized the General Post Office in Dublin, proclaimed the Irish Republic and raised the green and gold flag of Irish rebellion. In fierce and prolonged fighting which devastated the Georgian elegance of O'Connell Street round the General Post Office, some 450 Irishmen were killed and British deaths numbered about 100. By Friday the struggle was hopeless, and the Provisional Government of the Irish Republic surrendered.

Thus far, the Irish rebels had enjoyed singularly little Irish support. The hostility of the Dublin crowds when the leaders emerged from the G.P.O. was directed against Pearse and his followers rather than the British troops. It was the British commander in Ireland, General Maxwell, who transformed the entire situation: tried in secret, fourteen rebel leaders were executed one by one and their deaths were announced in calculated and clinically detached terms. Pearse and his comrades had achieved their martyrdom. Eamon de Valera avoided death on the technical grounds that he possessed no citizenship – though brought up in Limerick he was born in the U.S.A. of a Spanish father and an Irish mother.

The sympathies of the Irish were henceforth rallied behind

the murdered leaders. Not the least of the transformations wrought by Maxwell was the maturing of the genius of William Butler Yeats:

> And what if excess of love
> Bewildered them till they died?
> I write it out in a verse –
> MacDonagh and MacBride
> And Connolly and Pearse
> Now and in time to be,
> Wherever green is worn,
> Are changed, changed utterly:
> A terrible beauty is born.[1]

A form of agreement on Ireland was concocted in 1916 by the pragmatic talents of Lloyd George, who produced a deal between Carson and Redmond, the leader of the Irish Nationalist members of the House of Commons. The six predominantly Protestant counties of Ulster were to remain within the United Kingdom, whilst the remaining twenty-six counties were to have Home Rule, and there was to be a post-war Imperial Conference. The proposals were killed by the opposition led in the Lords by Lansdowne, and by the understandable refusal of Redmond to compromise. The break-down served still further to strengthen the hands of the Irish extremists, whilst Irish Nationalist M.P.s tended increasingly to opt out of the House of Commons and direct their attention to affairs in Ireland itself. Radical Liberal M.P.s regarded Asquith's withdrawal in face of Lansdowne's opposition as a show of weakness, a factor which was destined to be of great political significance in December 1916.

Ireland simmered until the end of the war, and resisted attempts to impose conscription in 1918. In the general election of 1918 Arthur Griffith's *Sinn Fein*, the party of independence, won all seats save four in Ireland (outside of Ulster) and set up in Dublin an independent Irish Parliament, the Dail, proclaiming the renewal of the declaration of independence of Easter 1916. In April 1919 the ranks of the Dail were swollen by the release of Irish prisoners from British gaols. A political situation perhaps impossible in any country save Ireland now arose: under the Presidency of Eamon de Valera the Dail simply ignored the existence of the British government. *Sinn Fein* worked on the assumption that as the authority of the Dail became established, British influence would simply wither away. By 1920, the executive functions of the Irish under the Dail had developed quite impressively, and Irish local author- ities, for example, were taking their instructions from W. T. Cosgrave's Ministry of Local Government.

The Irish extremists, however, were too impatient to wait for British power to wither: they determined to root it out. In January 1919 the remnants of the Republican Brotherhood founded the Irish Republican Army under the leadership of Michael Collins (a veteran of the Easter Rising) and the fervent Cathal Brugha, who clung obstinately to the Gaelic version of his name and was the proud possessor of the scars of no less than seventeen wounds received in battle. In the traditions of the nineteenth century Fenians, the I.R.A. received lavish support from the Irish colony in America, to whom de Valera paid a visit during 1919. Michael Collins was a remarkable leader of men and he developed a superb intelligence service which kept him always at least one step ahead of the British troops, who with the Royal Irish Constabulary outnumbered by ten to one the 5000 men which was the maximum number the I.R.A. could put into the field at any one time.

In 1920, however, with the dispatch to Ireland as reinforce- ments for the Royal Irish Constabulary of the notorious 'Black and Tans' (all too often recruited with every promise of violent sport to come) the methods of the British spilled over into open brutality, which was fully reciprocated by the Irish: 700 Irish lives were paid for by the deaths of 500 police and 200 British troops. Asquith visited the stricken country and was appalled: 'Things are being done in Ireland', he said, 'which would disgrace the blackest annals of the lowest despotism in Europe'.

The fact that Home Rule was not applied derived in part from Lloyd George's lack of genuine sympathy with the Irish. In 1920 he made yet another attempt at a settlement. The Government of Ireland Act of 1920 was forbidding in its com- plexity, and proved unacceptable to Ulstermen and *Sinn*

Feiners alike. The Act provided for two Home Rule Parliaments, in Dublin and Belfast, with both contributing to a Council of Ireland dedicated to the restoration of unity. It is noteworthy that such a proposal, in spite of the saving clause creating the Council of Ireland, virtually recognised the fact of partition as the solution to the Irish problem. Representatives from both parts of Ireland were still to be sent to Westminster.

George V was seriously concerned, and dogged in his determination to help solve the problem. He courageously opened the Belfast Parliament in June 1921 and made a warm plea for peace which marked the culmination of a campaign in both Parliament and the Press for a peaceful solution.

De Valera agreed to negotiate and a truce was made in July. Both sides stood firm in negotiation. The attitude of Lloyd George and his Conservative ministers was hardening again, and British offers of Dominion Status for the twenty-six counties of the south were met by the *Sinn Fein* demand for a united independent republic. De Valera himself had arrived at a formula of 'external association', broadly comparable with the relationship then between the United States and Cuba. Such a formula was in many ways a compromise between the British and the *Sinn Fein* positions. Any compromise which might appeal to Lloyd George was, however, effectively blocked by Bonar Law.

Negotiations for a Treaty opened in October 1921. De Valera stayed at home, and the Irish cause was in the hands of Arthur Griffith and Michael Collins, who whilst losing none of his courage was prepared to negotiate with British leaders like Smith whose forthrightness appealed to him: 'I trust them,' he said, 'I'm prepared to take their word.' There was much hard bargaining, with Lloyd George even prepared to resort to the threat of war, before Articles of Agreement were arrived at on 6 December 1921. The serious misgivings of the Irish about the division of the island were to some extent lulled by Lloyd George, who, perhaps even sincerely, promised that the Boundary Commission which would be necessary would virtually erode Ulster out of a separate existence. The Articles, by recognising the separateness of the twenty-six counties, to all intents and purposes spelt the end of the Union.

De Valera, who still wanted 'external association', opposed the Articles, but on 7 January 1922 the Dail approved them as the basis of a Treaty with the United Kingdom, whereupon de Valera resigned. But in June 1922 elections for the Dail showed a majority of some 72 per cent in favour of the Treaty. Ireland was not to be settled by mere votes, however, and another painful outbreak of violence followed, this time with the Irish fighting one another. The I.R.A. split, with the Regulars under Collins supporting the Dail whilst the Irregulars fought against the acceptance of the Treaty. Fighting broke out after Rory O'Connor and Irregulars seized the Four Courts in Dublin. Two outstanding recruits for the Irregulars were de Valera and Cathal Brugha. In the course of clearing Dublin of Irregulars, the Regulars inflicted wounds which at last proved mortal on Cathal Brugha.

Meanwhile, Michael Collins's intelligence service was no longer reliable and he was in constant danger of betrayal. He had remarked that in agreeing to the terms of the Treaty he was signing his death warrant, and he was killed in a violent battle on 22 August 1922 at the age of thirty-one. He was no ordinary battle casualty, for he was shot in the back of the head.

The civil war was efficiently, and at times ruthlessly, pursued by Willy Cosgrave, Richard Mulcahy and Kevin O'Higgins, and by the end of May 1923 the latest episode in the strife which has rent Ireland was over. In the meantime, the Treaty was put into force. A constitution submitted by the Dail was ratified by the Parliament of the United Kingdom in December 1922. The Irish Free State was created, and British troops were finally withdrawn by 17 December.

The Irish Free State achieved for the twenty-six counties autonomy in finance, justice, education and administration. The Royal Navy was guaranteed the use of ports at Queenstown, Berehaven and Lough Swilly. There was to be common citizenship with the United Kingdom, and the Irish Free State was to be a member of the Commonwealth, with Dominion Status. Virtually the sole remaining link with the Union was the Governor-General, and the first holder of that office also

provided a link with the days of the campaign for Home Rule
with the appointment of T. M. Healy.

Ironically, the Irish settlement ruined Lloyd George, for
Bonar Law and the rest were determined to make him pay for
the destruction of the Union. 'Ireland', writes Mr A. J. P
Taylor, 'ruined Lloyd George, as it had ruined Peel and
Gladstone. But at least he was ruined by success, they by
failure.'[2]

Ireland was moderately ruled in the years after the Treaty
but in 1932 Eamon de Valera returned to office. In the same
year he suspended the payment of land annuities due to the
United Kingdom and undermined the position of the Governor-
General. In 1933, appeals from Ireland to the Privy Council of
the United Kingdom were abolished, and two years later British
citizenship was abandoned. British citizenship was retained by
Irishmen resident in the United Kingdom – a convenient, if
distinctly 'Irish' arrangement. De Valera took advantage of the
opportunity offered by the abdication crisis to remove the
monarch from the Irish Constitution, and in 1937 the 'sovereign
democratic state of Eire' was proclaimed, still recognised by
Britain and the Dominions as a member of the Commonwealth
In 1949 the Irish Republic at last came into being. The long
struggle had come to an end – except for those Irishmen who
will never acknowledge the separation of Ulster.

CHAPTER SIXTEEN

Mediocrity and Illusion: Politics 1922–1929

... the second eleven ...
LORD BIRKENHEAD on the government of 1922

THE statesmen of the 1920s appeared to many of their contemporaries, and to some historians, as mere shadows of the
great figures who had dominated politics in the nineteenth
century and (in the person of Lloyd George) during the war.
This is no mere example of distance lending enchantment to the
view: although Mr Reginald Bassett has made out a strong case
for Ramsay MacDonald,[1] none of the others approached, in his
own time or in the context of history, the stature possessed
before them by Lloyd George or since by Winston Churchill.
Unhappily, the predominance of second-rate politicians coincided with the illusion that most, if not all, was right with the
world – an illusion fostered as the Great War faded into memory
and as a total of a million unemployed came to be accepted as
normal.

Bonar Law's premiership was consolidated by the general
election of November 1922, which returned 345 Conservatives,
142 Labour M.P.s, and 117 Liberals, who seem to have been
about equally divided between followers of Lloyd George and
those of Asquith.

Bonar Law's cabinet was traditionally Conservative in complexion and undistinguished in composition. Its most established political figure was probably Lord Curzon at the Foreign
Office; its most astute candidate for promotion was Senator

G

Baldwin, now raised from relative obscurity to the Chancellor-ship of the Exchequer. As far as the machinery of government was concerned, Bonar Law dispensed with the 'Garden Suburb, which had proved such an irritant to Lloyd George's colleagues as well as his opponents, but maintained the cabinet secretariat. Bonar Law appeared to be firmly established, with all the resources of power which had become available to a Prime Minister during Lloyd George's time. But his political strength was not matched by his physical condition. He was an ailing man when he took office, and was destined to be removed with stark suddenness.

Bonar Law had dropped Protection from the Conservative programme before the general election. The pressing economic question which confronted his government was the settle-ment of the debt with the United States. Baldwin went out to America as British representative, with instructions to settle only such debts as could be met from payments to Britain of debts owed by other countries. In spite of his instructions, he allowed the Americans to dictate very harsh terms, in-volving Britain in annual payments of £34 million for ten years and £40 million thereafter. The Cabinet overrode Bonar Law's wish to repudiate the agreement which Baldwin had made. The size of the American debt compelled Britain, whatever her diplomatic feelings in the matter, to exact reparations from Germany as far as she could. France was in any case determined to do so, and in 1923 occupied the Ruhr. The German economy, however, was in no condition to meet stringent demands, and the German currency collapsed. The speed and extent of the catastrophe is vividly familiar to those who collect the postage-stamps of the period.

In May 1923 Bonar Law realised that he was suffering from incurable cancer of the throat, and he resigned, ab-staining from recommending his successor to the King. The heir-apparent (and certainly presumptuous, if not presump-tive) was Lord Curzon, who had added to his already formidable reputation during his tenure of the Foreign Office. But he was unpopular. He had shown himself imperious in manner and inconsistent in loyalty, and many members of the Conservative Party little relished his advent to the premiership. Their anxieties were groundless: King George V was, as always, determined to do the right constitutional thing in a difficult situation. There is no evidence that Bonar Law had any preference or even much interest in the matter of his successor; the King believed that Bonar Law favoured Baldwin, and in any case there were serious objections to having a peer as Prime Minister.

Stanley Baldwin became Prime Minister and was duly elected leader of the Conservative Party, thus reversing the customary sequence of events. His rise had been rapid, but characteristically undramatic.[2] Drama, indeed, was uncongenial to him; but beneath his tranquil exterior, with his soothing pipe and his talk of his pigs and of the English countryside, beat the heart of a successful businessman and a subtle, tough politician. Lloyd George saw through the disguise, and paid Baldwin the compliment of calling him 'the most formidable antagonist whom I ever encountered'.[3] Actually, Baldwin genuinely cared for a quiet life, and he did much to foster the illusion that the twenties were normal, tranquil times – and that they would last. His greatest achievement certainly lay in his dealings with organised labour: his reassurances to them, based, as many of his political appeals were, upon the lulling formula 'You know my record', won over even as formidable an opponent as Ernest Bevin to a mood of resigned acquiescence, if not of conviction. Yet this was his most positive contribution to political and constitutional history: for all his failings it was well for the nation that Baldwin was in charge of its affairs in 1926.

Much of the dynamism and most of the dogmatism in Baldwin's Government stemmed from Neville Chamberlain.[4] Lloyd George described him, with cruel but perceptive relish, as 'a good mayor of Birmingham in an off year'. Where Baldwin was conciliatory, Chamberlain was combative. Essentially conceited, he displayed an irksome tendency to treat his colleages and opponents as if they were second-rate Birmingham city councillors. Such an attitude might – and did – get things done at the Ministry of Health, but was to prove disastrous when he would represent the nation in conversation with Adolf Hitler.

The one positive achievement of Baldwin's short first ministry was the work of Chamberlain at the Ministry of Health. In July 1923 yet another attempt was made to deal with the housing problem. Chamberlain's spirit is evident in its parsimony and in its apparent discrimination against the lowest-paid workers. A limited governmental subsidy (£6 million a year for ten years) was provided to help in the construction of houses which were essentially of utility design.

Prospects of further advance were suddenly thrown into the melting-pot in October 1923, when Baldwin declared that any real solution to the problem of unemployment must depend upon a protective tariff. Since Bonar Law had dropped Protection before his victory in the general election, an appeal to the country was necessary. Such a political gamble was not quite in keeping with Baldwin's love of the quiet life, and his real motives have never been satisfactorily explained: his biographer, Mr G. M. Young,[5] suggests that Baldwin saw a crucial issue such as Protection as a means of closely uniting the Conservative Party and of strengthening his own hold over it.

The general election returned 258 Conservatives, 191 Labour M.P.s, and 159 Liberals: something like a genuine three-party situation was thus created. In the absence of an overall majority, Labour now became the alternative government, provided it could rely upon the support of the Liberals. Baldwin had succeeded in reuniting the Liberals by fighting the election on an issue which was fundamental to their political principles, but they still occupied only third place.

On 21 January 1924 the Conservatives were defeated in the House of Commons. King George V once more acted with constitutional rectitude and summoned the leader of the next largest party to form a government. Since the general election of 1922, Labour representation in the House of Commons had been marked by a significant increase in moderate middle-class M.P.s, although there still remained a vocal and radical wing, broadly associated with the Clydeside constituencies. In 1922, Ramsay MacDonald had been re-elected leader of the parliamentary party, though he had won only a narrow victory over J. R. Clynes. He was in many senses the architect of the

Party and was at the height of his considerable powers, although his eloquence was already occasionally marked by the tortuous ambiguity which was later to prove so distressing.

Ramsay MacDonald's great love, and at this time his *forte*, was foreign policy, and he combined the offices of Prime Minister and Foreign Secretary. Haldane, denied the Woolsack until 1912 in the pre-war Liberal administration, now regained it. Philip Snowden, the Robespierre of the Party in its early days, became Chancellor of the Exchequer. George Lansbury, the conscience of the left wing, received no office at all.

The first Labour government was circumscribed by its dependence upon the Liberals; but it was even more gravely handicapped by the economic situation of the country and by the problem of an unemployment figure still over a million. J. M. Keynes, who called for the solution of the problem of unemployment by a bold policy of expansion through public works, was far in advance of contemporary economic thinking, and the Government lacked the political courage and the resources to follow his lead. Nor was the solidarity of the working-class movement strong enough to spare a Labour government the embarrassment of strikes, although Ernest Bevin was able to exert his powerful influence to have them called off.

At the Exchequer, Snowden was concerned to balance the Budget. He returned to Free Trade with the abolition of the McKenna duties, but he felt bound to exercise a disappointing restraint over expensive projects of social reform.

Thus, spectacular reforms were out of the question, at least for the time being. But at the Board of Education, C. P. Trevelyan managed to offset the most disastrous effects of the Geddes Axe. He also instituted the Hadow Committee, which, when it at length reported in 1926, set the pattern for future educational development by advocating a break at the age of eleven between primary and secondary education, thus firmly establishing the principle of 'secondary education for all' – a principle destined, however, to be compromised for too long by the inadequacy of financial resources.

In spite of the Treasury's stringency, the first Labour government managed to extend the housing programme through its

Minister of Health, John Wheatley (one of the Clydeside M.P.s). The governmental subsidy was increased, and the initiative in implementing the building programme was restored to local authorities, with a strict provision that houses must be built for renting. The confidence of the building industry was secured by the provision that the scheme would last for fifteen years. In fact, it lasted until 1932, but it gave the building industry the chance and the confidence to expand.

The Prime Minister's talents and energies were devoted to foreign affairs, where he maintained on behalf of Britain an attitude of strict impartiality, especially concerning relations with France and Germany. Like Lloyd George, he realised the need to mollify France. His most fruitful work in this context lay in persuading the two countries to accept the Dawes Plan – put forward by an American – which attempted to draw up a programme of reparations payments which Germany could actually carry out. Britain's share of the reparations served greatly to assist her in paying her own debt to the United States.

In the wider framework of diplomacy, Ramsay MacDonald was a devoted supporter of the League of Nations. He supported the Geneva Protocol – which in fact was never ratified – in which the signatories pledged themselves to seek arbitration in cases of international dispute and to strive for disarmament, whilst pledging mutual support in case of unprovoked aggression.

The Labour government's attitude to Soviet Russia was naturally of interest to supporters and opponents alike. The U.S.S.R. was formally recognised, and some hard bargaining ensued, since Britain wanted the payment of the pre-revolutionary Russian government's debts. The Soviet Union's price was a loan, backed by Britain. Haggling produced at first deadlock, then a compromise: a commercial treaty was to be signed at once, followed by Russia's payments of her debts and Britain's guaranteeing of the loan. Lloyd George fiercely denounced this diplomacy and sought once more to raise the spectre of Bolshevism.

It was, in fact, Communism which helped to bring down the Government and to ensure its defeat in the ensuing general election. Fears once more grew of sinister Communist influence behind the Labour movement. The defeat of the Government in the Commons was provoked by the ill-advised action of the Attorney-General, the distinguished advocate Sir Patrick Hastings, in first bringing charges, and then dropping them, against the Communist J. R. Campbell for an extremist article in which he had urged soldiers to refuse to take up arms against the working-class either at home or abroad. No doubt there was a case against him under the Incitement to Mutiny Act, but it was tactless to prosecute; by dropping the case, Hastings played into the hands of all the anti-communist groups in the House of Commons.

The 'red scare' again played its part in the election campaign when, just before polling-day, a letter was published in the *Daily Mail* purporting to come from Zinoviev, the president of the Communist International, giving instructions in revolutionary activities to the British Communist Party.

The general election of October 1924 was duly marked by a great swing to the Conservatives, who won 419 seats. Labour held 151 seats, and the Liberals were massacred, returning only 40 members. Asquith lost his seat, and retired to the House of Lords.

The first interesting feature of the second Baldwin administration was that it did not espouse a policy of Protection, which Baldwin had declared in 1923 to be so necessary. The second is the curious fashion in which the chief offices in the Government were distributed. The greatest surprise, not least to the person who received the office, was the appointment to the Chancellorship of the Exchequer of Winston Churchill, whose known loyalty to Free Trade seemed to close the door on Protection. A much stronger candidate for the Exchequer, though perhaps excluded by his obvious family connection with protection, was Austen Chamberlain. He became Foreign Secretary and his brother Neville returned to the Ministry of Health, where he spent perhaps his most fruitful years in politics. Birkenhead, perhaps the ablest lawyer in the Government, became Secretary for India. Was Baldwin trying to alter the whole complexion of Conservative government, or was he perhaps simply safeguarding his own position in a cabinet which he had hitherto conspicuously failed to dominate?

'Give peace in our time, O Lord', implored Baldwin in 1925 in response to a Conservative M.P.'s unsubtle proposal to declare war on the trade unions by outlawing the political levy. Peace was indeed to Baldwin a 'dear delight', both at home and abroad.

Abroad, during the twenties prospects of peace were bright in spite of French assertiveness. The war years and their aftermath were fading into the distance. In December 1925 Britain joined with Italy in guaranteeing the Treaty of Locarno, a non-aggression pact between France, Germany and Belgium. Austen Chamberlain declined to be associated with French diplomacy in eastern Europe, and regarded the Polish Corridor through Prussia to the sea as no business of Britain's. In the years which followed, hopes of peace were further consolidated: the European powers developed conciliatory attitudes, Germany was admitted to the League of Nations, and the Dawes Plan for the payment of reparations appeared to be working satisfactorily. The only real disharmony in which Britain was involved was the breakdown of naval talks in 1927 between Britain, the U.S.A. and Japan. In 1927, too, the nations came together in the Kellogg Pact to make a formal renunciation of war as a means of settling disputes.

Britain's influence in the world was naturally bound up with the strength of the Empire. An epoch-making Imperial Conference was held in 1926, which laid down the constitutional lines which were followed in making the great Statute of Westminster of 1931. The British Parliament was prepared formally to renounce its sovereignty over the Dominions: the Crown remained as the symbolic link between them. Departments of the Government were established to deal separately with Dominions and Colonies, although the same man, Leopold Amery, presided over both of them.

India remained a problem to be administered separately. In face of growing Indian claims for independence, the British government's policy clearly tended towards the granting of Dominion status. This certainly seems to have been the objective of Lord Irwin (later Lord Halifax), who became Viceroy in 1926. In 1927, Sir John Simon presided over a statutory Commission which began to inquire into the whole future of the government of India. Its report in 1930 did not go nearly far enough to meet the demands of the Indian leaders: meanwhile, British statesmen tended to misunderstand the true nature of the growing disturbances in India, which it was too easy to attribute to malign Soviet influences.

Growing optimism about the diplomatic situation along with the practical need for economies helped to bring about a consistent decline in expenditure on armaments, until by 1933 only 2½ per cent of the national income was devoted to them. So confident were the statesmen that until 1933 British strategic thinking was based on the assumption of a period of ten years of peace. But administrative machinery for the organisation of defence was consolidated. The Committee of Imperial Defence was restored and became the focus of the Government's defence policy. After the embarrassment of the Chanak affair, a Joint Chiefs of Staff Committee was maintained for the co-ordination of policy. Unfortunately, the existence of such a committee weakened the arguments for the creation of a Ministry of Defence, without which there was likely to be more inter-service bickering than genuinely co-ordinated policy. Rivalries, indeed, were intensified as the R.A.F. came to assert its claims. Its power and prestige, especially that of its bombers, was built up by its 'father', Lord Trenchard, in the decade after the war, and its status was recognised by the inclusion in the Cabinet in 1923 of the Secretary of State for Air, Samuel Hoare. The Royal Navy, with its immense traditional influence, managed to hold its own – and, indeed, to develop its base at Singapore innocent of all consultation with the R.A.F. – but the Army suffered most severely from the economies and the hidebound military theories of the period.

The atmosphere of international reconciliation and the return to normality were reflected also in what came to be one of the most controversial actions of the Government. In 1919, the Gold Standard as the basis of currency had been suspended for six years. In 1925, Winston Churchill took Britain back to the Gold Standard. Gold coins were not re-introduced, but the value of currency in gold was restored as the standard for international financial transactions. The resumption of the Gold Standard was not in itself highly controversial; what did cause argument was the return to the Gold Standard at the parity of 1919 (that is to say that the 1919 relation of the pound sterling to the dollar was restored). J. M. Keynes argued that in fact, since 1919, there was a 10 per cent difference in gold prices, favouring the dollar. This, then, amounted to a virtual revaluation of the pound against the dollar by 10 per cent. Long-term difficulties were obscured by the short-term advantages to Britain in overseas trade.

Churchill at the Exchequer maintained very much of an old-style Liberal policy, though his balancing of the budgets was achieved by a good deal of juggling between the various accounts – Philip Snowden was to remark that 'The Right Honourable Gentleman's financial methods have been such that had his Budgets been company balance sheets he would have found himself in the dock'.[6] Although the Government refused to raise the levels of unemployment benefits, Churchill in his first budget introduced the contributory old age pension scheme. He reduced income tax to 4s in the pound and maintained Lloyd George's expedients of death duties and supertax. By the mid-twenties, educational expenditure as a proportion of national income had doubled since 1914, and represented 2·2 per cent. Under the stimulus of Wheatley's Housing Act during the Labour government, and Neville Chamberlain's rigorous application of it, 100,000 houses were built in each year. There is ample evidence, too, that real poverty declined.

Yet the Government faced a grave economic and social problem: over a million people were still unemployed. The economy was in an unhealthy and unbalanced condition. Imports had recovered, and stood in 1925 at a level 10 per cent higher than in 1913. Industries catering for the home market had recovered, but exports had fallen seriously behind. in 1925, they were 25 per cent lower than the level of 1913: Much of the real difficulty lay in the need to expand exports in markets which were not themselves expanding. There was a ready assumption, however, that the problem of exports could be solved simply by cutting prices: and prices could be cut by reducing wages. The serious consequences of such a policy were not understood: wages were already lowest in the exporting industries, and further reductions would undoubtedly reduce home consumption too, by reducing the money available to buy goods.

There was a further serious consequence of such an attitude. The twenties had been marked by a conspicuous lack of political bitterness. The majority of Labour M.P.s, for instance, were now moderate in their views: Labour and Conservative politicians were moving towards political harmony. Economic policy based upon wage reductions, however, shattered the tranquillity of the political scene. The trade unions naturally resisted, and this time their resistance went to the limit. Far from 'peace in our time', Baldwin found himself, in 1926, confronted with a General Strike.*

The conciliatory attitude which Baldwin in particular had adopted during the General Strike was largely tarnished by the Trades Disputes Act of 1927. There was, however, some improvement in the economic situation: the home market continued to expand, and between 1927 and 1929, exports increased slightly, though they were still 16 per cent below the level of 1913. The balance of payments, however, taking into account 'invisible' exports such as shipping charges, insurance and investment abroad, now showed a surplus of some £100 million a year. In 1928 both sides of industry came together in the Mond–Turner talks in an attempt to improve industrial efficiency. Production increased by 14 per cent between 1924 and 1929, but in 1928 unemployment was still over the million mark. The national budget was balanced, but precariously so.

Meanwhile, Neville Chamberlain achieved significant reforms of local government, although his attitude to the wider national problem was ambivalent: his enthusiasm for economic reform was genuine, but was chilled by his opposition to

* See Chapter Seventeen.

increased expenditure. Such opposition was reflected in his stringent application of governmental control over local authorities: in July 1926, he put forward legislation to restrict local councils who practised 'Poplarism'. Following the lead of George Lansbury in Poplar, such councils were paying higher rates of wages and reliefs than were officially allowed.

In 1928, the powers of local authorities which had developed during and since the nineteenth century were further established. The old Poor Law was eliminated: Boards of Guardians, which had administered the Poor Law locally since 1834, were abolished, and their functions taken over by Public Assistance Committees of the authorities of the 62 counties and 84 county boroughs. By now, about 40 per cent of the income of local authorities was derived directly from governmental grants. The Government also paid a total of £24 million to make up the loss to local authorities when agricultural land was freed entirely, and industry and the railways from 75 per cent of rates.

In Parliament, during 1927 and 1928, much energy was expended and much excitement focused upon a proposed revision of the Prayer Book. The fact of Anglican establishment rendered the Church subject to the authority of Parliament. Proposals to amend some of the services in the Book of Common Prayer to accommodate trends towards High Churchmanship, although approved by the House of Lords, were twice rejected by the Commons. The irony that some members of the Commons were not Christians, let alone Anglicans, was not lost on the clergy, and there was a good deal of militant talk of disestablishment. Finally, however, either by a typically English compromise, or because issues of ecclesiastical fashion and politics no longer played the role they had exercised in the nineteenth century, Convocation gave authority for the new forms of service to be used. Such an action was illegal, but remained until the work of the Liturgical Commission in the 1960s.

The general election which was due in 1929 was held in May. It was the first general election based upon a democratic franchise. In 1928, the right to vote had been given to women over 21 on a basis of equality with men. The election was a genuinely three-cornered affair, with the Liberals striving to regain their lost fortunes. Each party put over 500 candidates into the field. Baldwin and the Conservatives fought with the insipid slogan 'Safety First'. Lloyd George and the Liberals (Asquith had resigned the party leadership in 1926 and died in 1928) though weak in constituency organisation, put forward a dynamic programme, breaking with the classic Gladstonian economics, taking up the theories of Keynes and foreshadowing the American New Deal. Lloyd George had infused new life into the party, not least by spending his own political fund; but he was still distrusted, and his claim that he could cure unemployment was not believed. Labour's programme was drawn up by no less a pundit than R. H. Tawney: *Labour and the New Society* was a moderate, rather academic document. It made its appeal to members of the electorate who found 'Safety First' uninspiring, and who probably were more ready to believe Margaret Bondfield's fatuous claim that unemployment could be cured by Labour in three weeks than to study the rather more complex reasoning of Lloyd George.

For the first time, Labour returned most M.P.s – 288; they still lacked an overall majority, since the Conservatives held 260 seats, and the Liberals, cruelly frustrated and very much the also-rans, held 59. Baldwin resigned, and Ramsay MacDonald became Prime Minister again on 5 June 1929.

CHAPTER SEVENTEEN

The Acid Test of the Social Revolutionaries: The General Strike

THE General Strike of 1926 was foreshadowed by many aspects of the economic situation after 1918: indeed the threat of such a strike was present, implicitly or explicitly, on more than one occasion between the end of the war and 1926. Stanley Baldwin, for one, expected such action sooner or later, and saw to it that he was better prepared for it than the union leaders themselves. Yet, paradoxically, the General Strike may also be interpreted as something of a surprise – a left-wing aberration in a period when the trends in organised labour's opinions were moving towards the right in the context of growing unemployment which followed the collapse in the early twenties of the post-war boom.[2]

In fact, British industrial and commercial supremacy had gone for ever, a fact which was temporarily obscured by the false boom after the peace settlement – a boom in prices rather than in production. So long as the apparent prosperity lasted, the unions were able to adopt a militant attitude. Whilst Lloyd George procrastinated in the face of the industrial unrest which was especially marked between 1919 and 1921, the trade union leaders recognised the meagre power of the mere fifty-nine Labour M.P.s who had been elected in the snap Coupon Election, and talked of 'direct action'. The syndicalists seemed to be coming into their own, and there were frequent references to the threat of a General Strike; but a practical organisation which could run such a strike was never worked out. As Mr Alan Bullock astutely remarks in his admirable biography of Ernest Bevin:

> This was all right so long as the General Strike was employed only as a threat and the Government found it expedient to compromise. But it was a dangerous game to play: when the Government made up its mind to call the unions' bluff, as it did in 1926, they had either to go forward – a course for which they were quite unprepared – or to retreat ignominiously.[3]

In 1919 there was a renewal of the Triple Alliance of the miners, railwaymen and transport workers: their plan was to gain mutual strength by agreeing beforehand on each union's demands, and then presenting them simultaneously. In the same year a cut in railwaymen's wages led to a rail strike. The clear need for closer co-operation between the unions led to the creation of the General Council of the T.U.C., which replaced the old Parliamentary Committee.

A triumph for the union movement was secured in 1920 by the remarkable performance of Ernest Bevin, who was dubbed 'the dockers' K.C.' after his evidence to the Shaw Inquiry into dockers' conditions of employment. Bevin was one of the most remarkable and significant Englishmen of the century, who applied his untaught and passionate genius to the improvement of working class conditions through trade union organisation. It was an ominous symptom of the confused and troubled post-war economic situation, however, that the 16s a day which Bevin won for the dockers lasted only until 1923, when mounting unemployment forced the dockers' wage down to 10s a day.

Ominous, too, was the disaster of 'Black Friday'. Early in 1921, attention was focused upon a basic national industry, coal. The mines were returned from governmental control to the owners, and the owners posted drastic wage-cuts. On 31 March 1921 the miners called for help from the Triple Alliance and on the following day a national coal strike began. The Triple Alliance called for a strike of its members (which might well develop into a General Strike) for 15 April. The miners' executive was in some confusion, however, and there was a drastic lack of liaison which angered the National Union of Railwaymen and led the Triple Alliance to call off its strike. The miners, who stayed on strike until 1 July, felt themselves betrayed by their fellow-workers.

' "Black Friday" was a severe defeat for the trade unions and a bitter one to accept; it was not, however, a "betrayal", and the responsibility must rest at least as much with the miners' leaders as with the other members of the Triple Alliance. Unfortunately, the lesson of 1921 was not learned, with the result that five years later the trade union movement was to suffer an even worse defeat for almost identical reasons.'4 However, on New Year's Day 1922 the potential of the trade union movement was increased by the creation of the Transport and General Workers' Union. It had 1500 branches and 300,000 members, and its architect was Bevin, who, as first General Secretary of the T.G.W.U., wielded immense power.

Trade union militancy, however, continued to be handicapped by unemployment. Membership fell by nearly two million from 1920 to 1921. The natural reaction in such circumstances is for trade union attitudes to move to the right. Professor Mowat makes the very significant point that the General Strike was thus not typical of working-class attitudes during this period.

The springboard for the General Strike was, once again, the mining industry, in which a crisis developed at the end of June 1925, by which time the artificial boom in coal which had followed the occupation of the Ruhr during 1923 and 1924 had subsided. On 30 June the mineowners posted notices to end an agreement made in 1924. Wages were to be cut, whilst profits were retained, and hints were made of the desirability of a return to the eight-hour working day. The owners' notices were posted two months after Britain returned to the Gold Standard: 'The miners', wrote Keynes, 'represent

·п ·:: flesh the "fundamental adjustments" engineered by the
·᛫᠎ᴜ.ɪry and the Bank of England. . . .'⁵

᛫.᛫: miners determined to fight, and were firmly supported
·ʏ ᴏᵉ T.U.C. A Court of Inquiry under H. P. Macmillan
·᛫᛫᛫ₐ largely in favour of the miners. On Friday 31 July the
Cabinet staved off a dangerous situation by providing for a
governmental subsidy and the appointment of a Commission
under Herbert Samuel.

Baldwin was attacked by some of his own right-wingers
for yielding to trade union 'intimidation'. But whatever else
he was doing, he was buying valuable time, for it seems likely
that in 1925 the Government was not yet prepared to cope with
a prolonged strike. In September 1925, the Organisation for
the Maintenance of Supply (O.M.S.) was created; but it
served to supplement preparations already made by the
Emergency Powers Act of 1920 and by Baldwin's early restoration of the Supply and Transport Committee. 'By 1926',
writes Baldwin's biographer, 'its arrangements were complete
and Baldwin sat quietly waiting on events'.⁶

That the situation was becoming critical was reflected
in the violence of the speeches of A. J. Cook, a leading syndicalist and secretary of the Miners' Federation. On 14
October 1925, acting under the authority of an Act of 1797
and at the instigation of the Home Secretary, Joynson-Hicks,
who 'saw a Communist under every bed',⁷ the Government
arrested 12 leading Communists and searched their houses.
Sentences ranging from six months to a year's imprisonment
put them safely out of the way in case of trouble.

The report of the Samuel Commission on 11 March 1926
leant broadly towards the miners and against the owners. It
proposed the nationalisation, not of the mines, but of royalties;
the reorganisation of the industry by the amalgamation of
pits; improved research and distribution; better working
conditions. It pointed to the immediate economic necessity
of a reduction in wages and advocated district settlements
rather than a national agreements. The owners were not noted
for their diplomacy: Lord Birkenhead recorded that 'it would
be possible to say without exaggeration that the miners' leaders

are the stupidest men in England if one had not had frequent occasion to meet the owners'.[8] By 13 April deadlock was reached. The miners had summed up their attitude as 'not a minute on the day, not a penny off the pay', and stood firm for a national agreement. Anything less was greeted with Herbert Smith's characteristic 'Nowt doing'.

Deadlock persisted when on 22 April the owners put forward terms which would have cut wages in the Durham and South Wales coalfields below the rates which had existed in 1914. Baldwin made a final and unsuccessful effort at a compromise at a joint meeting on 23 April.

On 30 April the lock-out notices took effect, and on 1 May the T.U.C. informed the Government that they had taken over the negotiations. A General Strike seemed imminent; once more the unions were unprepared. The General Council of the T.U.C. began detailed preparations for running a General Strike only three days beforehand. There was, moreover, bitter dispute over just what the miners had handed over to the T.U.C. They claimed that the organisation of the strike had been handed over, but not the authority to negotiate any concessions. In general terms, the T.U.C. wanted the Government to enforce the acceptance of the Samuel proposals; the miners took a firmer, though less practical, stand.

As either a precaution or a provocation, the Government announced its preparations, and proclaimed a National Emergency under the terms of the Emergency Powers Act. Ernest Bevin responded by claiming that 'war has been declared by the government',[9] and the call went out for a strike from midnight on 3 May.

Negotiations went on until the last minute, although they were complicated by the fact that the delegates of the miners themselves returned home. Finally, the Government broke off negotiations after printers had refused to print a *Daily Mail* leader – an action which members of the National Society of Operative Printers and Assistants took on their own initiative and which was eagerly seized upon by the militants in the Cabinet. Baldwin characteristically went to bed: he was later to deny that he did so in order to avoid the possibility of surrender by the T.U.C.

Now that the crisis had come, most of the advantages rested with the Government. Many historians agree – however reluctantly – that the conduct of policy during the General Strike was Baldwin's greatest triumph. He was well-prepared and had at his disposal the remarkable organising talent of Sir John Anderson (Permanent Under Secretary at the Home Office). The Prime Minister succeeded in holding in check the extreme right-wingers among his colleagues, some of whom sought to provoke a full-scale revolution in order to suppress it once and for all. 'Don't forget the cleverest thing I ever did', Baldwin reminded G. M. Young, 'I put Winston in a corner and told him to edit the *British Gazette*'[10] – which Churchill duly accomplished in a very vigorous and one-sided fashion! The unions' answer to the *Gazette* was the *British Worker*. Ernest Bevin strove manfully to compensate for lack of long-term preparation: he maintained communications by means of despatch riders. But the pressing need was for organisation at the level of local trade union groups.

The strike began quietly. Support was solid on the first day, but the Government's plans worked smoothly, and an ostentatious armed food-convoy from the docks to Hyde Park on 8 May was hardly necessary. Volunteer labour readily went to work, and students were widely employed. Although their spirit was that of rag week rather than of strike-breaking, there is some substance in Mr A. J. P. Taylor's assertion that 'this was class war, in polite form'.[11]

Later in the week, there was violence in Glasgow, Leeds and Barnsley, especially over the use of blackleg labour on buses, and there were further disturbances in the east end of London, and in Liverpool and the north-east. Elsewhere, however, there were demonstrations of goodwill between police and strikers.

There were constant negotiations behind the scenes. The King and the Archbishop of Canterbury, Randall Davidson, were trying to mediate, and Samuel reopened his Commission. But the miners still stood firm by their original claims.

Meanwhile on 6 May, Sir John Simon, regarded as something of a legal oracle, pronounced a General Strike illegal, and on 11 May Mr Justice Astbury followed suit in court. The effect of Simon's pronouncement has probably been exaggerated, but the key to the whole issue was undoubtedly that when the T.U.C. leaders realised the full revolutionary implications of the situation, they hastened to withdraw from it. If there was to be revolution in England, now was the time, but the leaders of the working class were neither prepared for it nor disposed to undertake it.

On 12 May the General Strike was called off. The T.U.C. leaders made little impact on a placid Baldwin. Bevin in particular was very unhappy: his efforts to win guarantees against victimisation were met with an enigmatic 'You know my record'. Once more the miners felt betrayed by their fellow-workers. There seems to have been genuine misunderstanding, in a situation complicated by the stubbornness of the miners on the one hand and the anxiety for a settlement at almost any price felt by J. H. Thomas in particular. The real point was that the General Council of the T.U.C. was prepared to accept the recommendations of the Samuel Commission as the basis for a settlement, and the miners were not.

Peace came as a surprise and an anticlimax – and as a great annoyance to many of the strikers. Victimisation followed hard on the heels of the settlement: railwaymen were especially badly treated, and many found themselves refused work unless they would accept markedly worse terms of employment. Such experiences led to local extensions of the strike. Baldwin spoke strongly against such victimisation and the situation became more stable, although no less than a quarter of the membership of the N.U.R. was still out of work as late as October 1926.

The strike in the coalfields lasted until December, and created a severe economic setback. Half a million other workmen were kept out of work. But the conditions among the miners, who in the end had to yield to worse terms, were so appalling that the Lord Mayor of London opened a Miners' Relief Fund.

So ended a threat of revolution in Britain. Baldwin, who had maintained a moderate and reasonable attitude throughout, appeared as the saviour of parliamentary government. The trade union movement was weakened: its total membership fell below 5 million. Experience of actual labour during the strike had enlightened many members of the middle class, and helped to bring about a measure of social reconciliation.

But the Conservatives had a harvest to reap: the failure of the General Strike was followed in 1927 by the Trades Disputes Act, which included the provision that a General Strike was illegal, and the stipulation that trade union members must in future 'contract in' if they wished part of their trade union subscription to be allocated to the 'political levy' for Labour Party funds. The Act served to strengthen the ranks of organised labour, who reacted strongly against legislation so obviously directed against them, and the Trades Disputes Act in part accounted for the improved fortunes of the Labour Party in the general election of 1929.

CHAPTER EIGHTEEN

Labour Betrayed? 1929-1931

I know a lot of you shook your heads over the National Government. If I might whisper in your ears – I may have shaken my own. Do you think that was the sort of thing we wanted? Not at all.

RAMSAY MACDONALD at Easington, 12 October 1931[1]

THE second Labour government took office at a cruelly inauspicious time, although the worst omens were not immediately apparent. Indeed, the situation seemed not unpromising. The international climate was friendly, domestic issues promised political harmony rather than rancour, and the Prime Minister was widely respected and admired.

The composition of MacDonald's administration reflected the moderate tone of politics generally. After some rather embarrassing haggling, Arthur Henderson became Foreign Secretary. His rival for the post, J. H. Thomas, was created Lord Privy Seal with special responsibility for dealing with unemployment, which was the burning issue of the day, and which Labour had been elected to cure: Miss Margaret Bondfield, who became Minister of Labour, had indeed declared that the problem could be solved in three weeks. The only left-winger in the Cabinet was the patriarchal George Lansbury, who became First Commissioner for Works. His influence within the Government was minimal. In fact, apart from MacDonald himself, the most influential figure in the Government was one who put the brake hard on any progressive measures which involved increased governmental expenditure: Philip Snowden was transformed from the socialist Robespierre into the Iron Chancellor. At the Exchequer, he was the unshakeable advocate of the old-style, classic (though increasingly outmoded) Treasury doctrines of economic and financial policy. In addition, he was passionately devoted to Free Trade. In an administration whose members floundered in the sea of economic misfortunes which struck them, Snowden, with his firm convictions and his ready flow of acid invective, found little difficulty in dominating his colleagues.[2]

The economic blizzard, however, was as yet the faintest cloud on the distant horizon. In its early days, the second Labour government enjoyed a period of success, notably in foreign policy. MacDonald's own prestige abroad was high, and Henderson became a popular and respected Foreign Secretary. In August 1929, at The Hague, Snowden made a characteristically outspoken defence of Britain's claim to her share of reparations. But the Young Plan, which provided for a more realistic assessment and collection of reparations, was accepted. Henderson's reputation and his devoted work for the League of Nations were recognised by his appointment to the presidency of the World Disarmament Conference which was called for February 1932.

MacDonald himself made a successful visit to the United States, and a measure of agreement was reached with the U.S.A. and Japan at the London Conference which met in 1930 to consider the limitation of navies. Britain, the U.S.A. and Japan agreed to restrict their navies in the ratio of 5:5:3, and Britain pledged herself not to have more than fifty cruisers. The good work of the Conference was somewhat vitiated by France and Italy, who refused to subscribe to the agreement, largely because Italy was insisting upon naval parity with France. Meanwhile in October 1929 the Government had resumed diplomatic relations with the U.S.S.R., this time in a less inhibited fashion than had been attempted in 1924.

Britain's imperial reponsibilities presented MacDonald's administration with opportunities and with serious difficulties. On 31 October 1929, before the Simon Commission on India had reported, the Viceroy, Lord Irwin, made a definite promise of dominion status for India. But the time had passed when dominion status would have satisfied the aspirations of the Indian leaders: in December 1929, the Indian Congress declared independence, and Gandhi led a great campaign of civil disobedience. In June 1930, the Simon Commission's report was published: it recommended responsible government in the provinces, and negotiations on the central governmental power in India. MacDonald called a Round Table Conference, which assembled in November 1930, but which was boycotted by the Indian Congress. Gandhi was, however, conciliated, and he attended a second Round Table Conference, but by that time Labour was out of office. Not everyone in Britain, let alone in India, was in favour of the Government's policy. Winston Churchill would not even accept the Conservative Party's version of it, and resigned from Baldwin's 'shadow Cabinet' in January 1931.

Elsewhere, the Government made less progress. Negotiations over the future of Egypt broke down, whilst Palestine presented a complicated and potentially dangerous problem. Jewish immigration, financed by the Zionist movement, provoked the Arabs into resistance. A White Paper published in October 1930 pronounced that immigration must cease. The Zionists were outraged at such a repudiation of the Balfour Declaration, and all of MacDonald's conciliatory skills were needed to stave off a crisis.

In domestic policy, there were some positive achievements before good intentions were swept away by the accelerating crisis. There was no outspokenly socialist legislation, but some mild compromises were made with the principle of state-intervention. The Coal Mines Act of 1930 fixed a $7\frac{1}{2}$-hour day, but left the mineowners to fix prices and quotas. A commission was proposed to reorganise the coal industry. In 1931, the Agricultural Marketing Act provided facilities for better organised pricing and marketing of farm produce. Herbert Morrison laid the foundations of what in 1933 became the London Passenger Transport Board, and Arthur Greenwood maintained the housing subsidies. But much more was blighted and killed off by the downfall of the Government. Trevelyan, for instance, failed to pass a bill to raise the school-leaving age to 15. Projects of electoral reform and attempts to repeal the Trades Disputes Act of 1927 were thwarted.

The crippling problem of unemployment remained to be dealt with. In June 1929, there were 1,164,000 unemployed. Under the pressure of economic events the figures rose uncontrollably: in June 1930, to 1,911,000, and by the summer of 1931 to 2,707,000. Traditional methods could do nothing to stem the tide, although the Cabinet was determined to stand firm by the rates of unemployment benefit. Radical measures, when recommended, were rejected.

A progressive solution stemmed from the studies of those ministers appointed to advise J. H. Thomas. In January 1930, proposals were put forward in the so-called Mosley Memorandum. Oswald Mosley advocated policies which were in part derived from Keynes and which went further than Lloyd George's proposals of 1929 and anticipated the New Deal which President Roosevelt was to inaugurate in the United States. Mosley proposed to prevent the effects of the world-wide depression from wrecking Britain. Imports were to be stringently restricted, whilst home agriculture was to be protected and subsidised. Food and raw materials were to be obtained through bulk purchase, wherever possible from the Dominions. The Government should control the banks and grant credit freely to enable industry to expand and absorb the unemployed, whilst the Government scrutinised investment and modernisation. There was to be an ambitious programme of public works – roads, slum clearance, and so on – financed by loans from the Government. The school-leaving age should be raised to fifteen immediately, and old age pensions should be payable at sixty. The scheme was far too *avant garde* to be accepted, especially by Snowden.[3] The Memorandum was rejected in May 1930; Mosley resigned, and carried his programme to the country at large and to the Labour Party Conference in particular. There, in a vote of 2,297,000, Mosley was defeated by only 205,000 votes. He formed a 'New Party', and then became a Fascist. One of the minor tragedies which sprang from the events of 1929-31 was the dissipation of the undoubted talents of Oswald Mosley.

The crisis which wrecked the Labour government in 1931 was not primarily concerned with unemployment, nor even with the economic situation in general. It was essentially focused upon financial confidence and the place of sterling in world markets. In fact, as Mr A. J. P. Taylor has pointed out, the terms of trade in 1930 moved 30 per cent in Britain's favour, with prices of imports falling whilst exports maintained their price-levels.[4] The weakness of the Government derived from its strict financial orthodoxy, especially that of Snowden, who was determined that the Budget must balance, and that the unorthodoxies of Churchill's tenure of the Exchequer must be redressed. In 1930, Snowden increased income tax to 4s 6d in the pound, and proposed a tax on land-values, whilst allowing the Safeguarding Duties to lapse. In short, the Budget was strictly in accordance with Snowden's rigid orthodoxy and his devotion to Free Trade.

In February 1931 the May Committee was appointed to inquire into possible governmental economies. Meanwhile, the effects of the appalling collapse of the Wall Street Stock Market in October 1929 were beginning to be felt.[5] On 11 May 1931 the great Austrian bank, Credit Anstalt, failed. Attempts to support it threatened the stability of the entire German economy. On 20 June President Hoover proposed a one-year moratorium on international credits. Britain agreed to a standstill on her German credits; she got no reciprocal protection from France. The London bankers were now threatened with the worst possible dividend of a policy which had been financially lucrative but vulnerable: they had lent over long terms at interests as high as 8 per cent or 10 per cent, especially to Germany, whilst borrowing, particularly from France, on short term at interests as low as 2 per cent. The French began making massive withdrawals of gold from London.

The situation, now largely a matter of confidence, was not helped by the publication of the report of a committee under Lord Macmillan, which was destined to exercise its positive influence later, with its arguments for a managed currency. Immediately, however, it drew attention to the fallacies of the established economic theories and pointed out that Britain's apparently healthy balance of trade was dependent upon 'invisible' exports (like insurance and shipping) which were particularly hit by the effects of the world-wide depression. Alarm and despondency were thus further increased.

The Government was not prepared to deal with the situation by methods other than the established ones. Nor should the ministers be too readily blamed for this shortcoming. As Mr Bassett has pointed out, there is a tendency to forget that the new, expansionist ideas which were so successful in the United States under President Roosevelt became fashionable only after these events.[6] Even Keynes was by no means settled in his arguments whilst the crisis had to be dealt with, and Ernest Bevin, in his advocacy of expansionist economics, was far more adventurous in his thinking than most of his trade union colleagues.

The Cabinet, then, was agreed upon the basic need to balance the Budget and preserve the pound. There were differences over method, and over the extreme to which economies should go. A recommendation from a Royal Commission that unemployment benefits should be reduced was rejected by a group of influential ministers, who took a firm political stand in spite of the economic argument that because of a fall in the cost of living the unemployment benefit had increased in value. Meanwhile, Snowden's emphasis upon the seriously unbalanced state of the Budget caused a further loss of confidence. His budget of April 1931 was essentially a stalling operation: he was awaiting the report of the May Committee, which would inevitably back him in much more stringent measures.

On 30 July 1931, Parliament adjourned for the summer. On the following day, the May Committee's report was published – a piece of timing by which Snowden ensured the postponement of parliamentary discussion of its recommendations. The proposals of the May Committee were drastic in the extreme, and certainly did nothing to alleviate the immediate crisis of confidence: Hugh Dalton records that Keynes called the report 'the most foolish document I ever had the misfortune to read'.[7] May's Committee calculated a budget deficit of £170 million. The annual payment of £50 million

into the Sinking Fund for redeeming the national debt was
regarded as sacrosanct. Deficiencies were to be met by £24
million in increased taxation, and by economies totalling £96
million, with a 20 per cent cut in unemployment benefit.

MacDonald and his colleagues went off on holiday, but
by 11 August the run on the pound had become so serious that
the Prime Minister was recalled to London. Attempts to
raise loans, particularly in the United States, now faced
pressures for evidence of serious retrenchment before money
would be forthcoming. Cabinet discussions which began on
20 August hinged especially upon whether retrenchment
should include cuts in the unemployment benefit. For the
T.U.C., Bevin expressed forthright opposition to such cuts
and the T.U.C's attitude may well have been decisive. On 23
August nine members of the Cabinet were determined to
resign rather than agree to the size of the cuts proposed.

There followed a political situation which was confused
at the time and has been worse confounded since by politicians and historians alike. The general impression that Labour
had been betrayed held sway until Mr Reginald Bassett
produced a study of 1931 which is masterly in its detail and
convincing in its argument.[8]

The hard facts are that on 23 August the Labour government resigned. On 24 August a National Government was formed.
Since a general election in such a time of crisis was unthink-
able, some form of coalition was inevitable. What caused
surprise was that Ramsay MacDonald remained as Prime
Minister. The idea that he should do so originated with Herbert
Samuel (who was acting as leader of the Liberals in the
absence of Lloyd George, who was seriously ill). Samuel's idea
was supported by Baldwin, and was regarded as congenial by
King George V, who had a high regard for the Prime Minister.
MacDonald took with him into the new Cabinet Snowden
and two other Labour members (Thomas and Lord Sankey),
together with four Conservatives (Baldwin, Chamberlain,
Hoare and Cunliffe-Lister), and two Liberals (Samuel and
Lord Reading). Mr Harold Macmillan has recently emphasised MacDonald's action in shielding the future careers of

younger Labour men by not taking them into his government.[9] He warned them, indeed, that by following him they would be putting their heads into a noose.

Why did the Prime Minister not resign and hand the burden to the other parties? Why, indeed, did he not resign earlier in the crisis? Mr Bassett finds the answer in MacDonald's high and idealistic view of Labour's mission: Labour ought to shoulder the burden, and therefore he prolonged his efforts to reach agreement with his colleagues. Many members of the Labour Party, including the dissidents in the Cabinet, felt sure that the Prime Minister would resign and leave the formation of a coalition to the other two parties. MacDonald himself probably thought the same on 23 August 1931. But who would become Prime Minister? Lloyd George, who might have risen to the occasion, was out of action and would scarcely have won Conservative backing, and it was by no means certain that the Liberals would support Baldwin. Thus the appeal to the Prime Minister in personal terms by the King must have carried great weight with him. There seems little real doubt that MacDonald was taken by surprise: the idea that he had plotted the betrayal of Labour in advance has no firmer foundation than MacDonald's undeniable enjoyment of aristocratic company and his ill-judged quip to Snowden (of all people) after forming the National Government that every duchess in London would be wanting to kiss him. The Prime Minister himself described the events of 23 and 24 August as 'very painful', and there is no serious reason to doubt his sincerity. Far from betraying Labour, he may, by shielding the younger Labour men and his refusal to allow the Labour government to run away from the crisis at an early stage, have done much to preserve the future of Labour, first in opposition and then as a potential government.

At the outset, MacDonald and his colleagues regarded the National Government as an interim measure to deal with the immediate crisis, after which the parties would revert to their normal alignments. This was clearly a miscalculation. Even more serious was MacDonald's gross underestimation of the bitterness and vigour of the opposition to his actions within the

Labour Party. In the early days of the National Government there was caustic mutual recrimination across the floor of the House of Commons as erstwhile colleagues sought to repudiate their earlier participation in Cabinet decisions. This goes far to account for the virulence of Snowden's attacks upon the Labour Party, in whose service he had devoted a lifetime. The T.U.C. pushed Labour into opposition. MacDonald naturally could not remain leader of the party, and was replaced by Arthur Henderson. On 31 August, the Hampstead Labour Party went so far as to expel MacDonald from membership.

As far as the immediate financial crisis was concerned, the creation of the National Government brought credits of £80 million, chiefly from the U.S.A. Snowden, in his autumn budget, duly balanced the accounts by reducing the payment into the Sinking Fund to £20 million, by increased taxation amounting to £76 million, and by economies of £70 million, to be achieved largely by cuts in salaries: public servants generally lost 10 per cent of their salaries, but policemen forfeited only 5 per cent, teachers as much as 15 per cent. Unemployment benefit was cut by 10 per cent.

On 15 September the sailors at Invergordon, incensed at an inept handling of their pay cuts, refused to put to sea. Confidence abroad was again disturbed: money in ever-increasing amounts was withdrawn, and by 19 September the latest credits were exhausted. Two days later, Britain went off the Gold Standard.

Clinging to the Gold Standard had in many ways been the root cause of the trouble, for gold supplies throughout the world were simply inadequate to meet vast expansions of population and commerce. But 'gold stood for stability'[10] and had hitherto been regarded as the supreme article of financial faith. Now events had overcome theory, and Britain had passed to a 'managed currency'. Most of the anticipated disasters never materialised. The external value of the pound fell by about 20 per cent, whilst internally its value was virtually unchanged. Thus the cost of living remained fairly stable, whilst foreign purchasers paid less for British exports and therefore bought more of them.

Strong arguments may be marshalled to explain MacDonald's

ormation of the National Government. It was, of course, harder to justify his leadership of it to the polls in October 1931. This, more than anything else, added intense bitterness to the resentment already felt by the majority of the members of the Labour Party. MacDonald seems to have hated to lead his own supporters against Labour. Not so Snowden, who attacked with a vitriolic relish. His election campaign broadcast on 17 October 1931 had great influence. Dismissing the manifesto of the Labour Party with contempt, he declared:

> I hope you have read the Election programme of the Labour Party. It is the most fantastic and impracticable programme ever put before the electors. All the derelict industries are to be taken over by the State, and the tax-payer is to shoulder the losses. The banks and financial houses are to be placed under national ownership and control, which means, I suppose, that they are to be run by a joint committee of the Labour Party and the Trade Union Council. Your investments are to be ordered by some board, and your foreign investments are to be mobilised to finance this madcap policy. This is not Socialism. It is Bolshevism run mad.[11]

At the polls, the National Government won a massive victory and the Labour Party was, at least temporarily, crippled. The National Government won 554 seats: 473 of them were Conservatives, 35 were Liberal followers of Simon, 33 Liberal followers of Samuel, and 13 Labour followers of MacDonald. Labour returned only 52 members, its leadership passing to George Lansbury, who was the only member with experience in the Cabinet.

CHAPTER NINETEEN

The Locust Years (1):
Piecemeal Solutions at Home

The lot of man is ceaseless labour,
Or ceaseless idleness, which is still harder,
Or irregular labour, which is not pleasant.

T. S. ELIOT, *The Rock*

THE consolidation of the National government in the general election of 1931 – the acknowledgement that a temporary political expedient had become an established political structure – threw party politics into the melting-pot. The election campaign, in which each party contributing to the Government had been able to put forward its own differing policies within the framework of the comprehensive government which MacDonald led, had foreshadowed the remarkable 'agreement to differ' which Neville Chamberlain was to propose as the reconciliation of conflicting principles concerning free trade and tariffs in 1932, and indicated the paradoxical situation in which politicians could cling to their political ideals whilst at the same time submerging them.

The bitter reaction against MacDonald in the Labour party made it abundantly clear that the Prime Minister's own political future was utterly dependent upon the continuation of the National government. He, Snowden, Thomas, Sankey, and the handful of National Labour M.P.s were 'traitors', and the Labour party, although it was to prove that it was not ruined by their 'treason', was for a time seriously weakened. The experience of 1931 had done much to destroy the trade union movement's confidence in the parliamentary party, now led by Lansbury

Cripps and Attlee, none of whom was particularly congenial to the rank and file membership of the trade unions. Certainly, the personal antipathy between Lansbury and Ernest Bevin did nothing to heal the breach, and it was indeed Bevin who was to drive Lansbury from the leadership.

MacDonald had asked the electorate and the parties for a blank cheque and had received it, but he was to find himself, as Joseph Chamberlain and Lloyd George had done before him, the prisoner of the Conservatives, who yet again had used a coalition as a springboard for their own political fortunes.

The Conservatives dominated MacDonald's Cabinet, both in numbers and in policies. They provided eleven out of the total membership of twenty. Baldwin, the Conservative leader, held the largely honorific office of Lord President of the Council, but was recognised as the heir-apparent to the Premiership; the elevation of Snowden to the House of Lords made way for the promotion of the strong man of the Conservatives, Neville Chamberlain, to the Chancellorship of the Exchequer. For a time, however, all was not well with the harmony of the Conservative party. There was a determined effort, led by the Beaverbrook and Rothermere newspapers, to oust Baldwin from the leadership, with the proclamation of the 'Empire Crusade'. Baldwin, however, proved unexpectedly resilient, and more than a match for the Press lords. Chamberlain, meanwhile, was content to dominate policy from the Exchequer, and to wait for the Premiership to fall into his lap in due time. The other embarrassment to the Conservatives, and one which was to grow with the years, was Winston Churchill, who cried from the political wilderness against official policy, first concerning India and then, on much better grounds, against the Government's foreign policy.

The Liberals were in a wretched state, split into three. The followers of Simon were out-and-out supporters of the National Government, tariffs and all; the Liberals led by Herbert Samuel were much more inhibited by the traditional Liberal gospel of free trade; Lloyd George led a family group of four in outright opposition and watched Ramsay MacDonald relive his own experiences in a Conservative-dominated coalition.

H

The Government had been elected to deal with the effects of the Great Depression, and its task was therefore fourfold: to solve the grievous social and economic problem of unemployment; to balance the Budget; to restore a favourable balance of payments; to restore confidence in the pound sterling. The National government was to achieve a fair measure of success; at the same time, great opportunities were wasted, and the success which was achieved was bought at the price of continuing unemployment. A society was produced in which those who were in work enjoyed a rising standard of living, but in which too many had no work at all. The 'dole' was at best a partial solution, especially when it was made dependent on the humiliation of the means test. There was a failure on the part of politicians like Chamberlain, in spite of the strictures of Archbishop Temple[1] and others, to appreciate that there is a dignity and fulfilment in labour for which even the most efficient soup-kitchen is no substitute. So the Government's economic and financial policies were piecemeal, with no real attempt at an imaginative solution of deep underlying problems, and no breadth of vision comparable with that of theorists like Keynes or practical statesmen like Roosevelt.

The solution on which many of the members of the Government, especially Chamberlain, had set their sights was the abandonment of Free Trade and the introduction of protective tariffs. Rumours of an impending protectionist policy provoked a great influx of imports, and led to an emergency measure in November 1931, the Abnormal Importations Act, which imposed an immediate duty of 50 per cent on a wide range of goods, and reserved to the Government the power to impose duties up to 100 per cent. British agriculture was similarly shielded.

A Cabinet committee under Chamberlain was set up to enquire into the balance of trade. Its recommendations were predictable, since it was packed with protectionists. There was no really searching enquiry, such as had been promised to the electorate during the general election; and in any case, there existed no really detailed and practical statistics on which the committee might have relied.

The Cabinet committee reported in January 1932, and the practical implementation of its recommendations was embodied in Chamberlain's Import Duties Bill, which came into effect on 1 March 1932. There was to be a general tariff of 10 per cent; but Empire goods and practically all raw materials and food-stuffs were exempt. An Import Duties Advisory Committee was set up under Sir George May, who had already made such a melancholy contribution to history in 1931. The Committee was empowered to recommend increases up to 33⅓ per cent. It might also recommend decreases, but rarely did so. Over the next few years, the general effect of the protective policy was that about a quarter of all imports were free of duty, whilst something like half paid 20 per cent.

In July 1932, at the Ottawa Conference, something very much like Joseph Chamberlain's Imperial Preference was at last put forward as governmental policy. What was created was far from being Free Trade throughout the Empire. The dominions accepted preferential treatment from Britain, and reciprocated, not by cutting their duties on British goods, but by increasing those on foreign produce. The system was extended in 1933 to include colonial produce, and in 1934 quotas – 'the bargaining power of the tariff'[2] – were introduced. The long-term economic effects of the Government's policy were that between 1930 and 1938, imports from the Empire increased from 25 per cent to 37·9 per cent of all imports, whilst exports to the Empire grew from 37·5 per cent to 45·6 per cent.[3] The immediate political consequence was to drive Samuel to resignation in September 1932, along with Snowden, who embarked upon a vitriolic campaign against Ramsay MacDonald and all his works. Snowden's success may be judged by the half-informed denigration of MacDonald which has persisted to the present day. The Conservative flavour of the National government was now even more pronounced: it now was virtually a Conservative administration, aided and abetted by MacDonald, Thomas and Sankey, and of course Simon's Liberal-Nationals.

In 1932, Chamberlain converted over £2000 million of War Loan from 5 per cent to 3½ per cent, thereby saving immediately some £23 million – an economy which totalled some

£86 million a year by 1936. He aimed, by a policy of 'cheap money', to stimulate expansion, and did succeed in creating a boom in housing: from 1934 onwards, more than 300,000 houses a year were being built – more than double the output of the 1920s. Industries catering for the home market also expanded. This expansion was achieved without unbalancing the Budget, although he had miscalculated in 1932, and still had a deficit in that year of £32 million. So there was none of that 'priming the pump' of the economy, for which Keynes was pleading, as the solution of the unemployment problem.

Britain did recover economically, partly as a result of governmental policies, and also because of a general revival of world trade, which by 1937 had revived almost to the level of 1929. The nation's share of that trade increased, but largely through growing imports; exports were at a level below 85 per cent of those of 1929. Britain was cushioned to some extent by a consistent fall in commodity prices. Her balance of payments improved from a deficit of £104 million in 1931 to a favourable balance in 1935, but too much of her income was derived from investment overseas, which was tending to be reduced as gold was exported.

Production also revived: in 1932, it had been 15 per cent below the figure for 1929; by 1937 it was 20 per cent above the 1929 level.[4] Two examples are indicative: steel production had been 9·6 million tons in 1929; in 1931 it had tumbled to 5·2 million tons; by 1937 it had reached 13 million tons. Coal, facing competition from other fuels, did not revive to a similar extent: from 244 million tons in 1930, it fell to 207 million tons in 1933, and revived to 241 million tons in 1937. The revival of the steel industry owed much to amalgamations and general reorganisation, the price exacted by the Import Duties Advisory Committee for a protective tariff. Shipbuilding never really recovered until the war, although in 1934, by the North Atlantic Shipping Act, the Government subsidised the completion of the Cunard liner *Queen Mary*.

Agriculture was heavily protected and subsidised, and between 1931 and 1937 its output volume increased by one-sixth. The Milk Marketing Board was set up, and subsidies were paid on milk for school children and for nursing mothers in the depressed areas. The price of wheat was guaranteed, and subsidies were paid on sugar-beet, barley and oats. By 1939, the annual cost to the Exchequer of this reinvigoration of agriculture was £100 million.

Agriculture indicates that the Government was prepared to undertake such direct responsibilities, and there were, indeed, three examples of nationalisation: the London Passenger Transport Board in 1933, coal royalties in 1938, and the creation of B.O.A.C. in 1939.

Yet unemployment persisted, and although the statistics were more favourable than in many other countries, they must stand as an illustration of the shortcomings of national policy generally during the 1930s. Between August 1931 and January 1933, the total was nearly 3,000,000 (23 per cent); in August 1933, it fell below 2½ million; in July 1935, below 2 million; and in July 1936, to 1,600,000 (12 per cent).

Meanwhile, the Government had passed two important pieces of legislation so far as Britain's imperial role was concerned. In November 1931 the Statute of Westminster gave legal recognition to the status already achieved by the dominions, whose Parliaments were enabled to legislate independently of British laws: these were to hold sway in the dominions only at the request of the dominions themselves. The Crown was to be the symbol of the free association of the members of the British Commonwealth of Nations; the succession and royal titles were to be subject to the assent of the dominions.

In 1935, the Government of India Act was passed. It was a step forward, though it did not meet Gandhi's demands at the second Round Table Conference in September 1931 for partnership and the immediate handing over to the Indians of control over foreign policy and defence. The Act of 1935, bitterly opposed by Churchill, provided for an all-India federation (which never came into existence), virtual cabinet government in the provinces, and a separate government for Burma.

Ireland added to the burdens of the National government. In 1932, de Valera succeeded the moderate Cosgrave, and set out to exploit the greater freedom given by the Statute of Westminster. In 1933 the oath of allegiance was abolished, the dignity and status of the Governor-General were deliberately reduced, and land annuities were withheld. Thomas, as Dominions Secretary, contested these moves, and economic sanctions were applied in retaliation for the withholding of land annuities: a small-scale tariff war followed. In 1935 de Valera repudiated British citizenship.

In June 1935 MacDonald, whose powers were failing, and who by now was revealing an embarrassing tendency to say less and less whilst speaking at great length, exchanged offices with Baldwin, whilst in November of the same year, the National Government was re-elected, with a total of 428 supporters in the House of Commons. Now led by Attlee, Labour revived, with 154 M.P.s, whilst the Liberals had 17 plus Lloyd George's family group of 4. There were 4 members of the I.L.P., and 1 Communist.

Baldwin, in his third term as Prime Minister, provided his customary lethargic leadership, although he was presented with one situation in which he might shine. In January 1936 King George V died. His successor, Edward VIII, had established something of a reputation as a Prince Charming, and had been reputed to display alarmingly radical tendencies when confronted, for instance, with the effects of the Depression in south Wales. But a crisis developed over his wish to marry Mrs Wallis Simpson, an American divorcee. Both the Church and the Government were opposed to such a marriage, and the King was mistaken when he thought he had found a solution in the proposal that he should marry Mrs Simpson without her receiving the title of Queen. The King had his supporters, notably Winston Churchill and Lord Beaverbrook, but Baldwin insisted that he must give up either Mrs Simpson or the throne. The King chose to abdicate. He made a broadcast address to the nation which was dignified and intensely moving; both qualities were conspicuously lacking in the unctuous performance of Archbishop Lang of Canterbury, who administered a distasteful clerical kick to an opponent who was not only down but out.

Edward VIII was succeeded by his brother, the Duke of York, who was untrained for kingship, shy, and afflicted with a stammer which his biographer thinks may well have derived from the harsh upbringing prescribed by his father.[5] But he was fortified by a charming wife and an idyllic family circle, and was destined to play his regal role supremely well in the ordeal of the war to come.

Baldwin retired in May 1937 and handed over to Neville Chamberlain, who applied his supreme self-confidence to the problems which now beset the nation.

CHAPTER TWENTY

The Locust Years (2): Shirking the Issues Abroad

Our enemies are little worms. I saw them at Munich.

ADOLF HITLER

THE story of British foreign policy in the 1930s is a sorry tale which assumes the proportions of tragedy, not merely because of its results, but because in many ways it was a genuine reflection of British attitudes, or at least of those of citizens who considered foreign policy at all. Too many Englishmen, at most periods in our history, have adopted the attitude of Stanley Baldwin, and have literally or metaphorically fallen asleep when foreign affairs were under discussion.[1]

Certainly it is true that the nation and its leaders were seriously – and understandably – preoccupied with the great issues of national survival and revival in the chronic economic crisis of the early thirties. Not merely did domestic affairs occupy men's minds, but they were directly relevant to some of the important diplomatic issues of the day. For instance, it was scarcely realistic to plan in terms of large-scale rearmament whilst the financial stringency of the time forbade the necessary expenditure.

There is no doubt, too, that a strongly pacifist sentiment made itself felt, especially during the early years of the decade. The glamour of the First World War had faded, and the literature and drama of the period spoke only of its futility. A play such as R. C. Sherriff's *Journey's End*, which enjoyed great success, still conveys its sombre and essentially pessimistic message, although much of its dialogue, with its emphasis on good chaps and the virtues of understatement and the stiff upper lip, is seriously dated by now. Men who had experienced the holocaust shrank from the prospect of their own exploits being repeated by their sons. There were many particular expressions of this general state of mind. In February 1933, the Oxford Union (a fashionable, albeit overrated sounding-board) carried by 275 votes to 153 the motion that 'this House will in no circumstances fight for its King and Country'. In October 1933, at a by-election in East Fulham, the Conservative candidate emphasised the need for rearmament: a Conservative majority of 14,521 was turned into a Labour majority of 4840. Whilst it is true that domestic issues such as the means test played a crucial part in the campaign, a strongly pacifist note had been sounded, and Stanley Baldwin, for one, regarded East Fulham as 'a nightmare'.

Opinion shifted only gradually. As late as June 1935, in the celebrated Peace Ballot, the majority of some $11\frac{1}{2}$ million citizens who took part still returned predictably pacifist answers to carefully loaded questions, but by that time the answers to the last of the questions in the ballot reflected a majority feeling in favour of collective security, even at the risk of war.

The great vehicle for diplomacy in the early thirties was still the League of Nations, in the context of which, in the absence of the U.S.A. and Russia, Britain still had the opportunity of playing a leading part. It was the nation's peculiar disadvantage, however, to be represented by two successive Foreign Secretaries whose cleverness outweighed their wisdom; both Sir John Simon and Sir Samuel Hoare tended to react to situations with responses so flexible as to have no backbone.

Support for the League was in any case half-hearted and the major issues were confused. There were two great hopes for peace: disarmament and collective security. But they were contradictory:[2] if one supported the League of Nations and disarmament, one effectively drew the teeth of the League's Covenant, for collective security without arms to enforce it was a mere paper formula. Conversely, individual national rearmament implied a contempt for the League. Collective

H2

security without rearmament was widely canvassed and accepted within the British Labour Party, for instance, whilst most of the strongest advocates of British rearmament tended to be found on the right of the Conservative Party.

Serious and sincere attempts to bring about general disarmament were made during the period. They foundered in the end, as similar efforts have done since, upon the rock of resentment at inspection of one's resources by other nations. The Geneva Disarmament Conference opened in February 1932 under the presidency of Arthur Henderson in an auspicious climate. The forces of occupation in the Rhineland had been withdrawn and reparations payments had been suspended in 1931 and would be abandoned in 1932.

The problem for the disarmers was, of course, Germany. There was a good deal of sympathy with the view that the Germans had been harshly treated at Versailles – as indeed they had. They now claimed equal status, and parity in armaments with France; in fact Germany had already rearmed beyond the prescribed limits. Britain was in a quandary: she sympathised with legitimate German grievances, but was in no position to guarantee France in case of German bad faith. A characteristically clever but meaningless formula was devised: Germany was granted 'equality of rights in a system which would provide security for all nations'. [3] The situation was complicated, though few at the time appreciated how drastically, when Hitler became Chancellor of Germany on 30 January 1933, in spite of the waning fortunes of the Nazi Party in the Reichstag. Those German politicians and businessmen who helped him to power were setting out to ride on a tiger.

The resumed Disarmament Conference set out to define the sizes of national forces. Germany was indeed given parity with France, to the indignation of Winston Churchill, who in discussing British defence needs produced the shocking heresy 'Thank God for the French Army!' Hitler was conciliatory, whilst maintaining the claim to parity. In October 1933 Simon and the French proposed a five-year period of inspection. Whether intentional or not, this was a trap into which Hitler declined to step. On the same day he withdrew from the

Conference and gave notice of Germany's resignation from the League of Nations. Those who had ears to hear remained deaf to this ominous and obvious warning-note. No man received more encouragement to become a compulsive gambler than Hitler: nobody called this bluff, and it killed disarmament. The Geneva Conference was adjourned *sine die* in May 1934.

Meanwhile, the potency of collective security was being put to the test elsewhere. In September 1931, the Japanese invaded Manchuria (an event which some contemporary historians have interpreted as the true beginning of the Second World War). China appealed to the League, the response of whose members was marked by a serious underestimation of the true scope of Japanese intentions and ambitions.

Britain proposed an inquiry and appealed for a cease-fire: the actions of the League were dilatory and its attitudes were confused. Early in 1932 the fighting was extended and the conflict spread to Shanghai. The Chinese invoked articles 10 and 15 of the Covenant, which should have led to the imposition of sanctions. In May a truce was agreed over Shanghai; the irony of appealing to the League was that nothing could really be achieved in the Pacific without the participation of the League's non-member, the U.S.A., and Britain failed to back up the American proposal of 'non-recognition' of Japanese conquests. Japan thus felt free to create the puppet-state of Manchukuo, and in February 1933, the Japanese resigned from the League and invaded China proper. The importance of the Manchurian episode spread beyond Asia: the League had failed an important test, and a dismal precedent had been set, of which the European dictators were only too ready to take advantage. As for Britain, she had been too ready to compromise with the aggressor, another precedent which she was to follow in her European dealings.

Hitler's advent to power produced an ambivalent response in Britain. Labour, of course, detested Fascism, but not strongly enough at this stage to modify the party's antipathy to rearmament. The Conservatives also disliked Fascism, but tended to regard it as an alternative to Communism, and thus perhaps as the lesser of two evils. That Hitler constituted a potential threat could not be denied, and Baldwin pledged the National Government to maintain parity with Germany in the air. The R.A.F. was thus to be extended, even if at the expense of the Army. In any case, projects of rearmament and such general plans to meet a war situation as existed were still largely on paper.

An important and unusual step was taken in March 1935 with the publication as a White Paper of the *Statement Relating to Defence*. Its contents clearly recognised the need for measures of rearmament and a withdrawal from reliance upon collective security. Still the British response was half-hearted – unlike Hitler's, for he used the *Statement* as a pretext for restoring conscription in Germany!

A limited attempt at some form of collective security was pursued in April 1935, when MacDonald joined Laval of France and Mussolini in the so-called Stresa Front, which sought to guarantee against breaches of the international order Even more questionable was a private agreement made with Hitler in June 1935, that the German Navy should be allowed to reach 35 per cent of British naval strength, with a special concession in favour of submarines! Germany could have 40 per cent of British submarine strength, with as much as 100 per cent if she faced danger from Russia.

After King George's Jubilee in May 1935, Baldwin became Prime Minister and Simon was replaced as Foreign Secretary by Sir Samuel Hoare, who had made a reputation for himself in the negotiations with India. Anthony Eden was being groomed for stardom and joined the Cabinet with special responsibility for League of Nations affairs.

Italy was pursuing aggressive designs on Abyssinia. Britain again proved too accommodating when dealing with aggression, although she was perhaps genuinely embarrassed by Mussolini's assertion that he wanted in Abyssinia only a position comparable with that of Britain in Egypt. Attempts to buy him off having failed, Hoare produced a despicable piece of verbal and political juggling. Like Simon, he was to prove adept at producing clever solutions which were no solution at all. Now he propounded the formula that Britain would support the

League wholeheartedly if all the other members were as whole-hearted as Britain was.

Understandably not discouraged, Mussolini attacked Abyssinia on 3 October 1935. Economic sanctions were applied, and Mussolini's aggression brought about the first really significant shift in British Labour opinion: the T.U.C. urged that Italy should be held in check even at the risk of war. The Labour Party Conference was more divided: George Lansbury as leader put forward the pacifist line, only to be crucified in a scathing personal attack by Ernest Bevin:

> I hope you will carry no resolution of an emergency character telling a man with a conscience like Lansbury what he ought to do. If he finds that he ought to take a certain course, then his conscience should direct him as to the course he should take. It is placing the Executive and the Movement in an absolutely wrong position to be taking your conscience round from body to body to be told what you ought to do with it.[4]

Bevin's attack, and his account of Lansbury's disloyalty to decisions of the National Council of Labour, swung the vote, in spite of the shudders at his brutality. He was unrepentant. He knew more of Lansbury's guile and subtlety than most of the delegates,[5] and he dismissed the episode – 'Lansbury has been going about in saint's clothes for years waiting for martyrdom: I set fire to the faggots'. The affair drove Lansbury from the Party leadership; it did not transform Labour's attitude overnight. The new leader of the Labour Party was Clement Attlee, and in the Commons he consistently opposed rearmament until 1939.

Amidst the alarms of Mussolini's attack upon Abyssinia, a general election was held in November 1935. Domestic issues again predominated in the campaign and in the minds of the electors. Baldwin – still haunted by the 'nightmare' of East Fulham – deliberately played down the necessary scale of rearmament: 'I give you my word that there will be no great armaments'. The National Government and its diplomacy were confirmed in office, although Labour gained 100 seats.

Pressure was mounting for more effective action against

Italy, particularly for an oil sanction which, if applied, must prove decisive. British diplomacy, however, was overshadowed by the fear that if war broke out, Britain would be left to fight Italy alone. Hoare produced another compromise, no more tasteful than the first. Britain and France (in the unprepossessing person of Laval) would see that Italy got the Abyssinian plains whilst the Emperor Haile Selassie, 'the Lion of Judah', was relegated to the mountains. Mercifully, the Hoare–Laval Pact was leaked to the French Press, and Baldwin diverted the righteous indignation which fell upon the Government on to the head of Sir Samuel Hoare, who was officially described as 'tired' and 'sick', and was replaced by Eden.

The problem of Italy remained unsolved. On 1 May 1936 Haile Selassie was driven into exile, and Mussolini, in the sort of fatuous gesture of which he was a master, proclaimed the second Roman Empire. In an appalling scene at Geneva, Haile Selassie protested to the League with great and touching dignity in the face of disgraceful derisive hooting by Italian journalists. A spineless end was written to a humiliating chapter when, at Neville Chamberlain's insistence, sanctions against Italy were withdrawn on 18 June 1936.

Hitler took his cue and played his greatest piece of bluff to date. On 7 March 1936 a token force of German troops re-entered the demilitarised Rhineland, Hitler apparently having reassured his nervous generals in advance that the troops would be withdrawn at once if they were opposed.[6] Later it became clear that this was the crucial moment, though few joined Churchill in recognising the fact at the time. This was the moment to call a halt to Hitler's European adventure and perhaps drive him from power in a disillusioned Germany. But France did nothing, so what would Britain do? Baldwin explained that she had no forces with which to oppose Hitler, and that in any case public opinion would be against such action. He may well have been right on the second count, and may well have overestimated the amount of force necessary on the first. He went on, though, to promise France and Belgium 'protection' if they were attacked by Germany – surely a far more dangerous contingency than the comparatively straightforward task of resisting in the Rhineland. Churchill, certainly, was confident that existing forces were more than adequate for that task.

A strong proposal for action against Germany came from Russia in the person of Litvinov, who proposed sanctions against Germany. The source was naturally regarded as suspect, and nothing was done. Hitler blandly announced that he had 'no territorial claims in Europe'.

Baldwin's prestige suffered under the impact of the further failure of collective security to which he had pledged himself during the general election campaign of 1935. Rearmament, meanwhile, went ahead, and its most significant progress was made in secret. It is perhaps not too much to suggest that in many respects the Battle of Britain was won in 1935 when Robert Watson Watt invented radar; it was developed through the enthusiastic advocacy of Henry Tizard and did something on behalf of Fighter Command to balance the R.A.F.'s emphasis on bombers.

In the summer of 1936 the Spanish Civil War broke out and overlapped into European diplomacy as the rebels received help from Italy and Germany and the Republican government received help from Russia. Direct British intervention was confined to the activities of volunteers, some 500 of whom lost their lives in the Republican cause. Both Britain and France were concerned above all to prevent a general European war on the issue, but the efforts of their 'Non-Intervention' Committee were vitiated by blatant Italian and German cheating. When action was taken, however, it worked. In the summer of 1937 unidentified submarines, which were in fact Italian, sank British, French and Russian ships which were carrying food and non-military supplies to the Republican government. Britain and France set up anti-submarine patrols and the sinkings ceased forthwith.

After the coronation of King George VI, Baldwin retired and Chamberlain entered into his inheritance. Eden remained as Foreign Secretary in an administration which was still strongly preoccupied with its domestic programme and which tended to incur the hostility of the permanent officials of the

Foreign Office. Chamberlain was dogmatic and opinionated. Well described by Mr A. J. P. Taylor as 'a meticulous house-maid'[7] in domestic policy, his interference (with that of his adviser, Sir Horace Wilson) in diplomacy was potentially dangerous and most certainly irksome to Eden.

Britain's strategical position was weakened in 1937 when the new Irish constitution was made and the three naval bases which had remained to the Royal Navy in southern Ireland were handed over to Eire. In Palestine, too, Britain faced trouble as hostility between Jews and Arabs increased, stimu-lated by the influx of Jewish refugees from Germany. In 1937 a Royal Commission recommended partition, which was found to be impossible. In May 1939 a White Paper prescribed the limitation of Jewish immigration into Palestine, and thus went back upon the Balfour Declaration.

Under Chamberlain rearmament now gathered pace as the Government sought to match Hitler's own account of his armed strength, which he characteristically exaggerated. In April 1937 Chamberlain proposed a special tax on profits from armaments, and provision was made for £460 million of the extra cost of armaments to be met by borrowing, rather than from immediate taxation. In 1938 craft and engineering restrictions were relaxed and preparations were made for switching production, particularly for changing to aircraft production. In February 1939, authorisation was given for aircraft production 'to the limit'.

Whilst he prepared for war, however, Chamberlain's policy bought peace – at a price, and for a time. This has given rise to the claims of his apologists that his policy was deliberately to buy time in which the country could rearm. This was an incidental result of his policy, but that it was his intention at the time is scarcely borne out by events. His policy, indeed, was marked by a fundamental error, in so far as he treated Hitler and Mussolini as orthodox statesmen. He seems to have believed that they were so, and was encouraged in his view by the reports of his ambassador in Berlin, Sir Nevile Henderson. Henderson may, of course, simply have told Chamberlain what he thought he wanted to hear. In any case Chamberlain should have been enlightened by the serried ranks of storm-troopers who were on display during his visits to Germany.

Chamberlain's fundamental belief may well have been that Germany was too strong to be crushed, and would inevitably dominate eastern Europe and the Balkans. He certainly shared with many British statesmen a low view of the potential strength of Soviet Russia. British opinion was still overshadowed, too, by a consciousness of the injustice of the Versailles settlement and by the sneaking feeling that there was some justice in the German claims. There was, too, a rather shamefaced envy of Germany's economic progress. *The Times*, under the editorship of Geoffrey Dawson, fostered the feelings that Germany had just claims, whilst Labour's attitude, though moving towards rearmament, was still equivocal. All these factors, coupled with the feelings of others than Neville Chamberlain that events in Czechoslovakia, for example, were 'a quarrel in a faraway country between people of whom we know nothing', provided the ingredients of disaster. The Empire, too, played its part: the Imperial Conference of 1937 was strongly in favour of appeasement.

Yet the true nature of the Nazi government could not be ignored. The intensification of the persecution of the Jews was vividly indicated in the increasing numbers of Jews who were seeking refuge in Britain and America.

Before Hitler presented another major crisis, other disputes remained to be dealt with. In November 1937 China again appealed to the League. The problem was handed over to a Nine-Power Conference in Brussels and Britain pledged herself to act if the United States did (an unlikely contingency).

In February 1938 trouble arose over recognition of Italy's position in Abyssinia. Chamberlain proposed to make it conditional upon Italy's withdrawal from Spain. Chamberlain consulted with the Italian ambassador over Eden's head and the Foreign Secretary resigned in protest, Lord Halifax taking over the Foreign Office. Eden did not now associate himself with Churchill, but his resignation provoked rumblings of Conservative discontent: twenty-six Conservatives abstained from voting after the debate on his resignation speech.

Hitler marched on. On 13 March 1938 he took over Austria. The question of the Sudeten Germans incorporated in Czechoslovakia since the Versailles settlement loomed on the horizon. The French wavered in their support of the Czechs, and Sir Nevile Henderson in Berlin was in favour of appeasing Hitler. The inevitable crisis came in September 1938. On 13 September the Germans in the Sudetenland staged an unsuccessful revolt against the Czechs, and two days later Chamberlain and Sir Horace Wilson flew to Berchtesgaden, where Hitler demanded self-determination for the Sudeten Germans. Daladier for France compelled Britain to guarantee the remnant of Czechoslovakia, and on 21 September, President Beneš of Czechoslovakia felt bound to agree to the separation of the Sudeten Germans rather than risk the withdrawal of all support by Britain and France.

Encouraged once more, Hitler stepped up his claims. Chamberlain again flew out, and at Godesberg on 22 September was confronted with Hitler's demand for the immediate occupation of the Sudetenland, which was modified into an agreement not to act before 1 October – which in any case was the earliest date by which his troops could be ready to move in.

The warning-signs were by now too vivid to be ignored. Labour and the trade unions now joined unequivocally in the growing support for the Czechs and demands for resistance were increasingly heard. Preparations for war went ahead. Air-raid precautions were instituted and gas-masks distributed to provincial centres ready to be handed out. The Foreign Office was still not clear in its attitude, but assumed that if the Czechs were attacked, France would make war on Germany, and Britain and Russia would help her. On 27 September, the Fleet was mobilised.

Then another attempt at conciliation was made. Appeals to Mussolini to mediate led to the four-power conference at Munich on 29 September. There was a marked lack of coordination between Chamberlain and Daladier, and the Munich conference produced a settlement virtually along the lines already laid down by Hitler at Godesberg: the occupation of the Sudetenland was to be spread over ten days.

After the Czechs had been thus sold out Chamberlain concluded a personal agreement with Hitler which affirmed the determination of their two nations not to go to war: Chamberlain waved the pathetic scrap of paper as he stepped from his aeroplane on his return, and spoke of his belief that it signified 'peace for our time'. If Chamberlain believed this, he deceived himself, and many of his countrymen shared in the deception. The relief with which the Munich agreement was widely greeted was soured somewhat by the resignation of Duff Cooper, the First Lord of the Admiralty, and by thirty Conservative abstentions when Labour divided the House of Commons on the issue.

The general anxiety over Czechoslovakia had given an increased impetus to rearmament and to the further implementation of existing plans. The target for the army was now a total of 32 divisions (6 Regular and 26 Territorial). Civilian preparations were also stepped up and in November 1938 the distinguished civil servant Sir John Anderson was made Lord Privy Seal and given responsibility for air-raid precautions. Plans were laid for the evacuation of children from London and coastal areas.

On 15 March 1939 Czechoslovakia disintegrated and tumbled into Hitler's pocket. Slovakia became 'independent' and a German protectorate was established in Bohemia and Moravia on the reluctant invitation of President Hacha. Though its fate might have been foreseen, the actual event greatly stiffened national resolve in Britain. On 17 March, in a speech in Birmingham, Chamberlain adopted a much firmer attitude towards German aggression.

Hitler now threatened Poland. He demanded that the free city of Danzig should be handed over to Germany, and that the Polish corridor to the sea should be seriously modified. There were ominous rumours of German troop movements. On 31 March Chamberlain announced to the House of Commons that if Poland were attacked Britain would support her, and on 6 April a mutual guarantee was agreed with Poland, the Poles having been too proud to accept a one-sided guarantee from Britain without themselves guaranteeing Britain's safety in return. Lloyd George pointed out that such a guarantee was to all intents and purposes futile, especially without the assistance of Russia, whose advances the Government had already spurned over negotiations on the security of Rumania.

On 26 April the Government announced the unprecedented step of conscription in time of peace. The measure was, however, only a half-hearted one, and could scarcely bear any immediate fruits. Meanwhile, pressures were increasing for the broadening of the composition of the Government, and particularly for the inclusion of Winston Churchill. A letter on the subject to *The Times* from Lady Violet Bonham Carter and other leading Liberals met with an editorial refusal to publish, yet another disgraceful episode in Geoffrey Dawson's editorship of the paper: the letter appeared in the *Daily Telegraph*.

Negotiations with Russia were pursued in a very half-hearted and dilatory fashion. Both sides were distrustful, but a warning-note for the British negotiators was sounded with the dismissal of the conciliatory Litvinov, and his replacement by Molotov. Russia swung to the other side: on 19 August she made a commercial agreement with Germany, and four days later, European diplomacy was shattered by the signing of the Nazi–Soviet Non-Aggression Pact.

Poland was now indeed in mortal peril, and German provocations in Danzig increased. Hitler had been led by Ribbentrop to expect that Britain would again back down and her refusal to do so embarrassed him, but his plans were too far advanced to be called off. On 1 September German troops invaded Poland.

Once more, the British Government delayed, even after sending a strong note to Germany requiring the removal of German forces from Poland. Mussolini was offering mediation; Britain, however, agreed to talk only if German troops were withdrawn. On 2 September Chamberlain spoke in terms of British action only if the Germans had not promised that they would withdraw – one step back from the assertion that Britain would hold back only if the troops actually were withdrawn. The House of Commons was indignant: Arthur Greenwood rose to speak for the Labour Party, and was greeted with a cry of 'Speak for England!' from the Conservative right-wing critic of Chamberlain, Leopold Amery. Greenwood successfully expressed the feelings of the House, and Chamberlain was forced into sending a formal ultimatum which expired at 11 am. British Summer Time on Sunday, 3 September 1939. The House of Commons had saved the dignity of the nation.

CHAPTER TWENTY-ONE

The Roaring Twenties
and the Pensive Thirties

I journeyed to London, to the timekept City,
Where the river flows, with foreign flotations.
There I was told: we have too many churches,
And too few chop-houses . . .
I journeyed to the suburbs, and there I was told:
We toil for six days, on the seventh we must motor
To Hindhead, or Maidenhead.
If the weather is foul we stay at home and read the papers.
In industrial districts, there I was told
Of economic laws.
In the pleasant countryside, there it seemed
That the country now is only fit for picnics . . .

T. S. ELIOT, *The Rock*

THE Great War of 1914–18 was a cataclysmic episode in the history of mankind. Its effects were far-reaching and revolutionary; not all of them were immediately apparent, especially in Britain.

In the economic context, for example, once the immediate post-war boom had collapsed, there was a dangerous tendency to blame the war for the economic malaise and to expect that, given time, conditions would improve. The truth was rather that the early symptoms of the country's economic sickness were apparent before the war.

Socially, despite the influence of the battlefield as a factor in integrating society, post-war Britain was far indeed from being a classless utopia. It has been estimated that in post-war Britain, 1 per cent of the population owned two thirds of the nation's wealth, whilst 75 per cent of citizens owned less than £100 each.¹

Politically, the war had undoubtedly stimulated tendencies towards democracy, as in the electoral reform of 1918 and the introduction of votes for women. The creation of a democratic franchise was not, however, immediately reflected in support for the Labour Party. But the confidence of the working class had notably increased. Higher wages and better working conditions were a dividend of war. In 1924 wage-rates were 11 per cent higher than in 1914, but already the important qualification had to be made that such rates applied to those fortunate enough to be in work.

By the 1930s the gloom of the effects of the great depression was intensified by the menacing shadow of political events abroad, and to the hardship of unemployment there was added the indignity of the means test. Especially unhappy was the spectacle of unemployment concentrated in the towns of the 'depressed areas'. At least in the countryside, the unemployed worker had the distractions offered by nature and by his own garden; in the towns which had made the traditional industries of Britain great there was little recourse for the unemployed save 'street corner idleness'. The new light industries which were catering for the home market escaped the effects of the depression, but they were not established in areas which needed them. Two-thirds of the working population of Jarrow were unemployed in 1934; as late as 1937 the unemployment figure in Wales was 22·3 per cent. London and the south-east revived much more quickly, and provided another stimulus to the drift of population to the South.

The problem of unemployment, which seemed to defy solution, provided material for economic and political theorists. In his classic *General Theory of Employment, Interest and Money* (1936) J. M. Keynes formulated the arguments on which he had been working and which he had been advocating since the war. Here were theories to control the cycle of trade and to make adventurous use of budget deficits. Not surprisingly, other theoretical solutions veered drastically towards the left. At this stage, not enough was known of the brutal nature of Stalin's régime, and Soviet Russia was often superficially regarded as a socialist paradise. There was support for the idea of a 'popular front' of the left, and Victor Gollancz's Left Book Club exercised considerable influence.[2] At the other extreme, Mosley's Fascists were aping their European counterparts and from 1934 onwards there were open clashes between Communists and Fascists, especially in the east end of London. The Spanish Civil War provided the opportunity for left-wing self-sacrifice in the International Brigade.

The population continued to rise, although much more slowly. In 1921 the population of Great Britain was 42,769,000, and ten years later reached 45 million: the rate of increase was 5 per cent in a decade, compared with 10 per cent in the ten years before the war. By 1938 the birth-rate was less than two-thirds of that of 1900, and the death-rate continued to fall. Tuberculosis, the scourge of nineteenth-century life, was in retreat against the forces of modern medicine: deaths from tuberculosis declined in England and Wales from 1066 per million in 1922 to 657 per million in 1937. Increasingly, the population was housed in the suburbs of towns and cities, in 'ribbon developments' of factories and poorly planned semi-detached homes.

The motor car was now firmly established as an ingredient in British life. Austin and Morris made small, mass-produced 'family cars'. Between 1922 and 1930 there was a threefold increase in the number of cars in Britain, which totalled over a million in 1930. By the outbreak of war in 1939 the total had almost doubled. Cars were not now merely used for holidays and weekends. They became normal everyday transport for many people. The 1930s witnessed increasing regulation of the motorist: in 1934, the driving-test was instituted, along with the imposition of a speed-limit of 30 m.p.h. in built-up areas. Later, 'Belisha beacons', now familiar as indicators of pedestrian crossings, were invented. But there was no really farsighted programme of road building to meet an entirely foreseeable need; a real chance to tackle the problem of unemployment by a valuable project of public works was largely ignored.

In public transport the motor bus was replacing the electric tram, but it was in civil aviation that most impressive developments were now taking place. In 1930, 22,045 passengers were carried in British-owned aircraft, and tourism as an industry was expanding rapidly in importance.

In everyday life, meanwhile, further extensions of educational opportunities were linked with increased governmental influence. Since 1918, the school-leaving age had been fourteen, but there was room for great improvement in facilities. In 1922, for example, no less than 25 per cent of classes in English schools contained over sixty pupils each. Governmental supervision was reflected in diverse ways: free places in secondary schools were made more readily available, whilst the Burnham Committee made teachers' salary scales uniform throughout the country, and the Government's involvement in the finances of education was further marked by the establishment of the University Grants Committee.

The serious literature of the period lost touch with society in general, although it does reflect much of the apathy which T. S. Eliot captured in *The Hollow Men*:

> We are the hollow men
> We are the stuffed men
> Leaning together
> Headpiece filled with straw. Alas!
> Our dried voices, when
> We whisper together
> Are quiet and meaningless
> As wind in dry grass
> Or rats' feet over broken glass
> In our dry cellar. . . .

The established novelists were Thomas Hardy, Arnold Bennett, Joseph Conrad and John Galsworthy, whose attitude was by now more conformist than in his earlier work. H. G. Wells was lapsing into increasing pessimism. Kipling, Bridges and Yeats were the most widely-read poets of the time. There was great creative writing, much of which reflected the influence of Freudian psychology. D. H. Lawrence preached against false moral values and against the rape of the countryside and its society by industrialisation, whilst Aldous Huxley was concerned for ethics in an increasingly scientific age. Neither was easy to read, but the two greatest novelists of the time, James Joyce and Virginia Woolf, in their rebellion against established forms and values were difficult almost to the point of impossibility. The unhappy paradox of a really large reading public coming into existence just when serious literature became so difficult goes some way to account for the great popularity of the lightweight, though skilful, works of P. G. Wodehouse, the crime stories of Edgar Wallace, and detective fiction generally.

The greatest poet of the age was T. S. Eliot, one of the outstanding revolutionary figures in the whole history of English literature. *The Waste Land* was published in 1923. Eliot's style is difficult; much of his work is clearly a pessimistic commentary upon the indecisiveness of his times, though his gloom is lightened by Christian faith. The workings of the middle-class conscience, and its reactions to the plight of the working class, may be found in the plays and novels of J. B. Priestley, notably in *English Journey* (1934) and in such writings of George Orwell as *The Road to Wigan Pier* as well as in the poetry of W. H. Auden, Stephen Spender and Cecil Day Lewis. An important publishing development was the advent of paper-backed books, with Penguin Books at sixpence a copy, introduced in 1935.

On the stage, Shaw's *St Joan* was movingly played by Sybil Thorndike, but the sharp edge of Shaw's satire was blunted by this time. More fashionable was the superficial philosophising and affected wit of Noël Coward, who added a touch of maturity to the antics of the 'bright young things'.

The theatre was in any case open to the challenge of the cinema, which was now making its own claims as an art form. Most of the films which drew increasingly large numbers of people away from the music halls and theatres were American, until an Act of 1927 protected the infant British film industry by providing for a quota of British films on the cinema circuits. And the greatest of the early stars, far outlasting and outshining the appeals of Rudolph Valentino and Mary Pickford, was a cockney, Charlie Chaplin, the first true genius of the cinema and one of the great comic actors of all time. Mr A. J. P. Taylor has, indeed, credited Chaplin with a wider appeal than that of Shakespeare. In 1929 the talkies began, and with them the great era of the cinema, which would last until the challenge of television. During the 1930s the British film industry was enhanced by the talents of Alexander Korda, and the war gave a further stimulus, with the need for really good propaganda. Films like *Pimpernel Smith*, *The Way Ahead* and *San Demetrio, London*, dated though they may be in technique, have a good deal to teach later generations about attitudes to oppression and to war.

The visual and plastic arts of the period matched the difficulty of the more obscure writers, but two great – if controversial – sculptors flourished: Jacob Epstein and Henry Moore.

A transforming influence in everday life was the development of broadcasting, the history of which is so perceptively narrated and analysed by Professor Asa Briggs in *The Birth of Broadcasting* (1961). Authority was vested from the beginning in the G.P.O. In 1922 the British Broadcasting Company was founded and four years later it became a public corporation. Broadcasting soon became more than merely a medium of entertainment. News broadcasts became an important feature of transmissions. The first and greatest Director-General of the B.B.C. was John Reith, a man strongly convinced of the moral responsibilities of broadcasters who imposed standards which verged upon the puritanical. He was caricatured as a moral censor, but he was right. In its early stages, the powers of broadcasting might well have got out of hand.

The B.B.C. had a real contribution to make to the cultural life of the nation. In 1930, for example, the B.B.C. Symphony Orchestra was founded and during the 1930s *The Listener* came to provide its invaluable weekly service of printed versions of broadcast programmes. In 1932 the voice of King George V was heard on Christmas Day in the first of the long series of annual broadcasts from the Monarch to the nation and the Commonwealth. Obviously broadcasting added greatly to the drama of events like the abdication crisis, with its memorable and moving broadcast by King Edward VIII. And the war was literally brought home to millions. None who heard it can forget, for example, the heartrending dispatch from Arnhem by Stanley Maxted, nor Robert Reid's account of the liberation of Paris. One of the war correspondents, Richard Dimbleby, became a truly national figure after the war, with the extension of broadcast commentaries and of television programmes.

Broadcasting inevitably challenged the Press. Northcliffe died in 1922 and his vast newspaper domains were divided. *The Times* passed into the hands of a trust in the family of Astor. In 1930 the *Daily Herald* became the subject of a joint venture by the T.U.C. and Odhams Press. But the outstanding popular newspaper by the outbreak of the war was probably the *Daily Mirror*, which under G. H. Bartholomew established itself with racy journalism and spicy illustration – a less crude sensationalism than that of the early days of Harmsworth.

The newspapers now fought an all-out war for circulation and the advertising revenue which only circulation could attract. Door to door canvassing, offers of free gifts, and even for a time free insurance policies, were the weapons. A most interesting venture began in 1938 with the publication of *Picture Post*, a high quality illustrated weekly which employed some brilliant journalists and photographers. *Picture Post* died under the post-war assaults of television, but its library of photographs is unsurpassed.

Life in general was marked by the further emancipation of women, who after a fashionable imitation of mannish appearance in the 1920s returned to femininity in the 1930s. The outward signs of class barriers began to break down with more uniformity in masculine attire and more informality in fashions generally. Facilities for games increased as never before: a favourite method of commemorating George V was by the provision of playing-fields. Hiking, and keeping fit generally, were popular pastimes, and 1930 saw the creation of the Youth Hostels Association. Gambling, particularly on horse racing and the football pools, flourished.

Dancing was popular, especially during the 'roaring twenties' – the era of the 'bright young things'. The thirties reflected a more sombre and pensive mood, although the mood was not predominantly religious. The Church had lost the hold it once possessed, in spite of the impact of one of the greatest Christian leaders of modern times, William Temple, who became Archbishop of Canterbury in 1942. His death before the end of the war was a national disaster, for he had much to contribute to the post-war world and especially to British society which, after the roaring twenties and the pensive thirties was to pass through the furnace of the Second World War.

CHAPTER TWENTY-TWO

The 'Phoney War' and the Fall of Chamberlain

> You have sat too long here for any good you have been doing. Depart, I say, and let us have done with you. In the name of God, go!
>
> OLIVER CROMWELL in the House of Commons, 1653
> LEOPOLD AMERY in the House of Commons, 7 May 1940

BRITAIN went to war on 3 September 1939 when the ultimatum which the House of Commons had coerced Neville Chamberlain into sending to Germany, expired at 11 a.m. The guarantee to Poland which the British Government had made in March 1939 was now to be put into effect, though how, and with what resources, was very much a matter for conjecture. Ambassador Kennedy of the United States was not alone in recognising the futility of the guarantee as far as Polish territorial integrity was concerned, but if nothing else it was a springboard for resistance to Hitler at last. Within a week the Dominions had followed the British lead. The British Empire and France now stood – however reluctantly or half-heartedly – against Nazi tyranny.

A by-product of Chamberlain's policy of appeasement – though surely not the main objective which some apologists have contrived to see in it – was that time was provided for important preparations to be made. The time was used with varying degrees of efficiency, and in general plans were better made on paper than they were carried out. The resources of manpower needed for vast administrative expansion and reorganisation tended to be underestimated, and some policies were only half-heartedly applied. For example, the creation of the Ministry of Supply in July 1939 was gravely weakened by the existence of the independent supply organisations of the Admiralty and the Royal Air Force, so that the new ministry worked only for the Army. Conscription at first had been introduced only in a form to provide for the future, and only one batch of men ever actually took part in the preliminary 'militia' training which had been prescribed.

Such preparations for war as had been made enabled some domestic rearrangement to be efficiently carried out. Gas-masks were promptly issued, and a blackout was imposed. Among new ministries, the Ministry of Information was established. A large-scale evacuation of children, some with their mothers, was organised. A million and a half people were officially moved out of supposedly dangerous areas, and some two millions more made their own arrangements for removal. The transportation of the 'official' evacuees was excellently organised, but details of billeting and financial and other long-term arrangements were much less satisfactory. The chaos which sometimes ensued inspired a harrowing play and at least one brilliant satire.[1] An important social consequence of evacuation, however, was an increase in mutual understanding – though not necessarily, at first, of mutual sympathy – between city-dwellers and country people. Another shortcoming of evacuation was that anticipation of where air-raids might occur tended to be somewhat inaccurate: in any case, during the early months of the war there were no air-raids, and by January 1940 about a million evacuees had been lulled into a false sense of security and had returned home.

Ration books had already been printed before the war, and a 'shadow' Ministry of Food was in existence. The actual application of rationing was stimulated by a popular enthusiasm for it, and it was organised on a basis of national registration, which also obliged every citizen to carry an identity card. Economic controls were established, placing a strong emphasis upon purchase within the sterling area, and a most significant precedent was created when the Government introduced food-subsidies to offset a rise in prices.

The conduct of the war itself was seriously lacking in dynamism. Chamberlain was never a war minister in either spirit or action. He failed to persuade Liberals or Labour to join his Government, which he did at least succeed in broadening by the inclusion of two opponents of appeasement in Anthony Eden (who became Dominions Secretary) and, significantly, Winston Churchill as First Lord of the Admiralty. 'Winston is back' went out the ebullient signal to the Fleet. Yet what Chamberlain conspicuously failed to convey was the necessary sense of urgency and vitality. Any national enthusiasm which might have existed for a crusade against tyranny remained largely unexploited.

In fact, the early stages of the war were marked by a bland optimism on the part of the Government, based upon the comforting illusion that Germany was teetering on the brink of economic collapse. This no doubt explains, amongst other things, the curiously old-world response of the Secretary of State for Air, Sir Kingsley Wood, when it was suggested that his bombers, which, after an early raid on the Kiel Canal, were dropping nothing more potent than leaflets, might perhaps set fire to the German forests. 'Are you aware,' he demanded, 'that it is private property? Why, you will be asking me to bomb Essen next.'[2]

Four divisions of the British Expeditionary Force were sent to France under the command of General Gort – who was on notoriously bad terms with the War Minister, Leslie Hore-Belisha – and placed under the supreme command of the French General Gamelin. Whilst the Germans were occupied in Poland, French patrols crossed into Germany, but withdrew to the deceptive security of the Maginot Line when challenged. Hore-Belisha was the victim of a conspiracy by the generals when he complained of inadequate British defences along the Franco-Belgian frontier. Chamberlain dutifully sacrificed him and he was replaced by Oliver Stanley in January 1940. Meanwhile, in an attempt to undermine Italian influence, forces were built up in North Africa, under the supreme command of one of the ablest and most amiable of British generals, Sir Archibald Wavell.[3] Though action there was delayed, the Middle East was destined to become a highly significant theatre of war.

At sea, the belief in Germany's economic vulnerability led to an emphasis upon the traditional weapon of the blockade. But the effectiveness of the German U-boats threatened to turn such a strategy inside-out, in spite of the immediate introduction of the convoy system. Within nine months, 800,000 tons of merchant shipping were lost, although the loss was more than replaced by using reserve shipping and by new launchings. The fighting ships suffered too. In September a U-boat sank the aircraft-carrier *Courageous* and in November an unprecedented disaster occurred when the battleship *Royal Oak* was torpedoed actually within the defences of Scapa Flow. But in December the Royal Navy achieved the first real victory of the war. The German surface-raider *Graf Spee* was attacked in the Atlantic by the cruisers *Ajax*, *Achilles* and *Exeter*, and forced to run for shelter into the neutral port of Montevideo. When the time-limit allowed by international law expired, the *Graf Spee* was scuttled in face of a gathering fleet of overwhelming strength.

The war situation was confused in November by a Russian attack on Finland and by pressure for a campaign to help the Finns. Churchill had a scheme to mine the route by which iron ore was carried from Sweden to Germany, and such a plan might have been co-ordinated with a move through north Norway and Sweden to assist Finland. By the time such an operation was ready, however, the Finns had made peace in March 1940. But on 9 April the Germans occupied Denmark and the Norwegian ports, so the British campaign was revived. It was badly bungled at Narvik, which was not taken until 28 May. There a vital lesson was to be learned, for air power proved to be the crucial factor.

It was the mishandling of the Norwegian campaign which brought about the downfall of the Chamberlain Government. An historic debate was opened in the House of Commons on 7 May. Called at the instigation of the Opposition, the debate was distinguished in its early stages by the virulence of attacks from the Conservative right wing upon the Government's

I

handling of the war. Sir Roger Keyes, resplendent in his uniform of Admiral of the Fleet, blistered the conduct of the Norwegian campaign, and a high point of drama was reached when Leopold Amery, who had long been a friend and supporter of Chamberlain, reiterated the stinging words first heard in the House nearly three centuries earlier: 'You have sat too long here for any good you have been doing. Depart, I say, and let us have done with you. In the name of God, go!'[4] On 8 May the Opposition declared their intention of forcing a division on what had by now become a serious motion of censure. Chamberlain, not uncharacteristically, turned it into a personal matter and appealed to his friends. He aroused the righteous contempt of a shadow from the past. David Lloyd George, whilst attempting to shield Churchill, whom he warned not to allow himself to become an 'air-raid shelter' for his colleagues – for Churchill was standing loyally by Chamberlain – poured scorn upon the Prime Minister:

> It is not a question of who are the Prime Minister's friends. It is a far bigger issue. He has appealed for sacrifice. The nation is prepared for every sacrifice so long as it has leadership, so long as the Government show clearly what they are aiming at, and so long as the nation is confident that those who are leading it are doing their best. I say solemnly that the Prime Minister should give an example of sacrifice, because there is nothing which can contribute more to victory in this war than that he should sacrifice the seals of office.[5]

After Churchill had clashed violently with the Labour benches in the final speech of the debate, the Government had a majority in the division of 81. But more than 30 Conservatives voted with the Opposition and a further 60 abstained. Chamberlain was virtually defeated, and he sought unsuccessfully to form a national government. Once more the House of Commons had saved the soul of the nation.

Two men were possible successors: Lord Halifax, the Foreign Secretary, and Winston Churchill. There were many Conservatives with long memories who preferred Halifax, as well as a significant proportion of the Labour Party, with whom

Churchill's controversies over the years had flared up again during the debate. On 10 May, the day on which the German onslaught in the west was opened, Chamberlain met both men. On this, perhaps the most important event in his life, the usually garrulous Churchill sat silent. At last Halifax abdicated his claim on the grounds that his position as a member of the House of Lords would make the conduct of such a war very difficult. On the evening of 10 May the King commissioned Winston Churchill to form a government. Churchill's hour had come, and he met it with tranquillity. He recalled that he slept soundly, with no need of comforting dreams, for 'facts are better than dreams'.[6]

CHAPTER TWENTY-THREE

Churchill in the Great Tradition

I have nothing to offer but blood, toil, tears and sweat. You ask, What is our policy? I will say: It is to wage war, by sea, land and air, with all our might and with all the strength that God can give us . . . You ask, What is our aim? I can answer in one word: Victory – victory at all costs, victory in spite of all terrors; victory, however long and hard the road may be.

WINSTON CHURCHILL in the House of Commons, 13 May 1940

ALTHOUGH Winston Churchill never referred to the elder Pitt's proud and worthy boast at the outbreak of the Seven Years War – 'My lord, I am sure I can save this country and nobody else can' – it is perhaps not too fanciful to wonder whether it was in his mind when he took office. Churchill wrought a transformation: those who remember 1940 recall a curious sense of exhilaration in face of mortal danger, as if the broad daylight of truth had scattered the mists of self-deception and inane optimism. 'Nothing to offer but blood, toil, tears and sweat' was strangely more digestible than scraps of paper and 'peace for our time'; Churchill's uninhibited slanging of 'Corporal Hitler' and his 'gang of Nazis' (the last mispronounced with contemptuous relish) was distinctly more palatable than insipid diplomatic references to 'Herr Hitler'.

What manner of man so transformed the British attitude? Winston Churchill was one of the remarkable men of history, and such creatures beggar all attempts at easy definition. He was an aristocrat by birth, haunted by the early death of his father, who promised so much and fulfilled so little. Winston was determined to live his life to the full before a similar fate overtook him. Sadly out of tune with the traditional education offered by Harrow, he was none the less captivated by the magic of words, the joys of literature and the excitement of history.[1]

He joined the Army, which was a fashionable occupation for the junior scions of the aristocracy, and turned to journalism, which was not. He insolently upbraided Kitchener for his behaviour in the Sudan, and his own exploits in South Africa early made him a national hero.

When he turned to politics he became, predictably enough, a Conservative M.P. But like Lloyd George, he was never a party politician in the usual sense. Nothing is more certain than that, but for the coincidence of his genius and the national crisis of 1940, Churchill would never have been Prime Minister of a Conservative, or of any other sort of government. Indeed, he remained as great an embarrassment to many orthodox Conservatives in the years after the war as he had been in the decade preceding it.

Churchill's defection to the Liberals in 1904 and his return to the Conservatives in the twenties have been stigmatised as mere political opportunism, but such judgements are superficial. The truth is that no party could hold him; this may have been a weakness of party, or of Churchill, but beside men of his stature most party politicians appear mere hacks.

Yet political genius is many-sided: its very volatility may produce grievous and dangerous errors of judgement as well as moments of sublime perception. For example, there is no doubt that after his dynamic and progressive social reforms as President of the Board of Trade under Asquith, Churchill's attitude to organised labour and the use of strikes assumed a complexion which was pregnant with genuine menace. Baldwin was right when he remarked that his greatest achievement during the General Strike was to put Winston into a corner and tell him to edit the *British Gazette*. But when crisis came Churchill's genius overrode his prejudices. Perhaps his most far-sighted ministerial appointment was that of Ernest Bevin to the Ministry of Labour, though no two men ever had less in common. And the humanity of the man overcame all: at least as revealing about Churchill as his precipitate haste to summon troops to deal with strikers were his tears as he stood amidst the ruins of East End homes during the German blitz on London.

The biographer might multiply his shortcomings. His tenure of the Chancellorship of the Exchequer during the twenties was highly controversial, and J. M. Keynes could write without too great injustice of *The Economic Consequences of Mr Churchill*. His attitude to India, motivated by old-style high imperial principles, was so misguided as to make him a reactionary even by Conservative standards.

In person, he could be arrogant, bullying – conversations and Cabinet meetings often proved to be monologues – and unjust, as he was to Wavell and Auchinleck, for instance. But this was a small price to pay for his particular brand of genius. If in his personal attitudes he is perhaps reminiscent of Pitt the Elder, he matched that great statesman in many of his appointments to command in the field of battle. It is true, of course, that in 1940, as in the days of Pitt the Younger, it was Britain as a whole who 'saved herself by her exertions' and did much to 'save Europe by her example', but such exertions and such an example did not arise spontaneously: it was Winston Churchill more than any other individual who called them forth. His weapon was the old-established political artistry of the orator. As President Kennedy was to put it, 'he harnessed the English language and sent it into battle'. Reports of his speeches in the House of Commons, and above all his broadcast addresses to the nation, struck a responsive chord in the hearts and minds of his fellow-countrymen. It is difficult to hear them on record, a quarter of a century and more after they were first delivered, without a nostalgic and moving echo of the emotions which they aroused at the time.

Churchill avoided the administrative confusion which had marked Asquith's government during the First World War from the outset. He at once appointed himself Minister of Defence, without attempting to set any limits to his function, and established a small War Cabinet, which he set out to dominate. 'All I wanted', he wrote, 'was compliance with my wishes after reasonable discussion'.[2] Neville Chamberlain led the House of Commons and became Lord President of the Council (until October 1940, when he retired mortally ill and was replaced by Sir John Anderson). Clement Attlee was made Lord Privy Seal (and formally became Deputy Premier in February 1942). Lord Halifax remained as Foreign Secretary until he became Ambassador to the United States in December 1940 and was succeeded by Anthony Eden. Arthur Greenwood, a respected pillar of the Labour Party, held office in the War Cabinet until February 1942. Such was the original War Cabinet. Various alterations and additions were made as the war proceeded, the most noteworthy early recruits being Lord Beaverbrook, who was made Minister of Aircraft Production in August 1940 and held various appointments within the War Cabinet until February 1942, and Ernest Bevin, who entered the War Cabinet in October 1940 as Minister of Labour – a vital office in a full-scale war waged by a democratic country. Sir Kingsley Wood (Chancellor of the Exchequer) also joined the War Cabinet at the same time.

Churchill's first appointments to the service ministries were politically comprehensive, with Anthony Eden at the War Office, A. V. Alexander (Labour) as First Lord of the Admiralty, and Sir Archibald Sinclair (leader of the Liberal Party) at the Air Ministry.

Churchill's advent to power coincided with crises of the severest magnitude. Early on 10 May the Germans, without declaration of war or even the fabrication of a pretext, poured over the frontiers of Holland and Belgium. British and French troops advanced into the two countries at considerable strategic risk to their own heavy armour, but the German forces were overwhelming and in face of *Panzer* thrusts and the devastation of Rotterdam from the air, the Dutch surrendered on 15 May. On the same day the R.A.F. bombed the Ruhr for the first time. French strategy was based upon the static defensive networks of the Maginot Line, which ceased at the Belgian frontier and ignored the complication of troops transported over it by air. In any case, the Line was probably compromised by infiltration and treachery on the frontier. French political and military authorities during the thirties had turned a deaf and irritated ear to the arguments of Brigadier Charles de Gaulle, who had pressed for a mobile strategy of the sort which the Germans were now practising with such success. As early as 14 May the concentrated German forces broke the French defences at Sedan and the whole defensive strategy collapsed. Without reserves, the French army was powerless, and in no more than five days the German *Panzers* reached the sea near Abbeville. The French supreme commander, Gamelin, was dismissed, and replaced by Weygand, who lived in a dream-world of paper strategies. By 27 May any attempt to collaborate with the French in such a situation had collapsed, and the evacuation of the B.E.F. was ordered.

The B.E.F. retreated on Dunkirk. Calais was valiantly held until the last possible moment to protect its flank, whilst some of the younger divisional generals, notably Alan Brooke and Alexander, fought a masterly withdrawal against appalling odds. The fall of Calais and the collapse of Belgian resistance opened both flanks.

The evacuation from Dunkirk was widely regarded as a miracle. In response to broadcast appeals, 860 vessels of all shapes, sizes and ages set out to cross the Channel to join the Royal Navy in carrying off the cream of the British Army. On the beaches, the soldiers formed orderly queues for the boats whilst the German dive-bombers were hampered by fighters in the air and by the soft sand which muffled the explosions of their bombs on the beaches. The operation lasted from 27 May until 3 June: 338,226 soldiers were evacuated, including nearly 140,000 Frenchmen. Virtually all the equipment of the B.E.F. was lost; but the men were saved, and they formed the nucleus of the vast army which was to be built up during the remainder of the war.

Further attempts by Churchill in person, and by the dispatch of two divisions to France to stiffen French resistance, were in vain. Weygand and Pétain were determined upon an armistice, and Pétain – a pathetic remnant of the hero of Verdun of 1916, now callously exploited by the politicians – had his way on 22 June. Eleven days earlier the Italians had declared war.

Now might have been the time for careful consideration of how to make the best settlement possible. Such a course was never considered: a German peace offer was contemptuously brushed aside, and Churchill's bland assumption that 'of course . . . we shall fight on' was widely accepted.

An immediate strategical problem posed by the French surrender was the fate of the French Fleet, which, if it fell into German hands, could become a vital factor in the war at sea. French ships in British ports were taken over, but the Mediterranean Fleet at Oran was less co-operative, and on 3 July British ships sank two battleships and a battle-cruiser in harbour. The operation was painful to all concerned, not least to Churchill; the French government broke off relations, which freed the exiled de Gaulle from some of his embarrassments in trying to rebuild French strength overseas. 'Free French' forces became a significant factor in the struggle, along with the forces of other governments in exile. The prickly pride of de Gaulle – 'the heaviest cross I have to bear is the Cross of Lorraine', said Churchill later – was to cause diplomatic anxiety, but his spirit contrasted wholesomely with that of the miserable French government established at Vichy.

Events had made it very clear that the decisive immediate struggle was to be in the air. For a time the German successes had outrun their expectations and their organisation, and they were unprepared for an invasion of Britain at once. Before such a task could be undertaken they had to achieve superiority in the air to counteract the threat of the Royal Navy in the Channel. So the Battle of Britain was born.

Fighter Command of the R.A.F. as it existed in 1940 was largely the creation of a determined and far-sighted officer, Air Marshal Dowding, who resisted political pressures for spectacular operations and husbanded his precious resources in men and machines. The imperious vitality of Lord Beaverbrook stimulated aircraft production, but shortage of pilots became a pressing problem which could only be dealt with in the longer term. Fighter Command won the Battle of Britain on the ground as well as in the air by masterly plotting of enemy aircraft, and by direction of the R.A.F. fighters made possible by a chain of radar stations. Confident that the radar screens would warn of the approach of enemy aircraft, the fighters were spared the wearisome task of constantly flying in search of their targets.

During July the *Luftwaffe* persistently attacked convoys in the Channel, and Fighter Command held back much of its strength for the inevitable major conflict to come. The R.A.F. lost 150 planes in destroying twice as many Germans, and losses of planes – though not of pilots – were more than compensated by 500 new aircraft which came off the production lines.

Direct air attacks on south-eastern England began on 13 August, when waves of bombers under fighter escort crossed the coast in daylight. Soon the Spitfires and Hurricanes demonstrated their effectiveness both to the *Luftwaffe* and to the anxious men of Kent, who watched from their fields the vapour trails above their heads in the clear skies of the most glorious summer weather for years. Within five days 236 German aircraft had been shot down for the loss of 95 British planes. The *Luftwaffe* was compelled to attempt the destruction of the fighter bases, and the battle had reached a crucial stage when, on 7 September, the *Luftwaffe* switched its attack, and commenced the blitzkrieg upon London. Baldwin's pre-war nightmares of terror rained from the skies over London was realised, whilst the whole nation lived under the threat and the conviction of imminent invasion. The decisive day in the Battle of Britain was a Sunday, 15 September, when some 60 German aircraft were destroyed for the loss of 26 R.A.F. fighters. Contemporary estimates exaggerated the German losses fourfold – a splendid, if unintentional, boost for national morale. Two days later, the German invasion was postponed, and within a month it had been cancelled 'for the winter'. German attacks continued from the air. There was no respite in the night-bombing of London between 7 September and 2 November, after which provincial targets like Coventry were assaulted. The great blitz lasted until 16 May 1941, and inflicted enormous, if haphazard, destruction and the loss of 30,000 civilian lives. But morale remained unbroken.

Meanwhile, the whole fabric of domestic government had been drawn tighter. Ernest Bevin dominated the forces of labour and was instrumental, by persuasion rather than by compulsion, in securing a magnificent industrial effort: a seventy-hour week, for example, was worked in the aircraft factories. Purchase tax was instituted, and income tax raised to 8s 6d in the pound. Civilians thus contributed from their pockets to the war effort, and also prepared actively to resist invasion. A Local Defence Volunteer force was organised in May 1940, and in time became a Home Guard of over a million men. A second evacuation of London was organised, and some families went overseas; but the royal family refused to go, and the King himself prepared to resist the invader by practising with a revolver in the grounds of Buckingham Palace.

The inevitable economic confusion on the home front was vigorously tackled: the creation of a Ministry of War Transport in May 1941 cleared congestion on the railways; industry was closely organised; the Board of Trade imposed 'utility' standards, and introduced clothes rationing on a system of 'points' which was adopted by the Ministry of Food in the rationing of such items as jam and tinned foods. Kingsley Wood's budget of 1941 was strongly influenced by J. M. Keynes and was revolutionary in its attempt to close the gap between governmental revenue and expenditure. Food subsidies were maintained, income tax allowances were cut and the rate of income tax was increased to 10s in the pound. 'Post-war credits' were instituted as a form of compulsory saving, and voluntary personal saving was encouraged. The threat of a serious labour shortage was offset by the direction of labour and by the compulsory recruitment of women, both of which expedients were skilfully managed by Ernest Bevin.

Domestic organisation and the increased efficiency of rationing did much to avert a serious shortage at this stage of the war, but at sea the menace of the U-boat and the surface raider had to be countered. At the beginning of the war, fears of widespread U-boat attack tended to be exaggerated, but as U-boat production increased the menace grew, especially with the German possession of the French Atlantic ports and the denial to the Royal Navy of the ports of an obstinately neutral Ireland. The first great crisis came in the spring and early summer of 1941, and Winston Churchill dramatically proclaimed the Battle of the Atlantic. In April 700,000 tons of shipping went down, and it was only in the autumn that the situation was eased through the increased efficiency of the convoy system and of R.A.F. Coastal Command, together with the growing aggressiveness of the neutral U.S.A. Like the victims of the blitz from the air, the merchant seamen subjected to blitz from beneath the waves sustained their morale unbroken, in spite of the loss of some 50,000 merchant seamen during the war.

The other German threat at sea came in the even more dramatic form of the surface raider, of which the supreme example was the *Bismarck*, a beautiful vessel of 45,000 tons. In May 1941 the *Bismarck* and the battle-cruiser *Prinz Eugen* were at sea. The Home Fleet set out in pursuit with ships from Gibraltar. In the first engagement the *Bismarck*'s heavy armour resisted attack although her oil supply was damaged, and her excellent gunnery damaged the battleship *Prince of Wales* and blew up the great battle-cruiser *Hood*. The *Bismarck* then escaped into the vastnesses of the Atlantic. On 26 May she was spotted by aircraft from the *Ark Royal* and hampered by torpedoes. She was sunk in the grand manner by concentrated gunnery of British battleships on 27 May. The fight with the *Bismarck* was really the last classic set-piece naval battle. Henceforth, sea warfare was rapidly transformed by the use of aircraft, and aircraft-carriers tended to assume the key-role which had for so long been played by the great guns of the battleships.

The contribution of a supposedly neutral U.S.A. against the U-boats was symptomatic of a very special relationship. Seldom has the idea of neutrality been so blatantly compromised as it was during these years by President Roosevelt, with whom Churchill had established a close and fruitful personal contact even before he became Prime Minister. Once convinced that Britain had the power and the will to resist, and once re-elected to the Presidency in 1940, Roosevelt was increasingly generous with such resources as American industry at that time could provide. Half a million 'surplus' rifles were supplied, and in August 1940 fifty old American destroyers were exchanged for base facilities in Newfoundland and the West Indies. British reserves of dollars rapidly diminished, and the great question was for the future, when the dollars would all be spent. The answer came with 'Lend-Lease', which was accepted by Congress in March 1941, and provided for supplies without immediate cash payment. Benefits were slow in coming, but immediate anxiety was over. In the long term, however, Britain's commerce was seriously weakened, for American industrialists took care to give no help which might stimulate British exports. Britain's future in world trade was perhaps the dearest price she paid for her dedication to 'victory at all costs'. J. M. Keynes weighed the balance when he said 'We threw good housekeeping to the winds. But we saved ourselves and helped to save the world'.[3]

British strategy was conditioned by hopes of German economic weakness, and a full-scale campaign of propaganda was undertaken in the hope of weakening the German will, whilst Bomber Command now began the concentrated attacks on industrial and thus on civilian targets for which the *Luftwaffe* had set the pattern. Air Chief Marshal Sir Arthur Harris played a part in the history of Bomber Command comparable with that of Dowding in Fighter Command. Harris's appointment as C.-in-C. Bomber Command in February 1942 led to an intensification of the bombing offensive, about the effectiveness of which some doubts were already being expressed.[4]

Invasion of the continent was out of the question in these days of the war, and if hopes of German economic vulnerability were fulfilled, it might prove unnecessary. The focus of strategy was the Mediterranean. Arrangements were made to reinforce the troops in Egypt, with a view to protecting Middle Eastern oil supplies from a German threat which may well have been illusory, and to striking against Italian forces in both Libya and Abyssinia. After a strategic withdrawal of British troops from British Somaliland, Italian armies invaded Egypt in September 1940 but halted at Sidi Barrani when they found their lines of communication across the Mediterranean were vulnerable to British attack. Admiral Cunningham, commanding the British

Fleet in the Mediterranean, failed to lure the Italian Navy to battle in spite of its numerical superiority, but on 11 November 1940 carrier-borne British aircraft eliminated half of the Italian fighting ships in harbour at Taranto.

General Wavell, commanding on land, made a poor personal impression upon Churchill, but in December 1940 launched an attack with a mere 25,000 men under General O'Connor against the vastly superior Italian army at Sidi Barrani. The Italians disintegrated and by the first week in February 1941 the whole of Cyrenaica fell to Wavell's troops, along with 113,000 prisoners and 1,300 guns.

Mussolini had overstretched Italian resources, for in October 1940 he had invaded Greece. That campaign also failed. In both theatres of war, the Germans had to come reluctantly to the help of the Italians, and in both they were dramatically successful. The British attempt to aid the Greeks was a disaster, whilst the German *Afrika Korps* under General Erwin Rommel, the best of the German generals, swept back through Cyrenaica in the first fortnight of April 1941. On 7 May Churchill had to face criticism in the House of Commons. He turned the attacks into a vote of confidence and won by 477 votes to 3.

But the Prime Minister was seriously dissatisfied with his commanders in the Middle East, in spite of another victory by Admiral Cunningham at the battle of Matapan on 27 March 1941, when three Italian heavy cruisers and two destroyers had been sunk, and of Wavell's success in driving the Italians out of Abyssinia. A dismal postscript, however, to the campaign in Greece was written with the loss of Crete on 27 May. Churchill pressed an offensive on the reluctant Wavell, whose fate was sealed with the collapse of an attack which he launched on 15 June 1941. A week later, Wavell was posted as C.-in-C. India, and replaced by General Auchinleck. A minister of state (Oliver Lyttelton) was established in Cairo.

On 22 June 1941 the whole war situation was transformed when the German armies invaded Russia. Churchill, the arch anti-socialist, proclaimed the common cause of Britain with Russia (and the still neutral United States!) against Nazi tyranny. But prospects were gloomy, for there seemed little chance of Russian success in a conflict for which Stalin was ill-prepared, in spite of forceful warnings he received of a forth-coming attack (British agents had even told him the date of the invasion). If Russia's vast economic resources fell into the hands of the Germans, prospects of a German collapse from within seemed slight indeed.

It was hoped that the U.S.A. might be drawn even more actively into the war, but American opinion remained firmly against open participation. Churchill met Roosevelt in August 1941, off Newfoundland. The meeting produced the Atlantic Charter, a proclamation of democratic principle. Behind the scenes more practical steps were taken to stimulate greater American contributions to the common cause.

The Russians withdrew in face of a tremendous German onslaught, which was marked by particular brutality towards the civilian populations. There was no German breakthrough, however, and the Caucasus was for the time being out of danger. Auchinleck thus felt free to attack, and Rommel strategically withdrew the *Afrika Korps* from Cyrenaica by January 1942. But on and over the Mediterranean the situation was perilous: the Royal Navy suffered serious losses, including the sinking of the *Ark Royal*, and Malta lay open to German air attacks.

Meanwhile, another decisive change was soon to be brought about, as Japan became increasingly aggressive towards Malaya. On 7 December 1941 doubts were at an end. The U.S.A. was flung into war by a devastating surprise attack by Japanese aircraft on the American Fleet at Pearl Harbor. Hitler then declared war on the U.S.A. The Japanese speedily follow-ed with an invasion of Malaya.

Two days earlier, the German offensive in Russia ground to a halt. The loneliness of Britain was over as the resources of the world were mobilised for war on an unprecedented scale.

CHAPTER TWENTY-FOUR

The World in Arms 1942-1945

Do not underrate England. She is very clever. If you plunge us all into another Great War she will bring the whole world against you, like last time.

WINSTON CHURCHILL to Ribbentrop, 1937[1]

THE extension of the war, although it eventually brought vast resources into play against the Axis powers, at once confronted Britain and her Allies with problems of policy and organisation. The role of Britain, and of Winston Churchill, gradually became transformed from that of leader against tyranny into that of the 'honest broker' amongst associates. By the end of the war, perhaps even the capacity to play a mediating role in the making of policy had been eroded.[2]

At once, disaster struck in the Far East. As the Japanese armies poured down the Malayan peninsula towards Singapore, two great capital ships, the *Prince of Wales* and the *Repulse*, advancing along the coast out of range of air-cover, were spotted on 10 December 1941 by Japanese aircraft and sunk. Churchill conveyed the solemn tidings to a House of Commons whose mood matched the gloom of the nation.

More bad news followed thick and fast. In January 1942 Rommel's *Afrika Korps* drove Auchinleck's forces out of Cyrenaica and once more threatened the Suez Canal. On 12 February, the Royal Navy and the R.A.F. proved unable to prevent the escape up the Channel of two formidable German surface-raiders, the *Scharnhorst* and the *Gneisenau*. Three days later, on the other side of the world, Singapore surrendered: the garrison had been reinforced right up to the last moment, and 60,000 men passed into a Japanese captivity which was to be marked by callous exploitation and brutal ill-treatment. In March 1942 the defence of the East Indies collapsed in face of the Japanese campaign in the Java Sea. Burma was overrun and the whole area of the Indian Ocean, including Ceylon and the mainland of India, seemed to be threatened with imminent invasion. In fact, the Japanese had reached the limit of their immediate ambition, but the threat seemed very real at the time.

The early months of 1942 were in many ways the most perilous period of the war, and Britain came nearer to disaster than when threatened with direct invasion in 1940. The U-boats were enjoying a dangerous measure of success, and Britain was faced with shortages of food and fuel. In March 1942 the extraction level from wheat was raised to 85 per cent, and for the duration of the war 'white' bread remained a dingy grey colour. A developing coal shortage was met by governmental control over distribution, but a wage increase for miners failed to bring about increased production.

Faced with crisis, however, the community in general maintained a firm resolve. Almost everybody felt involved in the war – this is perhaps the most striking contrast with the period of 1914-18 – and united in what they felt was an essential resistance to tyranny and aggression. Civilians, as well as acting as Home Guard, A.R.P. wardens and firewatchers, were encouraged to 'Dig for Victory' and 'Make-do and Mend'. Paradoxically, in a financial sense, many people were better off; whilst the cost of living rose by 43 per cent between 1938 and 1943, the average wage increased by 65 per cent but of course taxation was higher.

The direct involvement in the war of both the U.S.A. and the U.S.S.R. introduced the need for co-ordinated planning, and frequent meetings took place between the leaders of the Allies, particularly Britain and the United States. The first such meeting, the Arcadia Conference, began in Washington on 13 December 1941, and produced on New Year's Day 1942 a declaration of united resolve, which embodied the title 'United Nations' for the Allied powers. In practical terms, agreement was reached on co-operation between the chiefs of staff, in which American resources came to assert an American predominance; it was also resolved that the elimination of Germany from the war should take precedence over campaigns in the Pacific.

Meanwhile, Churchill was faced with growing criticism over the unsatisfactory way in which the war was progressing. But he outshone all possible rivals: in a vote of confidence in the House of Commons on 29 January 1942 Churchill triumphed by 464 votes to 1. Reshuffling of the Cabinet in February 1942 made Beaverbrook Minister of War Production; his methods aroused the hostility of Ernest Bevin and Beaverbrook gave way and was replaced by Oliver Lyttelton.

In the spring of 1942 renewed emphasis was placed upon a massive bombing offensive as the short answer to the problem of eliminating Germany, in spite of serious doubts as to the efficacy of such a policy. There was now little pretence of concentrating upon military or industrial targets: on 30 May, for instance, one thousand bombers raided Cologne. The *Luftwaffe* retaliated by raiding historic cities like Bath and Exeter.

At the same time the Russians began to demand direct action on the continent to draw off German armies from the Russian front. Molotov's cry for a second front was dutifully echoed by the tiny British Communist Party, which had already executed a remarkable exercise in mental gymnastics to transform its opposition to capitalist war so long as the Nazi–Soviet Pact lasted into demands for all-out resistance to Fascism as soon as the Russians became involved.

In June 1942 Churchill was again in Washington. His pressure for an American landing in North Africa was seriously compromised by British reverses in the desert and by the humiliating surrender of Tobruk. At the opening of July Churchill again had to face a motion of censure, and this time there were 25 votes against him; 476 M.P.s supported him. In face of disaster which derived from incompetence in field command, Auchinleck now personally took over the command of his armies in the field, and executed a well-organised withdrawal to El Alamein, whose defences he successfully held against strong German attacks during early July. The Prime

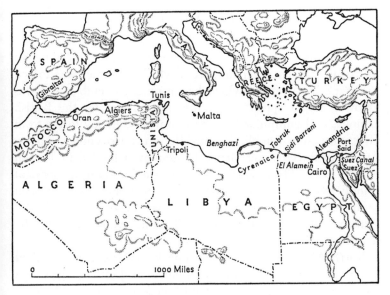

IV. The Western Desert, 1940–3

Minister, however, was not satisfied and went to Egypt in person. In August 1942 Auchinleck was relieved of his command and replaced by the most promising and least perturbable of the younger generals, Sir Harold Alexander. Sir Bernard Montgomery was appointed to the command of the army in the field, the 8th Army. He was flamboyant and controversial in personality, but masterful in command and painstaking in preparation for battle. Rarely have the personalities of two generals proved so complementary.

It was in August 1942, moreover, that a clear demonstration was made of the difficulty of landing a second front on the mainland of Europe without meticulous preparation and a massive build-up of forces. On 19 August an attack was made on Dieppe. Canadian troops were landed but there was a disastrous lack of naval and air support, and the exploit was a costly failure.

On 30 August the defences at El Alamein were again held against Rommel, and Montgomery began to build up his forces for a great counter-stroke. He refused to be hurried by political pressures, and it was not until 23 October that he opened his set-piece attack with a colossal artillery bombardment which was followed by a concentrated thrust at Rommel's strength. After wearing down the enemy, Montgomery began to execute an encirclement, from which Rommel was forced to escape by a retreat which began on 4 November and was followed up at speed across the open desert by the British armour, and culminated in the removal of enemy forces from Cyrenaica and Tripoli. Meanwhile, on 7 November, Anglo-American forces under General Eisenhower landed in French North Africa. The campaign there was not without its political complications, deriving from rivalries among the French commanders. The Germans retaliated by occupying Vichy France, but the French fleet in Toulon evaded capture by scuttling itself.

North Africa provided the venue for the next great Allied conference, which met at Casablanca in January 1943 and produced the doctrine of unconditional surrender as the only terms upon which a German armistice was to be negotiated. It was also agreed that Sicily should be invaded as a pre-liminary to a possible campaign on the Italian mainland. United States bombers were to collaborate in the strategic bombing offensive, although it was by no means clear by now whether the bombing was still intended to eliminate Germany or to serve as a prelude to a great invasion of the continent. Meanwhile, the grave shortage of shipping reduced monthly sailings to the Indian Ocean to 40 instead of 100. This not merely weakened the war effort against the Japanese, but had other tragic consequences. There was, for example, a terrible famine in Bengal in which a million and a half people died of starvation.

The war in North Africa ended on 12 May 1943: the campaign yielded 250,000 Italian and German prisoners. On the same day, Churchill began further talks in Washington, urging an attack on Sicily and the Italian mainland.

The year 1943 saw the culmination of the battle of the Atlantic, where the situation was transformed from near-disaster to triumph. Two hundred and sixty American de-stroyers were committed to the war against the U-boats, and R.A.F. bombers were introduced as escorts for convoys.

Portugal also compromised a none-too-benevolent neutrality and granted the use of bases in the Azores. In March 1943 no less than 477,000 tons of shipping were lost, with only 12 U-boats sunk. In July the statistics were much more favourable: 123,000 tons of shipping lost in exchange for 37 U-boats sunk. By the last quarter of the year, the end was in sight. Between October and December only 146,000 tons of shipping went down and 53 U-boats were sunk. The last remaining threats from the surface-raiders were also eliminated. On 22 September 1943 the *Tirpitz* was crippled by midget submarines in a Norwegian fjord, and on 26 December the *Scharnhorst* was sunk by H.M.S. *Duke of York*. The year as a whole showed a welcome improvement in British imports, which totalled some 27 million tons. A greater anxiety on the home front was that a shortage of manpower was now making itself felt in industry.

The brighter prospects which began to appear in 1943 were reflected in more active preparations for the rehabilitation of the nation once the war was won. In February the Ministry of Town and Country Planning was created, and during the year the great planner Sir William Beveridge produced his ideas for social insurance based upon flat-rate contributions. The scheme was more comprehensive than any of its predecessors, but still did not go far enough to satisfy a good many Labour M.P.s. In November 1943 a Ministry of Reconstruction was established under Lord Woolton. The outstanding social reform emerged, however, in the following year. R. A. Butler's Education Act of 1944 established the principle of secondary education for all children and provided for the raising of the school-leaving age to 15, to be followed by a rise to 16 (due in 1972). On the basis of tests to be taken at the age of 11, each child was to be allocated to a secondary school appropriate to his or her age, ability and aptitude. Secondary schools were to be of three main types – grammar, technical and modern.

One most interesting, though controversial, wartime provision was not maintained after the war. Under the threat of invasion, plans had been made for regional government by commissioners. Lacking the stimulus of such a threat, successive post-war governments have fought shy of implementing genuine measures for regional government, although a good deal of lip service has been paid to the principle.

Meanwhile during 1943 the bombing offensive continued. As the attacks mounted in intensity and were concentrated on particular areas, they lost something of their effectiveness by a lack of discrimination. Between March and June the Ruhr was under attack; from July to November the assault switched to Hamburg, then until March 1944 to Berlin.

On 9 July 1943 Allied armies began the invasion of Sicily. The effects of the landing, together with forces of resistance within Italy, led to the downfall of Mussolini on 25 July 1943. On 3 September the Italian government surrendered unconditionally, but the Italian campaign was by no means over, for now the Germans poured troops into the peninsula. It was at this stage that disagreement between Churchill and the Americans became intense: Churchill pressed emphatically for an extension of campaigns in the Mediterranean; the Americans favoured a genuine second front in the west. At the Tehran Conference in late November 1943 Churchill was overruled by the combined opinions of Roosevelt and Stalin. Roosevelt was sure he could handle Stalin and was perhaps distrustful of Churchill's motives in wanting to put troops into the Balkans before the Russians could arrive there.

An attempt was made in January 1944 to ginger up the Allied campaign on the mainland of Italy by a landing at Anzio, but it failed, and the front continued to be very slow-moving. Rome fell only on 4 June 1944.

Two days later, on 6 June, Allied forces began landing on the coast of Normandy. General Eisenhower, in supreme command, had spent agonising days watching the weather-charts; he took a calculated risk on a break in stormy weather and it succeeded.

Unlike some other combined operations, the invasion of the continent was meticulously planned and prepared. A massive build-up of forces in southern England was shrouded in great secrecy, and elaborate schemes were undertaken to deceive the enemy about the real area in which the landings were to take place.[3] The ingenuity of man was applied to the

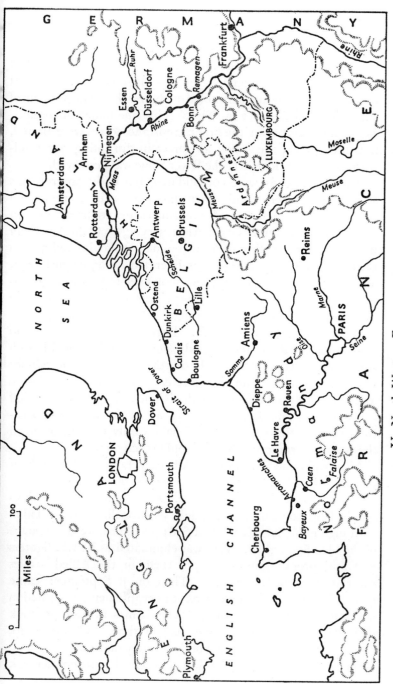

V. North-Western Europe, 1944–5

natural problem of feeding and supplying the armies once they had landed. On the assumption that natural harbours would be destroyed, an artificial harbour – 'Mulberry' – was towed across the Channel and assembled on the beaches. The problem of supplying fuel was met by 'Pluto' (pipe line under the ocean). Before landings began, the French resistance forces were alerted, and they joined the Allied air forces in disrupting communications. Every bridge over the River Seine was destroyed.

The beachheads were consolidated, but early progress was slow. Montgomery held down the enemy in a prolonged static battle, which helped the Americans to break out on 25 July. In mid-August German forces trying to cut the American lines of communication were surrounded at Falaise and 50,000 prisoners were taken. Paris was liberated on 25 August 1944, and on 1 September Eisenhower took over in person the command of the armies. Montgomery was in dispute with the Supreme Commander. He strongly advocated a sharp, concentrated thrust northwards; Eisenhower disagreed, and distributed his forces more evenly along the front. British 30th Corps advanced rapidly to the north, aiming for the Rhine: in mid-September, an imaginative attempt by airborne forces to seize the bridges over the Rhine in Holland succeeded at Nijmegen, but failed gallantly at Arnhem, where paratroops and glider-borne forces fought vainly to hold on until the Guards' Armoured Division could reach them.

Meanwhile the Germans struck back at London. Throughout the war there had been much rumour of 'secret weapons'. Now they made their appearance. On 13 June the first flying-bombs fell upon London. Pilotless, jet-propelled aircraft laden with high explosive, they killed 6184 people before the menace of the 'doodle-bug' (the V.1) was eliminated as R.A.F. fighters and anti-aircraft guns destroyed them or the Allied armies overran their launching-sites. Then on 8 September came rockets (V.2s) – far more dangerous because neither prediction nor interception was possible. The armies in Europe took their launching-sites, but only just in time, and not before 2754 people were killed and morale severely shaken.

In the Far East, Japanese forces received a severe setback

when General Slim's 14th Army, which regarded itself, with a good deal of justice, as 'the forgotten army', won a victory at Imphal in June 1944 to open the way for the reconquest of Burma and thus – in time – of Singapore.

The Allies continued to confer, and political as well as military matters began to assume a prominent place in their discussions. At Moscow in October 1944 Churchill conducted some very blunt bargaining, but gained Stalin's agreement to share political influence in the Balkans, by which Britain was to have influence in Greece. Stalin appears to have kept his part of the bargain not to help Communist rebels in Greece, and Britain intervened, as the agreement entitled her to do, against them.

There was a serious, and alarming, setback to the campaign in the west just before Christmas 1944. On 16 December, the German field-marshal von Rundstedt counter-attacked strongly through the Ardennes in a last desperate attempt to stave off the invasion of Germany and to throw the Allied armies into confusion by seizing Antwerp.

He almost succeeded, but the Allies responded by increasing their air attacks. American bombers were achieving marked success in their precision-bombing of enemy oil installations. More questionable were the effects of British bombing attempts to ruin German morale by massive attacks on Berlin and by an assault on Dresden on 14 February which could only be explained by terror. The whole validity of Harris's strategy was by now open to serious question: his political masters began to desert him, and treated him shabbily after the war.

In March 1945 Allied armies crossed the Rhine. The Americans crossed at Remagen on 7 March, and on 23 March, Montgomery's troops poured over into the Ruhr. In April, the Italian campaign was reaching its climax as Alexander's troops crossed the Po. Events now moved rapidly towards the collapse of the Nazi régime, but not before a bitter blow fell with the death of President Roosevelt on 12 April 1945 – an occasion which gave Hitler great encouragement, but little respite. Mussolini was shot by Italian partisans on 28 April, and the campaign in Italy ended on the following day.

On 30 April 1945, with Russian troops fighting their way through Berlin, Hitler killed himself. His body was soaked with petrol and burned. Nominal leadership of Germany passed to Grand Admiral Doenitz. The Germans unsuccessfully attempted to divide the Allies by offering a separate peace in the west; but on 4 May 1945 German forces in north-western Europe surrendered unconditionally and three days later the unconditional surrender came into force on all fronts.

Social and economic chaos which might have followed the ending of hostilities in Europe was staved off largely by bodies such as the United Nations Relief and Rehabilitation Association. Political disruption was harder to deal with: the ties which had bound incompatible ideologies together during the war were falling apart.

The last great conference took place in Potsdam. Before it was over, Winston Churchill had ceased to be Prime Minister. The wartime coalition had dissolved on 23 May and Churchill had formed a 'caretaker' government whilst the general election was organised. Polling took place on 5 July, but because of the delay in collecting the votes of servicemen the count was not held until 26 July. The results showed an overwhelming victory for Labour. Churchill retained his own popularity, but, as Mr Taylor has written,[4] 'the electors cheered Churchill and voted against him'.

The vote was less against Churchill than a retrospective condemnation of the government of the 1930s. War had produced social upheaval and had broadened social sympathies in an unprecedented way. People wanted reform and they believed that Labour would carry it through; they did not trust the Conservatives' promises of reform. Labour was better organised for the election than the Conservatives: they produced a pungent and appealing manifesto – *Let Us Face the Future* – whilst the Conservatives relied far too much upon the magic of Churchill. The country was plastered with posters proclaiming that a vote for their local candidate was 'a vote for Churchill', but too many electors remembered that Churchill had been driven into the wilderness by the Conservatives in the 1930s, and that nothing short of a great war could ever have given him office.

The war in the Far East had still to be won. Rangoon was taken at the beginning of May 1945, and the Americans were patiently leap-frogging the Pacific islands. But the end came suddenly and in stark terror, which could not but fill the victors themselves with dark fears for the future of humanity. The greatest secret weapon of all was unleashed. On 6 August 1945 an atomic bomb was exploded over the Japanese city of Hiroshima, and three days later another blasted Nagasaki. On 14 August Japan surrendered unconditionally. The awesome shadow of the mushroom-shaped cloud still hangs over mankind, and a later generation may perhaps too readily condemn the statesmen for their decision to use such a weapon. Yet powerful arguments were brought to bear upon President Truman and his advisers, and uppermost in their minds was probably the appalling cost in lives of a long-drawn out campaign to defeat the Japanese. The thought that the atomic bomb would bring the war to a speedy conclusion was an attractive one, especially to laymen who had no conception of the disastrous and poisonous long-term effects of radiation following an atomic explosion: Clement Attlee, for example, testified later that he had never even heard the term 'fall-out'.

So Britain turned to face the future, but with a crippling burden, for American lend-lease ceased abruptly with hostilities, and the British economy was saddled with a debt of £4198 million as the price of saving the world from tyranny.

CHAPTER TWENTY-FIVE

Social Revolution – British Style: Labour in Office 1945–1951

When society requires to be rebuilt, there is no use in attempting to rebuild it on the old plan.

JOHN STUART MILL, 1859

THE Labour Government was swept into power on the strong electoral tide which ran against the memories of the thirties and the 'men of Munich' and in favour of an optimistic spirit for 'facing the future'. There were high ideals at work, both in the country at large and within the new government itself. Though nobody stooped to borrow Lloyd George's slogan, there was a genuine determination on this occasion to produce 'a fit country for heroes to live in'.

In the House of Commons the Government's hold was formidable. There were 393 Labour M.P.s, 213 Conservatives (and their allies, including the so-called Liberal Nationals), a mere 12 Liberals, 3 members of the I.L.P., 2 Communists, 1 Irish Nationalist and no less than 14 Independents.

The talent at the disposal of the Prime Minister was also redoubtable: he created a Cabinet of 20, but gave broad supervisory reponsibilities to his senior colleagues. Clement Attlee himself retained the Ministry of Defence along with the Premiership until the forces had been demobilised, after which responsibilities for defence policy and its co-ordination were passed to A. V. Alexander. First impressions of Attlee could be seriously misleading: nothing could be further from the truth than Hugh Dalton's early assessment of him as 'a little mouse'. Certainly he was no match for Churchill or indeed several other statesmen of the time as an orator, but beneath his quiet exterior there was an astute political judgement and a resolute will. He successfully resisted a plot to oust him from the leadership, and was a strong leader of the Cabinet, ruthless in pruning political dead wood: a dismissed colleague, seeking a genteel explanation for his removal, was likely to be told: 'Because you don't measure up to the job!' And Attlee had little patience with the more irrational and sentimental attitudes of his own left wing: a naive and uninformed critic of the Army, for example, was curtly told in cabinet after confessing his ignorance to the veteran of Gallipoli: 'well, shut your bloody mouth, then.'

Ernest Bevin, as Foreign Secretary, dominated all external affairs. Forthright, unpolished, and unashamedly emotional at times, his transparent honesty made its impact overseas, and a speech to the United Nations in which he set out his simple aims for a world at peace, where passports should be a thing of the past, made a lasting impression. His simplicity of mind might on occasion be perverted by bias, which undoubtedly added to his difficulties in handling Palestine.

Herbert Morrison, born and bred in the politics of London and a most astute political manager, was given the office of Lord President of the Council, with responsibility for supervising the Government's schemes of nationalisation. Another established figure in the party, Arthur Greenwood, was made Lord Privy Seal, and given the task of co-ordinating the social services. Economic policy was the responsibility of Hugh Dalton, who was Chancellor of the Exchequer until 1947, and of the austere and intellectual Stafford Cripps, who moved to the Exchequer from the Board of Trade. Probably the most controversial figure – as he was all his life – was Aneurin Bevan, whilst among the younger men obviously destined for political eminence were Hugh Gaitskell and Harold Wilson.

In spite of its undoubted resources in parliamentary votes and political talent, Attlee's government took office in a climate which was brutally inclement for the flowering of political idealism. In the post-war situation, the nation laboured under serious shortages of materials and resources, notably in shipping, industrial plant and housing. Problems were made much worse by financial crisis of the severest kind, deriving from the sale of foreign investments in the early stages of the war, and intensified by the abrupt cessation of lend-lease.

Although the actual process of demobilisation was very skilfully and fairly carried out, with each man usually provided with a job and given a gratuity and a 'demob suit' of clothes, servicemen returning from the war discovered that wartime conditions at home had not been transformed overnight. Rationing persisted, and was even extended – in 1946 to bread and in 1947 to potatoes. De-rationing was a long-drawn-out process: bread, potatoes and jam were freed in 1948; clothes and footwear in 1949; milk and soap in 1950. The rationing of tea and sugar was destined to outlast the Labour Government, until 1952; and butter, fats, bacon and meat remained 'on the ration' until 1954. Although rationing was fair, there was a good deal of resentment at evasions of it by the 'black market' in the hands of men stigmatised in the jargon of the time as 'spivs'.

Nature, and some lack of adequate preparation, added to hardship. The winter of 1946–7 was excessively severe, and appalling weather produced chaos in transport, which contributed in turn to a serious shortage of fuel, especially coal. Electricity cuts were widespread, and industry was hard-hit, so that an unemployment figure of 400,000 spasmodically and temporarily leapt to 2 million.

Abroad, the diplomatic situation was menacing. The Russians showed a disappointing and alarming unwillingness to maintain in peace the co-operation which had existed in time of war. Diplomacy came to be dominated by the 'Iron Curtain' – dividing the Communist East from the West – and the 'cold war', which soon chilled the early hopes of the United Nations Organisation and drew Britain and Western Europe even more closely to the protective power of the United States.

The Government struggled to overcome this multiplicity

of problems. The immediate financial crisis was staved off by a loan of 3750 million dollars negotiated by Keynes, whilst in the longer term the need was recognised to increase exports by 75 per cent on the pre-war level (this figure was achieved by 1950). At the Exchequer, Hugh Dalton, in an effort to stimulate public investment and expansion, pursued a policy of low interest rates – 'cheap money' – which nearly proved disastrous, since it had the foreseeable effect of encouraging speculation and hence produced serious inflation. Stafford Cripps was constitutionally incapable of such folly (Dalton had in any case abandoned his scheme by 1947) and his policy was marked by severe restraint. Both Chancellors maintained high rates of direct taxation, some of the proceeds of which were returned to the community in general in the form of food subsidies and extended social services. Cripps had to deal with another serious crisis which followed his restoration of the convertibility of sterling in 1947. The danger was averted, once more with American help, this time in the form of Marshall Aid, whilst a longer term prescription was the creation of O.E.E.C. (the Organisation for European Economic Co-operation). Britain's position was temporarily strengthened, too, by American importations of raw materials from British colonies. Clearly, Britain's economic links with, and dependence upon, the United States' economy were closer than ever before: it was a very sensitive relationship, so much so that a small-scale depression in the U.S.A. in 1949 sparked off yet another crisis in Britain, which could be dealt with only by the devaluation of the pound in relation to the dollar. From 4.03 dollars to the pound, the exchange-rate tumbled to 2.80 dollars. The delicately balanced financial situation demanded a very close restraint upon foreign exchange generally, and the expenditure of dollars in particular. Severe restriction was maintained throughout the lifetime of the Labour Government and beyond.

The key to economic salvation lay, of course, with industry and its exports. The short-term effects of devaluation, with consequent lower prices of British exports, helped to attain the target of 75 per cent above the pre-war level by 1950. But

British industry soon began to feel the effects of foreign competition, especially from the revivified industries of Japan and
Germany, much of whose plant had to be completely renewed:
a more effective procedure than the restoration of old plant as
often happened in Britain. Textiles ceased to be the basis of
British exports, which was as well, since it was in textiles that
foreign competition was particularly effective. Cars (again
faced with serious and increasing rivalry), aircraft, chemicals
and electrical goods were the most promising exports.

Strong emphasis was naturally placed upon increased productivity in industry. An *Economic Survey* was published each year
to provide statistical information and stimulus, and the British
Productivity Council was established. Generally speaking,
the relations between labour and management in industry
were better than before the war, with notably improved
procedures of consultation, but a disturbing feature was a
marked increase in disputes between different unions within
the same industry. Old-fashioned emphasis on 'demarcation'
and 'differentials' indicated the need for a reappraisal of attitudes and probably for a reorganisation of trade unionism,
especially within large-scale industries which employed members
of many different unions.

Working conditions, and the living conditions of working
people, were incomparably better than before the war. Wages
remained high – although rising prices, especially in the
early fifties, made rapid inroads into them – and the 2.1 per
cent of the population whom Rowntree found in 1950 to be
below his 'poverty line' were largely accounted for by the
plight of old-age pensioners, who certainly could not keep pace
with the rising cost of living.

Foreign policy was concerned with strenuous efforts to
preserve the peace which had been won. Once again close
links with the U.S.A., especially on the basis of Marshall Aid,
were essential, as was emphasised by two crises in 1948. The
Communist seizure of power in Czechoslovakia in that year
was a marked addition to the strategic and economic strength
of the empire which Stalin was building in Eastern Europe,
and the Russians brought about an open trial of strength in

1948 by denying the western powers access to their zones in Berlin, which, of course, lay deeply inside the Russian-controlled eastern zone of Germany. The western powers responded to the challenge with a massive and successful 'air lift' which maintained supplies to western Berlin and greatly encouraged its population with a demonstrative assurance that the city would not be abandoned to the Russians.

A practical demonstration of solidarity, which marked the grievously rigid division of Europe into two armed camps, was made in 1949 with the creation of the North Atlantic Treaty Organisation (N.A.T.O.). The United States committed itself to involvement in European affairs as never before by joining in a military alliance with most of the countries of Western Europe, along with Italy, Greece and Turkey, and Canada. Nor was this any wishy-washy agreement of the pre-war type: a supreme headquarters (S.H.A.P.E.) was established in Paris, and a joint military effort was closely prepared. Attempts at closer political co-ordination in Western Europe were made with the establishment in Strasbourg in 1949 of the Council of Europe, but it lacked any executive authority. The fact that its strongest advocate was Winston Churchill has led to speculation whether, had he been in office, his great European reputation would have enabled Britain to assume a leadership in European life. It is possible, but given the economic problems of the time and the strength of the Russian threat, both of which threw Europe into dependence upon the United States, it must remain doubtful.

Two further events in 1949 transformed the world situation. Russia discovered, partly by her own efforts and partly through treason, the secret of the atomic bomb, and thereby nullified the West's greatest insurance against aggression; and the Chinese Communists won their long civil war against the Nationalist régime of Chiang Kai-shek.

Chinese Communist influence had already made itself felt in 1948 with the infiltration of the Malayan peninsula, where a guerilla war was begun which lingered on for years until the Chinese Communist threat was removed.

The greatest test, however, both of Chinese strength and of

K

the determination and resources of the United Nations, came in 1950, when South Korea was invaded by forces from the north, increasingly aided by Chinese 'volunteers'. Russia boycotted the United Nations, which at least had the positive effect of preventing her vetoing of effective action. President Truman stood firm; the U.S.A. provided the greater part of U.N. forces, though troops of many nations, including Britain, took part. The fighting-line was stabilised by 1951, but it was a further two years before an armistice was agreed.

Meanwhile, there were other diplomatic troubles for Britain, especially in the Middle East. Britain still held a mandate over Palestine, where there was incessant strife between Jew and Arab, marked particularly by calculated acts of terrorism against the British by Jewish secret forces who were striving to wring from Britain an honouring of the Balfour Declaration. British troops were withdrawn in 1948. Arab armies attacked the newly created state of Israel, which has since lived a vigorous but precarious existence amidst hostile neighbours. The wider effect of events in Palestine marked the serious undermining of British prestige in the Middle East, which by the 1950s jeopardised British influence in Persia, Egypt and the Sudan.

In such a troubled world, defence policy was of crucial importance. It was not one of the strengths of the Labour Government. The two basic issues were whether to extend and develop British work on atomic weapons as a staple of defence, and how far, in the absence of satisfactory voluntary recruiting, to impose conscription. Policy on the period of compulsory national service vacillated in relation to the situation at any given moment. In 1947 the period was 18 months, reduced under back-bench pressure to one year. In 1948 it was restored to 18 months and then, with the Korean War, in 1950 extended to two years.

The Government's record in imperial matters was marked by a happy coincidence between idealism – the belief that colonial peoples should be led to independence – and necessity – the impossibility of maintaining a vast empire with limited British resources. It was in Asia that the two factors most obviously coincided. Malaya and Singapore had to be held against the Communist menace, but Burma gained independence in 1947 and left the Commonwealth entirely, whilst Ceylon, independent in the same year, remained within the Commonwealth. The independence of the Indian sub-continent was obviously due, but the issue was vexed by communal rivalries, intensified by religious conflict between Hindus and Moslems. The attitudes of a century were reversed, and it was now the British government which pressed for an early settlement: Attlee declared in February 1947 that whatever happened, Britain would hand over power in June 1948. This forced the hands of the Indian leaders, Gandhi and Nehru for the Hindus and Jinnah for the Moslems. An inspired appointment was that of Lord Mountbatten, the hero of the South-East Asia campaigns in the war, and a member of the Royal Family, as the last Viceroy of India. By skilled and patient diplomacy and with the co-operation of the Indian leaders, a solution was achieved, albeit at the price of partition. The state of Pakistan (in two parts) and the republic of India were created: both remained members of the Commonwealth. Distressing and bloody racial strife followed partition, and the problem of predominance in Kashmir still remains, but it is likely that bloodshed and disorder would have been much worse had the solution not been pushed through.

In Africa, the granting of independence began in the 1950s; the broad lines of development were laid down, and above all a responsibility was recognised to help 'underdeveloped' countries.

At home, there were positive – though frequently controversial – achievements to record. Under Morrison's supervision, the programme of nationalisation which had been promised was carried through. The Bank of England was nationalised in 1946, and on 1 January 1947 the National Coal Board took over the collieries 'on behalf of the nation', as the noticeboards proudly proclaimed. In the same year two civil airlines, B.E.A. and B.O.A.C., were created, and the British Transport Commission took over the railways and canals and some road transport (organised by British Road Services). In 1948 the

British Electricity Authority, and in 1949 the British Gas Council, came into being. Both were administered through regional boards. Iron and steel were nationalised in 1949, but the House of Lords exercised its delaying-power to defer the implementation of the take-over until 1951. This provoked a bill to reduce the delaying-power of the House of Lords from two sessions to one.

There was naturally opposition to nationalisation on political and economic grounds, although it was difficult to oppose the nationalisation of the Bank of England, and many Conservatives were ready to admit the need to take over the mines and railways. Strongest opposition was focused upon the nationalisation of iron and steel, which could claim to be efficient anyway, and of road transport. There were, of course, weaknesses. The ideal of 'workers' control' of industry was as far away as ever, and administrative personnel often remained the same as under private enterprise. Moreover, an illogical competition existed between nationalised industries, each of which was expected to be self-sufficient: electricity and gas were the obvious examples here – as they still are.

In 1946 James Griffiths was responsible for the consolidation of existing legislation in the National Insurance Act. The most dynamic and controversial figure was Aneurin Bevan at the Ministry of Health. He introduced two Housing Acts, in 1946 and 1949, but his housing policy was largely unsuccessful and fell short of the annual target of 200,000 new homes. In spite of a promising piece of legislation in the New Towns Act of 1946, which provided for imaginative and planned development to accommodate the 'overspill' from London, too much of the housing development after the war was ill-planned and piece-meal. Blocks of unsightly and cramped flats were erected; as a temporary expedient prefabricated bungalows were used which were not intended to last for more than ten years: they proved more durable, and perhaps more comfortable than was foreseen, and many of them are with us still.

Bevan's greatest achievement, in face of serious political and professional opposition, was the creation of the National Health Service. Free medical and dental services were provided, with doctors and dentists being paid a fee for each patient they were prepared to look after. The organisation of hospital services was placed in the hands of regional boards, and ambitious 'health centres' were planned, but were blighted by economic restrictions. The whole scheme proved unexpectedly expensive, largely because the provision of free drugs, medicines and appliances like dentures and spectacles produced a rush of customers – 'a free wig on the National Health' became a stock music hall joke of the period. Professional objections continued and reached a crisis by 1966, threatening the whole structure. But it is undeniable that the health of the nation improved: infant mortality markedly declined, infectious diseases were controlled and then largely eliminated, and tuberculosis was virtually wiped out. For this, the National Health Service ought to share at least some of the credit.

Educational services were, as always, inhibited by financial stringency. But the Government made a real effort to carry out the provisions of the Butler Act of 1944, and in 1947 the school-leaving age was raised to fifteen. There were already critics of the process by which a too-rigid selection of secondary school pupils was made at the age of eleven, and, especially in London, there were experiments in 'comprehensive' secondary education, but they made slow progress.

Other legislation is noteworthy. In 1946 the Trades Disputes Act of 1927 was repealed, and henceforth trade unionists not wishing to contribute to the political levy for the funds of the Labour Party had to contract out. In 1946, looking to the future, and incidentally preparing a field in which Britain was to lead the world, the Atomic Energy Act was passed. In 1948, by the Representation of the People Act, constituencies were redrawn to take account of movements of population, and the plural vote for owners of business premises and university graduates was abolished; with the latter most of the chances for election of Independent M.P.s were swept away. In 1948, too, the Monopolies Commission was established to preserve the public interest against a conspicuous form of unfair trading.

The general election due in 1950 was held in February. Support for Labour had slumped, largely because of austerity and from a general satiety: too much reform tends to be politically indigestible. 315 Labour M.P.s were returned, 297 Conservatives and 9 Liberals. The Government was now seriously inhibited by its narrow majority, which was naturally exploited by a reinvigorated opposition. Parliamentary sessions were marked by acrimonious debates and by high attendance in the division-lobbies.

Troubles came thick and fast. Involvement in the Korean War, and the world-wide effects of that conflict together with high prices for raw materials and the transport of goods, forced up prices, threatened another financial crisis, and provoked a political cleavage in the Government. Hugh Gaitskell, now Chancellor of the Exchequer, proposed to levy a charge of half the cost of spectacles and dentures supplied under the National Health Service. Aneurin Bevan and Harold Wilson (regarded at this stage of his career as a left-winger) resigned from the Government. Attlee went to the country in September 1951 and lost, though still only narrowly: the Conservatives won 321 seats, Labour 295, and the Liberals touched rock-bottom with 6. Labour retained a majority of the votes cast, but too many of them were 'wasted' – concentrated in highly industrialised constituencies with vast Labour majorities: Bevan once remarked that in his constituency of Ebbw Vale they didn't count the Labour votes, they weighed them!

So Britain returned to Conservative government. During the six years of Labour rule, noteworthy social and cultural developments had taken place. Political enthusiasm markedly declined from its high peak at the end of the war, and fewer people bothered to go to the polls in 1950 and 1951. The movement of population from the country to the town and from the north to the south continued. Eighty per cent of the people now lived in towns, and the cleavage between the north and the south now became more conscious: the absurd belief that the real life of the nation was concentrated in London and the south-east, and that north of the Trent one entered a sort of twilight world, was reflected, for example, in a grotesque inflation of the cost of housing around London – a tendency which has continued in an intensified fashion to the present day. The motor car began to make its impact as never before, and exposed the parlous shortcomings of the nation's roads, as, indeed, of its transport system generally.

Cultural life revived. The theatre was buoyed up by imported musical shows from America, of which *Oklahoma* was the first, and best, example. In literature, the influential novelists – Graham Greene, Evelyn Waugh, and the latter-day George Orwell – reflected a distinct tendency to the right in politics, in contrast with the left-wing literary enthusiasms of the 1930s. The B.B.C. developed its contribution to the artistic life of the nation with the creation of its Third Programme in 1946 and with its patronage of the hugely successful Henry Wood Promenade Concerts. It retained its monopoly over the growing medium of television, which had yet to make its overpowering impact on the social habits and cultural standards of the people.

Covent Garden and Sadler's Wells came back to life, and 1946 witnessed the first performance of an undoubted masterpiece in the English operatic repertoire, Benjamin Britten's *Peter Grimes*. The first Edinburgh Festival was held in 1947. The Arts Council at home and the British Council abroad sought to stimulate cultural activity. The culmination was the Festival of Britain, which was held in 1951 to celebrate the centenary of the Great Exhibition and to provide an enlivening and optimistic springboard into the future. Its most permanent legacies, apart from the Pleasure Gardens in Battersea Park, were the National Film Theatre and the architecturally controversial Royal Festival Hall.

CHAPTER TWENTY-SIX

The Return to Conservatism
1951–1964

'A sound Conservative government,' said Taper, musingly. 'I understand:
Tory men and Whig measures.'

DISRAELI, *Coningsby*

THE narrow Conservative victory in the general election
of 1951 restored to power an ageing Winston Churchill (he
was now 77) and a Conservative Party which had been re-
vitalised and modernised by Lord Woolton and by progressive
planners like R. A. Butler. In the new House of Commons
there were 321 Conservatives, 295 Labour members and 6
Liberals.

The new administration was disposed, both by genuine
conviction and by the exigencies of its narrow majority, to
maintain the social reforms inaugurated by Labour whilst
naturally eschewing policies which savoured too obviously of
socialist dogma. For example, the steel industry was denational-
ised, although the Iron and Steel Board set up in 1953 ensured
a continuing measure of governmental supervision. Control
over much of road transport was removed, but British Road
Services still represented an important section of the industry.

The first Chancellor of the Exchequer, R. A. Butler, cut
food subsidies, but governmental spending on education was
increased, and the levels of pensions and family allowances were
also raised. At home, the 1950s reflected a general European
prosperity, and there is no doubt that most members of the
community shared in the national well-being. In time, the
slogan 'You never had it so good', distasteful though it might

be to the moralist and the grammarian, undoubtedly made an obvious appeal to the electorate. Yet social justice was not everywhere apparent. In spite of increases in pensions and allowances, pensioners were beyond the pale of affluence, as their incomes failed to keep pace with rising prices. Homelessness, especially in the big cities, remained an urgent problem, which was tackled with skill and determination by the responsible minister, Harold Macmillan, who set and achieved a target of 300,000 new dwellings each year.

The national economy was far from relieved of the anxieties and alarms which have periodically beset it during the twentieth century. Prosperity was based upon expansion and the growing exploitation of technical and scientific advance. Tremendous imagination and real progress were reflected, for instance, in the creation of the Atomic Energy Authority, and the use which the British Electricity Authority was prepared to make of atomic power stations. It is no exaggeration to say that Britain led the world in the peaceful exploitation of atomic energy. British agriculture provides another example of the achievement of prosperity by a combination of modern techniques and governmental protection.

The basic problem, however, was to hold in check a vicious spiral of increasing prices which chased the increased wages upon which the prosperity of the individual was founded. In other words, prosperity had to be real rather than merely illusory, and prosperity had to be paid for by increased productivity and increased exports. In 1950 exports were 177 per cent higher than in 1946, but during the early 1950s too little advance was made from that level. Basic exporting industries, particularly woollen and cotton textiles, actually declined in face of stern competition, notably from the Far East.

Successive chancellors grappled with this economic Apollyon, but Conservative politicians tended to fight shy of too closely-knit economic control which might be too reminiscent of socialist theory. They sought the reconciliation of Conservative free enterprise with a necessary degree of economic planning. Whilst no Conservative sought to undo the Welfare State which had been built, there were increasing suggestions that welfare

K2

services should be made to pay more for themselves rather than being a direct charge upon the Exchequer.

Foreign affairs were dominated by the U.S.A. and Russia. Winston Churchill was still a great international figure, but it is probably true to say that by this time the opportunity for British leadership in Europe had gone for ever. The Iron Curtain – Churchill's own phrase – dominated European politics, and there seemed little prospect of easing the chill effects of the cold war, although the death of Stalin in 1953 might perhaps offer a long-term glimmer of hope. The close links with the United States which had been written into the N.A.T.O. agreement remained essential in view of the undeniable threat from Russia. In 1952 and 1953 both the U.S.A. and Russia exploded hydrogen bombs. Britain, in what is likely to remain the most controversial major decision on policy since the war, decided to enter the contest. A British atomic bomb was tested in 1952 and a programme was launched in 1955 to produce a hydrogen bomb. Meanwhile, open warfare had been maintained in Korea, where a final truce was made only in 1953. The acid test of Britain's old-style role as a world power was destined to come in 1956, however, over Suez.

Politically, the fortunes of the Conservatives were fostered by increasing evidence of disarray in the ranks of the Labour Party. There was open conflict between the supporters of Aneurin Bevan – the 'Bevanites' – and the official leadership of Attlee, Morrison and Gaitskell. Conservatives optimistically looked forward to the day when the Labour Party would tear itself to pieces in doctrinal and constitutional strife. They reckoned without the resilience of Attlee and of his successor, Hugh Gaitskell, but there is little doubt that during the 1950s the troubles of the Labour Party, with the great trade unions backing the official leadership and the constituency parties rallying round Bevan, constituted a marked advantage for the Conservatives.

In 1952 King George VI died after a long fight against serious illness: 'he walked with death and did not fear; and at the end, death came as a friend', said Churchill in a moving obituary broadcast. Yet the death itself was surprisingly sudden, and the new Queen Elizabeth flew home from a visit to Africa. The general optimism of the 1950s was embodied in much ebullient talk of a 'new Elizabethan age', which seemed a reality as, just before the Queen's coronation in 1953, news arrived of the conquest of Mount Everest. In 1955 Winston Churchill – now a Knight of the Garter – retired. His successor was ready-made in the person of Anthony Eden.

The general election of May 1955 reflected prevailing political trends. The Conservative position was strengthened at the expense of Labour: 345 Conservatives were returned, 277 Labour members and 6 Liberals.

No man had been more obviously groomed for the Premiership than Anthony Eden, and few politicians have built such a reputation for calm judgement and statesmanlike action. Yet his Premiership was disastrous, dominated as it was by the ill-conceived and appallingly executed enterprise at Suez.

The full story of Suez has yet to be told, and much of what has been spoken and written must inevitably be speculative. Yet some broad lines of the story seem indisputable to the historian, if not to the politicians who took part.

In 1953 Britain had given up her influence over the government of Egypt, and in 1954 Eden, then Foreign Secretary, had negotiated an agreement that British forces should leave the Canal Zone, in the teeth of ferocious opposition from right-wing Conservative M.P.s. Fears of Russian influence in Egypt seemed confirmed in 1955 when the Egyptians made an agreement for the supply of arms from Czechoslovakia. The whole situation in the Middle East was made more tense by Israeli fears that the Arabs intended to attack and eliminate the state of Israel, and British opinion was further alarmed early in 1956 when Glubb Pasha, the famous British commander of the Arab Legion in Jordan, was dismissed. At the time this was thought to be the result of Egyptian pressure, but it may well not have been so.

President Nasser, who by this time was firmly established as the dictator of Egypt, needed money for the construction of the great Aswan Dam. Negotiations with the United States

were abruptly broken off by the Secretary of State, John Foster
Dulles, and Nasser felt insulted. There was clearly a lack of
liaison between Dulles and Eden, and the British Premier
seems to have overestimated the identity of interest between
Britain and the U.S.A. Middle-Eastern oil was far less important to the United States than to Britain. Meanwhile,
France felt involved in Egypt, both because of her historical
associations with that country, and because the Egyptians
were giving aid to the Algerian rebels against France. From
1955 onwards France developed closer relations with Israel,
and supplied her with arms, especially aircraft.

On 26 July 1956 Nasser nationalised the Suez Canal Company. Overnight, he gained enormous prestige in the Middle
East and achieved from the profits funds for the Aswan Dam.
British reaction was prompt and vigorous, and the Press was
extremely violent. Herbert Morrison attacked Nasser's action,
and Gaitskell compared the Egyptian dictator with Hitler
and Mussolini. This reaction is interesting, since there seems
little doubt that Eden himself was already thinking of the situation in the context of pre-war diplomacy and the failure of
appeasement.

During August, British and French forces in the Mediterranean were reinforced and a mission to Cairo by the
Australian Prime Minister, Robert Menzies, failed to persuade
Nasser to agree to international control of the Canal. Early
hopes that the Egyptians would prove unable to run the Canal
without British help were groundless: by September, the Canal
was working most efficiently, using Russian and American
pilots. During September, too, there was much discussion
between British and French representatives. Opinion in Britain
was divided: Gaitskell, in spite of his antipathy to Nasser,
was asking for governmental assurances that force would not
be used. But it should not be supposed that Gaitskell voiced
the unanimous feeling of Labour supporters throughout the
country, for this was an issue which divided on emotional,
rather than on clear-cut party lines.

Tension seemed to decrease during October. Britain and
France had agreed to take the dispute to the United Nations,

and meetings were held with the Egyptians whilst the Security Council was in session. The American position was unclear. President Eisenhower did not share the British view that the nationalisation was illegal, and he was opposed to the use of force. This was not the only time during his Presidential career that he failed to make his opinion clearly understood. Tension was heightened again by Egyptian attacks on the Israelis over the Gaza Strip, and by the return to office in Israel of David Ben Gurion, the renowned strong man of Israeli politics.

The great dispute over what happened next centres on whether or not there was collusion between Britain, France and Israel. On 16 October there was a secret meeting between French and British leaders in Paris at which such collusion may have been decided. On 22 October Ben Gurion had a secret meeting at Sèvres with French leaders, and there are persistent suggestions that on the following day Selwyn Lloyd, the British Foreign Secretary, joined the discussions, but Selwyn Lloyd has consistently denied this. On 29 October the Israelis began a brilliant armoured and paratroop invasion of Egyptian territory. On 30 October Britain and France issued an ultimatum demanding that Israeli and Egyptian forces should withdraw to positions ten miles from the Canal: the fact that this ultimatum conceded a huge Israeli advance and constituted an Egyptian retreat from their own territory was not lost on observers at the time, and strengthened suspicions of collusion between Britain, France and Israel.

Israel quickly accepted the ultimatum, and Egypt just as readily rejected it. Britain and France had threatened to occupy key positions. In the Security Council, the rift between Britain and the U.S.A. was openly revealed when Britain vetoed an American resolution against the use of force. R.A.F. bombers in Cyprus were prepared for action and Egyptian civilians were warned to take cover.

On 31 October Anthony Nutting, the British Under-Secretary of State at the Foreign Office, resigned. On the eve of the Presidential Election in the United States, Eisenhower, outraged at the lack of consultation, spoke strongly against any British and French action. Meanwhile, the Egyptians had put the Canal out of action by sinking blockships, and British and French forces, in spite of much talking, were still not moving. On 2 November an American resolution in the United Nations General Assembly for a cease-fire received 64 votes against those of Britain, France, Australia, New Zealand and Israel.

Amidst all this confusion, a European tragedy was enacted. A rising in Budapest against the Hungarian Communist régime was crushed by Russian armour by 4 November. Britain, embroiled in her own undertakings, stood powerless to speak with the voice of political moderation and morality.

Opinion at home and in the Commonwealth was bitterly divided. Eden still spoke against appeasement, but Gaitskell strongly expressed his opposition to Eden in a television broadcast. Canada proposed sending a United Nations force.

At last, on 5 November, paratroops were landed at Port Said and Port Fuad. Every effort was made to prevent civilian casualties. By now, threatening noises were to be heard from Russia. A cease-fire came into effect on 6 November.

Economic pressures were also being brought to bear. There was a run on the pound and Eisenhower, duly re-elected, threatened to stop American support for sterling. The Chancellor of the Exchequer, Harold Macmillan, insisted that the campaign must be called off in order to avert an economic disaster.

The cost of the Suez affair was 650 Egyptian dead and 900 wounded, in exchange for 26 British and French casualties. In terms of money, the campaign cost Britain £250 million. Pipe-lines were blown up in the Middle East, and petrol rationing was imposed in Britain. Thirteen thousand British subjects were expelled from Egypt and British property was seized. Moreover, Britain suffered a serious loss of prestige in the Middle East, especially in Iraq, on whose security the Baghdad Pact depended. The humiliation of Britain and France gave great encouragement to extremist nationalist politicians.

For humiliation this certainly was. Those people in Britain who saw the whole episode as a macabre reincarnation of Palmerstonian diplomacy were naturally humiliated. Those who followed Eden, and saw Nasser as another Hitler (with vague whisperings of Russian plots in the background) were in turn humiliated by the sheer ineptitude of the whole enterprise. Even on Palmerstonian terms the campaign was a fiasco. Above all, it was a demonstration that nineteenth-century diplomacy was out of fashion: the United States, the United Nations, and the Commonwealth had to be taken into account in the twentieth century.

Late in November 1956 Anthony Eden's health collapsed. It now seems clear that he had been seriously ill throughout the crisis, which may well account for the strange departures from his normal political methods. In January 1957, crippled by illness and hounded by the opposition in the House of Commons, he resigned. Since Eden was the leader of the Conservative Party, there was no ready-made successor. There were only two real contenders. In normal circumstances, the stronger candidate might well have been R. A. Butler. After consultation, however, the Queen appointed Harold Macmillan.

Beneath a rather Edwardian exterior, which seems to have been a cloak for shyness, the new Prime Minister was a talented and subtle politician, and an experienced statesman. He had been a rebellious Conservative in the 1930s, opposing both the lethargy of the Government's domestic programme and the ineptitude of its diplomacy. His family had once burned an effigy of Neville Chamberlain on Guy Fawkes' Night. Since the war, he had been a successful Minister of Housing and an imaginative Chancellor of the Exchequer. He had a highly developed concern for the American alliance, got on well with Eisenhower and even better with John F. Kennedy. Generally he was a skilled negotiator abroad and a formidable political opponent: with his suave, off-hand manner, he could devastate an opponent, whether it were Khrushchev, hammering with his shoe at the United Nations, or Gaitskell, quivering with righteous indignation in the House of Commons. Macmillan now set about salvaging the country and the Conservative government from the wreckage of Suez. The measure of his success may perhaps be judged from the result of the general election of 1959.

In 1959 the Labour Party achieved the melancholy distinction of losing seats at four consecutive general elections. The Conservatives increased their overall majority in the House of Commons to 100. Electorally, at least, the boast of the posters that 'Conservative Freedom Works' appeared to be justified.

The defeat in 1959 led to further recrimination and division within the Labour Party, and especially between those who thought that Labour's only political future lay with the abandonment of such specifically socialist aims as nationalisation ('Clause 4') and those who maintained that it was essential to stand by the pure socialist doctrine. Disputes also raged over the official Labour attitude to the nuclear deterrent. The Campaign for Nuclear Disarmament was particularly vociferous in opposing Hugh Gaitskell on this fundamental issue, but what was really significant was the attitude of some of the influential trade unions, several of which shifted from their support of the party leadership and adopted a policy of unilateral nuclear disarmament by Britain. Aneurin Bevan was now probably the key figure, but he never explicitly stated his own point of view, and died in July 1960. Hugh Gaitskell provoked a storm of abuse when, at the Labour Party Conference in 1960, he declared his intention to 'fight and fight again' to reverse the unilateralist vote of the Conference. He withstood a challenge to his leadership from Harold Wilson, and his fight was successful at the Conference in 1961.

When future historians consider the 1950s and 1960s they are likely to place their strongest emphasis upon the transformation of Britain's Empire into the multi-racial Commonwealth which, if all its aspirations and ideals were fulfilled, would be an object-lesson to the world. Between 1945 and 1964, the numbers of souls directly under British rule fell from 500 million to 15 million. Generally speaking, the peoples who achieved their independence had been well prepared: few transfers of British power have been marked by the sort of catastrophe which occurred in 1960 when the Belgians ditched their responsibilities in the Congo. British administrators and governments gave aid, financially and otherwise, to British territories both before and after independence. The high imperial ideal envisaged as early as the eighteenth century by Edmund Burke was sometimes realised, although on occasion controversy and animosity were unavoidable.

The troubles which beset Britain in the last days of her Empire should not, of course, be minimised. She waged a stubborn – and brilliantly successful – campaign to fight against Communist infiltration before Malaya was safe to receive independence in 1957. Singapore became independent in the following year. The independence of Cyprus in 1959 was preceded by bitter and bloody controversy and communal strife.

It was perhaps in Africa that the most momentous progress was made. The period began in a frightening fashion, with an outbreak in 1952 of terrorism in Kenya organised by the pseudo-religious Mau Mau. In 1953 the Central African Federation was created from Southern Rhodesia, Northern Rhodesia, and Nyasaland. The Federation was highly controversial, with the Africans justifiably fearing domination by the whites of Southern Rhodesia. Some African colonies campaigned fiercely for their independence, whilst others waited more patiently. Ghana (formerly the Gold Coast) became independent in 1957, and Nigeria three years later. Tanganyika, ably led by Julius Nyerere, became independent in 1961, Uganda in 1962 and Kenya at the end of 1963. The Central African Federation came to an end in 1963, and in 1964 independent Malawi (Nyasaland), and Zambia (Northern Rhodesia) came into existence. The question of the independence of Southern Rhodesia ominously remained to be dealt with.

Meanwhile the intransigence of the South African government in its iniquitous policy of *apartheid* was an increasing embarrassment to the Commonwealth. In 1960 Harold Macmillan, on a visit to South Africa, openly warned South Africans of the need to take into account the 'wind of change' which was blowing through Africa. In 1961 South Africa was proclaimed a republic and left the Commonwealth.

The early 1960s saw changes in the general social climate,

and such changes were naturally reflected in the politics of the time. The cheerful optimism of the 1950s was now exposed to challenge. Antagonism to nuclear policy and to the bland assumption that Britain had a 'nuclear role' to play was manifested in the mass marches of the C.N.D. and organised civil disobedience by members of the Committee of 100. There was increasing evidence of dissatisfaction with the way in which Parliament worked, and pressure for the creation of committees of investigation on the American model, to impose a check upon the efficiency of ministers and the Civil Service. Challenges to the established educational system grew in intensity, and 'satire' became a fashionable occupation for ex-undergraduates. The transformation of the White House by the youthful idealism of President Kennedy seemed to contrast unfavourably with the established hierarchy in British politics.

Affluence was undeniable. The standard of living of the majority of the population continued to rise, and the tendency was reflected in such luxuries as holidays abroad, which had been undreamed of by ordinary folk before the war. Teenagers came to be regarded as something of a distinctive species. They enjoyed prosperity as never before, and provided a ready market for commercial exploitation and for the advertisers, whose resources had been extended since 1955 with the advent of commercial television.

Yet, amid such affluence, poverty and loneliness and homelessness cruelly persisted: in 1963, $8\frac{1}{2}$ million citizens were receiving National Assistance. Social problems were complicated by some resentment against immigrants from the Commonwealth and by the persistence of poor living conditions in certain areas. The drift to the south continued.

The Government showed an awareness of such problems and a concern for long-term planning. The early 1960s were fruitful in governmental Committees and Enquiries into such diverse topics as higher education (Robbins), the railways (Beeching) and transport and town planning (Buchanan).

The greatest problem was still the economic health of the nation. Early in 1961, there was serious concern over the slow rate of growth of national productivity and the unfavourable balance of trade. Selwyn Lloyd, at the Exchequer, produced a supplementary budget in July 1961 which imposed a severe measure of deflation. Bank rate was raised to 7 per cent: surcharges were imposed; a 'pay pause' was devised which clamped down on increases due, amongst others, to Post Office workers and teachers. In 1962 the long-term principle of a 'guiding light' for wage and salary increases was propounded, and the National Economic Development Council was created.

The Government had by now forfeited much of its popularity, and the suggestion of reviving fortunes for the Liberal Party was triumphantly confirmed at a by-election in March 1962 when Eric Lubbock captured the apparently impregnable Conservative stronghold of Orpington. The Prime Minister reacted in July 1962 with a sweeping reorganisation of his Cabinet. Among the dead wood which came under the axe was Selwyn Lloyd himself: 'Greater love hath no man than this', remarked Jeremy Thorpe, 'that he lay down his friends for his life'.

Harold Macmillan was enjoying more success in his role as a world statesman. In January 1960 he delivered his famous speech in Cape Town on 'the wind of change', and in September of the same year he won his personal triumph over Mr Khrushchev at the United Nations General Assembly. In October 1962 major war over Cuba seemed a real possibility. The reaction in Britain of the C.N.D. and its associates was illogical, for they campaigned hysterically against President Kennedy for his refusal to allow the extension of Russian atomic weapons on his own doorstep. The inherent anti-Americanism of the C.N.D. response was disturbing, but it was the last large-scale C.N.D. demonstration. In July 1963 Macmillan achieved one of the ambitions of his diplomacy, and helped to write a constructive postscript to the alarms and anxieties over Cuba: the major powers initialled a Test-Ban Treaty agreeing to stop testing atomic weapons in the atmosphere.

Another cause of controversy was the attempt of the Government to join the E.E.C. (the Common Market). Since 1959 Britain had formed part of the European Free Trade Area (the 'seven') and had built up her campaign to enter the Common Market. Edward Heath was put in charge of British negotiations. The Government encountered opposition from left and right, and in 1962 Hugh Gaitskell came out against British attempts to join the Common Market. President de Gaulle seemed likely to block British entry. In December 1962 Macmillan concluded the Nassau agreement, which bound British defence more closely to the United States, and in January 1963 de Gaulle imposed his final veto on British entry into the E.E.C.

In January 1963 tragedy struck at the Labour Party and at British politics in general with the sudden death of Hugh Gaitskell. Harold Wilson was elected as his successor.

Ten months later the Conservative Party also had a new leader. Forces of scandal and rumour had added to the problems of the Government. There were several serious breaches of security, and the Prime Minister was cruelly embarrassed by the behaviour of the War Minister, John Profumo, who, after persistently denying a scandalous association, at length confessed it and resigned. Wild rumours were rife for a time and the Government was on bad terms with some sections of the Press.

On 10 October Harold Macmillan announced his wish to resign through his ill health. After over a week of manœuvring, what were called 'the customary processes' of the Conservative Party resulted in the appointment to the Premiership of the Earl of Home, who renounced his peerage and became Sir Alec Douglas-Home. His difficult task was to establish his position within the party and in the nation as a whole before the general election was due during 1964.

The general election was held off until 15 October 1964. In the meantime the Government passed an important measure, with the abolition of Resale Price Maintenance – not altogether to the satisfaction of all sections of the Conservative Party itself. On the whole, however, the omens were unfavourable. Sir Alec, who was a very amiable personality, scarcely matched the political pre-election subtleties of Mr Wilson. There were serious industrial disputes, including a major strike at the great steel works at Port Talbot, and a systematic 'go-slow' in the power industry. The Conservatives promised an enquiry into the workings of the trade unions if they were re-elected. In the first elections for the Greater London Council, which had been brought into being in the hope of breaking the Labour control over the L.C.C., Conservative expectations met disaster. Labour dominated the new G.L.C. by 64 seats to 36. At a Commonwealth Conference the increasingly embarrassing problem of Rhodesia was shelved. Against such a troubled background the nation went to the polls.

The general election restored Labour to power after an interval of thirteen years – but only just. Labour returned 317 members, Conservatives 304, and Liberals 9.

Britain Today

HAROLD WILSON became Prime Minister after the general election of 1964 and declared the Labour Party's intention to govern, in spite of its slender majority. In a critical economic situation, the new administration succeeded in carrying on the government of the country until March 1966, when the Prime Minister appealed to the electorate for a confirmation of Labour's mandate. The electors returned 363 Labour M.P.s, 253 Conservatives and 12 Liberals, an overall Labour majority of 97, and a vote of confidence in the Government over the Conservatives, now led by Edward Heath.

Contemporary politics are too clouded in controversy to admit of ready-made historical judgements. The legacy of the Conservatives and the degree of skill shown by the new Labour government are matters for future historians. But some general observations may be made, and some questions asked, about the nature of the problems facing the Government and the nation.

What part has Britain to play in the contemporary world? It was the Empire above all which made Britain into a great world power in the past. The days of Empire are past, although responsibilities remain, as the bitter controversy over the future of Rhodesia clearly emphasises. Such imperial responsibilities are not to be shirked, unless Britain's role in the new Commonwealth is to be abdicated. But can the nation retain its status in a changing world, and is it even desirable that it should attempt to do so? Can the vast national expenditure upon defence, and especially nuclear weapons, be justified by claims to an independent role in a nuclear age?

Britain's future clearly demands involvement. Can Britain retain a special relationship with the United States and become at the same time fully involved in the economic and political life of Europe? Can the nation afford not to be part of the European Economic Community? Or is it to be Britain's particular function in the contemporary political and economic world to serve as a bridge between the United States and Europe?

If Britain's pretensions to the status of a great power are even to approach realism, national prosperity must be soundly and genuinely based upon industrial productivity. Truly remarkable technological progress must be matched by advances in industrial and managerial methods. Both employers and trade unionists must seriously reconsider their traditional techniques and attitudes.

Perhaps the most serious issue of all concerns what Professor J. K. Galbraith has called *The Affluent Society*. Assuming that affluence can really be afforded, what use is to be made of it? Contemporary society is at the mercy of commercial techniques. Commercial exploitation is all too often an end in itself, and a vast advertising industry has developed in order to persuade people to spend, regardless of real need. Television has provided an unparalleled and vivid means of communication which intrudes into every aspect of national life, and too frequently stultifies rather than stimulates standards of aesthetic and social good taste. A literate population is a prey to a 'Pop' culture, in which culture is frequently indistinguishable from commerce.

Today's society is divorced as never before from religious sanctions. The Church has lost the authoritative voice with which it once spoke, and there is some danger of ethical and moral standards emphasising permissiveness at the expense of responsibility. A contemporary morality remains to be worked out as the effects are felt of unprecedented educational opportunities, just as social justice has developed along with a growing realisation of need and as expanding resources have become available to enlightened governments.

The roots of contemporary politics and society are to be found in the pages of history. The pattern of the future lies with the present generation, as it applies its talents and its judgements to unprecedented opportunities and problems which derive from the wisdom and the folly of the past.

Notes

CHAPTER ONE

1. Elizabeth Longford, *Victoria R.I.* (Weidenfeld & Nicolson, 1964) p. 567, quoting Kingsley Martin.

2. Quoted in Longford, op. cit. p. 437.

3. See R. C. K. Ensor, *England 1870–1914* (Oxford, 1936) pp. 103 ff.

4. See Ensor, op. cit. p. 267. Most of the statistics in this chapter are derived from Ensor.

5. Ensor, op. cit. p. 273.

6. Ensor, op. cit. p. 130.

7. William Morris, quoted in Ensor, op. cit. p. 155.

8. W. H. Gardner, introduction to the 3rd ed. of *The Poems of Gerard Manley Hopkins* (Oxford, 1950) p. xiii.

9. See Lord Birkett, *Six Great Advocates* (Penguin Books, 1961).

10. Ensor, op. cit. p. 310.

CHAPTER TWO

1. Gladstone's speech at West Calder, 2 Apr. 1880. Quoted in Robert Rhodes James, *Rosebery* (Weidenfeld & Nicolson, 1963) p. 105.

2. H. Pelling, *The Origins of the Labour Party* (Oxford, 1965) p. 1.

3. A. J. P. Taylor, *The Trouble Makers* (Hamish Hamilton) p. 69.

4. Quoted by A. J. P. Taylor, op. cit. p. 86.

5. Lady Frederick Cavendish's Journal, quoted by Philip Magnus, *Gladstone* (John Murray, 1954) p. 302.

6. Gladstone to Mrs O'Shea, Aug. 1885, quoted by Magnus, op. cit. p. 333.

7. e.g. Asa Briggs and Steven Watson, in the B.B.C.'s *Not So Much a Programme*, on the occasion of the death of Sir Winston Churchill.

8. Magnus, op. cit. p. 445.

CHAPTER THREE

1. Robert Rhodes James, *Rosebery* (Weidenfeld & Nicolson, 1963), upon which much of the material in this chapter is based.

2. Quoted in Rhodes James, op. cit. p. 17.
3. Quoted in Rhodes James, op. cit. p. 52.
4. Rhodes James, op. cit. p. 76.
5. Quoted in Rhodes James, op. cit. p. 447.
6. Quoted in Rhodes James, op. cit. p. 465.
7. Rhodes James, op. cit. p. 489

CHAPTER FOUR

1. Quoted in Cecil, *Salisbury*, vol. 4, p. 401.
2. Lady Gwendolen Cecil, *The Life of Robert, Marquess of Salisbury* (Hodder & Stoughton, 1921).
3. Quoted in Cecil, op. cit. vol. 3, p. 180.
4. Quoted in Cecil, op. cit. p. 169–70.
5. For a masterly account of the power of Sir Charles Russell, see Lord Birkett, *Six Great Advocates* (Penguin Books, 1961).
6. See J. A. S. Grenville, *Lord Salisbury and Foreign Policy* (University of London Press, 1964).
7. See Grenville, op. cit. chapter 2.
8. Winston S. Churchill, *The River War* (Longmans, 1899) pp. 211–12.

CHAPTER FIVE

1. Winston S. Churchill, *London to Ladysmith* (Longmans, 1900), pp. 133–6.
2. Élie Halévy, *Imperialism and the Rise of Labour* (Benn, 1926) p. 27.
3. Quoted in Halévy, op. cit. p. 75.
4. Halévy, op. cit. p. 84.
5. Chamberlain to Sir Robert Meade, 24 Oct. 1896.
6. Halévy, op. cit. p. 30.
7. Elizabeth Pakenham, *Jameson's Raid* (Weidenfeld & Nicolson, 1960) p. 331.
8. Sir Evelyn Wrench, *Alfred Lord Milner* (Eyre & Spottiswoode, 1958) p. 106.
9. Quoted in R. C. K. Ensor, *England 1870–1914* (Oxford, 1936) p. 247 n.
10. Quoted in Halévy, op. cit. p. 78.
11. Halévy, op. cit. p. 92.
12. Halévy, op. cit. p. 79.
13. Cecil, *Life of Salisbury*, III, p. 191.
14. Halévy, op. cit. p. 95.
15. Quoted in R. Rhodes James, *Rosebery* (Weidenfeld & Nicolson, 1963) p. 423.
16. Violet Bonham Carter, *Winston Churchill as I Knew Him* (Eyre & Spottiswoode/Collins, 1965) p. 72.

CHAPTER SIX

1. Kenneth Young, *Arthur James Balfour* (Bell, 1963).
2. Winston S. Churchill, *Great Contemporaries* (Odhams, 1947) p. 195.
3. Alfred Gollin, *Balfour's Burden* (Blond, 1965) pp. 7 ff.
4. Quoted, Robert Rhodes James, *Rosebery* (Weidenfeld & Nicolson, 1963) p. 445.
5. Quoted, Robert Rhodes James, op. cit. p. 196.
6. Quoted, Gollin, op. cit. p. 7.
7. Alfred Gollin, *Balfour's Burden: Arthur Balfour and Imperial Preference* (Blond, 1965), on which much of this chapter is based.

CHAPTER SEVEN

1. Quoted, Philip P. Poirier, *The Advent of the Labour Party* (Allen & Unwin, 1958) p. 139.
2. Quoted, H. M. Pelling, *The Origins of the Labour Party* (Oxford, 1965) p. 209.
3. John Burns, *The Liverpool Congress* (Green, MacAllan & Feilden, 1890) p. 6.
4. Quoted, Pelling, op. cit. p. 204–5.
5. Poirier, op. cit. p. 58.
6. G. B. Shaw, *Sixteen Self Sketches* (London, 1949) p. 58.
7. Poirier, op. cit. p. 29.
8. Pelling, op. cit. p. 207.
9. Quoted, Poirier, op. cit. p. 103.

CHAPTER EIGHT

1. Quoted in R. C. K. Ensor, *England 1870–1914* (Oxford, 1936) p. 515.
2. Barbara Tuchman, *The Proud Tower* (Hamish Hamilton, 1966) p. 356.

CHAPTER NINE

1. Barbara W. Tuchman, *The Proud Tower* (Hamish Hamilton, 1966) p. 367.
2. Colin Cross, *The Liberals in Power, 1905–14* (Barrie & Rockliff with the Pall Mall Press, 1963).
3. December 1905, quoted in Cross, op. cit. p. 19.
4. Quoted in Cross, op. cit. p. 27.
5. Roy Jenkins, *Asquith* (Collins, 1964) p. 195.
6. Quoted in Jenkins, op. cit.

7. Sir Philip Magnus, *Gladstone* (John Murray, 1954) p. 402.
8. Quoted in Tuchman, op. cit. p. 386.
9. Quoted in Jenkins, op. cit. p. 212.
10. David Lloyd George, *War Memoirs* (Odhams Press, 1938) p. 614.

CHAPTER TEN

1. Quoted in Barbara Tuchman, *August 1914* (Constable, 1962) p. 304.
2. Quoted in Tuchman, op. cit. p. 97.
3. Tuchman, op. cit. p. 191.
4. Quoted in Tuchman, op. cit. p. 67.
5. For an interesting study of Moltke, see Corelli Barnett, *The Swordbearers* (Eyre & Spottiswoode, 1963).
6. Again, see Barnett, op. cit.
7. Such is the argument, strongly and convincingly put forward, of Roy Jenkins, *Asquith* (Collins, 1964).

CHAPTER ELEVEN

1. Quoted in Roy Jenkins, *Asquith* (Collins, 1964) p. 410.
2. A. J. P. Taylor, *English History, 1914–1945* (Oxford, 1965) p. 49.
3. Taylor, op. cit. p. 46.
4. See Jenkins, op. cit.

CHAPTER TWELVE

1. A. J. P. Taylor, *English History, 1914–1945* (Oxford, 1963) p. 73.
2. John McCrae. The poem was first published in *Punch*.
3. President Wilson's Fourteen Points:
    1. There were to be open covenants of peace, openly arrived at.
    2. The establishment of absolute freedom of navigation, in both peace and war.
    3. The removal, wherever possible, of economic barriers, and the establishment of equal trading conditions.
    4. There was to be an absolute guarantee that all national armaments would be reduced to the lowest possible level consistent with domestic safety.
    5. There was to be a free, open-minded and impartial adjustment of all colonial claims . . . 'the interests of the populations concerned must have

equal weight with the equitable claims of the government whose title is to be determined'.

6. All Russian territory was to be evacuated.
7. Belgium to be evacuated and restored without any limitation upon her sovereignty.
8. All French territory was to be restored, and the 'wrong done to France by Prussia in 1871' over Alsace-Lorraine was to be put right.
9. National frontiers were to be established in Italy.
10. The peoples of Austria–Hungary were to be given the opportunity of autonomous development.
11. Occupied territory in Rumania, Serbia and Montenegro was to be evacuated, and Serbia was to be given access to the sea.
12. Turkish parts of the Ottoman Empire were to be secured. But other areas under Turkish rule must be given the opportunity of autonomous development. The Dardanelles were to be permanently opened, under an international guarantee.
13. An independent Poland must be established, with free access to the sea.
14. 'A general association of nations must be formed under specific covenants for the purpose of affording mutual guarantes of political independence and territorial integrity to great and small states alike.'

CHAPTER FOURTEEN

1. See above, p. 166.
2. Trevor Wilson, *The Downfall of the Liberal Party* (Collins, 1966).
3. Figures from C. L. Mowat, *Britain between the Wars* (Methuen, 1955).
4. Figures from Mowat, op. cit.
5. Wilson, op. cit. p. 222.
6. Wilson, op. cit. p. 230.

CHAPTER FIFTEEN

1. Yeats, written on 25 Sep. 1916. *Collected Poems of W. B. Yeats* (Macmillan, 1968).
2. A. J. P. Taylor, *English History 1914–1945* (Oxford, 1965) p. 161.

CHAPTER SIXTEEN

1. R. Bassett, *1931 Political Crisis* (Macmillan, 1958) pp. 28 ff.
2. See G. M. Young, *Baldwin* (Hart-Davis, 1951).

3. Quoted in A. J. P. Taylor, *English History, 1914–1945* (Oxford, 1965) p. 205.
4. See Keith Feiling, *The Life of Neville Chamberlain* (Macmillan, 1946).
5. G. M. Young, op. cit. ch. VI.
6. Quoted in Colin Cross, *Philip Snowden* (Barrie & Rockliff, 1966) p. 244.

CHAPTER SEVENTEEN

1. Quoted in G. M. Young, *Baldwin* (Hart-Davis, 1951) p. 117.
2. See, for example, C. L. Mowat, *Britain Between the Wars* (Methuen, 1955).
3. Alan Bullock, *The Life and Times of Ernest Bevin* (Heinemann, 1960) p. 100.
4. Bullock, op. cit. p. 179.
5. J. M. Keynes, *The Economic Consequences of Mr Churchill* (L. & V. Woolf, London, 1925) p. 23.
6. Young, op. cit. p. 110.
7. A. J. P. Taylor, *English History, 1914–1945* (Oxford, 1965) p. 242.
8. Quoted in Mowat, op. cit. p. 300.
9. Quoted in Mowat, op. cit. p. 305.
10. Young, op. cit. p. 116.
11. Taylor, op. cit. p. 245.

CHAPTER EIGHTEEN

1. Quoted in R. Bassett, *1931 Political Crisis* (Macmillan, 1958) p. 338.
2. See Colin Cross, *Philip Snowden* (Barrie & Rockliff, 1966).
3. See Cross, op. cit. pp. 246 ff.
4. A. J. P. Taylor, *English History 1914–1945* (Oxford, 1965) p. 284.
5. See J. K. Galbraith, *The Great Crash* (Hamish Hamilton, 1955).
6. R. Bassett, op. cit. pp. 338 ff.
7. Hugh Dalton, *Call Back Yesterday* (Muller, 1953) p. 290.
8. R. Bassett, op. cit.
9. Harold Macmillan, *Winds of Change* (Macmillan, 1966) chapter 9.
10. Lionel Robbins, *The Great Depression* (Macmillan, 1934) pp. 77–8.
11. Quoted in Bassett, op. cit. pp. 444 ff.

CHAPTER NINETEEN

1. See F. A. Iremonger, *The Life of William Temple* (Oxford University Press, 1948).
2. C. L. Mowat, *Britain Between the Wars* (Methuen, 1955) p. 437.

3. H. M. Pelling, *Modern Britain* (Nelson, 1960) p. 113.
4. For these and other detailed statistics, see Mowat, op. cit.
5. John Wheeler Bennett, *King George VI* (Macmillan, 1958).

CHAPTER TWENTY

1. See G. M. Young, *Baldwin* (Hart-Davis, 1951) p. 63.
2. See A. J. P. Taylor, *English History, 1914–1945* (Oxford, 1965) pp. 368 ff.
3. Cf. C. L. Mowat, *Britain Between the Wars* (Methuen, 1955) p. 425.
4. Quoted in Allan Bullock, *The Life and Times of Ernest Bevin* (Heinemann, 1960) p. 568.
5. See Bullock, op. cit. p. 570.
6. But see D. C. Watt, 'German Plans for the Reoccupation of the Rhineland: A Note', in *The Journal of Contemporary History*, vol. 1, no. 4 (1966), for an interesting if not entirely convincing modification of the usual view.
7. Taylor, op. cit. p. 406.

CHAPTER TWENTY-ONE

1. See A. J. P. Taylor, *English History, 1914–1945* (Oxford) p. 171.
2. See Stuart Samuel's, 'The Left Book Club', in *The Journal of Contemporary History*, vol. 1, no. 2 (Weidenfeld & Nicolson).

CHAPTER TWENTY-TWO

1. *No Room at the Inn*, by Joan Temple, and *Put Out More Flags*, by Evelyn Waugh.
2. Edward Spears, *Prelude to Dunkirk*, p. 32, quoted in A. J. P. Taylor, *English History, 1914–1945* (Oxford, 1965) p. 459.
3. For a sympathetic biography of this attractive personality, see John Connell, *Wavell, Scholar and Soldier* (Collins, 1964).
4. See Winston Churchill, *The Second World War*, vol. 1 (Cassell, 1948) p. 594.
5. Churchill, op. cit. pp. 594–5.
6. Churchill, op. cit. p. 601.

CHAPTER TWENTY-THREE

1. For an exhilarating account, see Lady Violet Bonham Carter, *Winston Churchill as I Knew Him* (Eyre & Spottiswoode/Collins, 1965), and, of course, Winston Churchill, *My Early Life* (Odhams, 1947).

2. Churchill, *The Second World War*, vol. IV (Cassell, 1951).

3. Quoted, Taylor, *English History, 1941–1945* (Oxford, 1965) p. 513.

4. See Taylor, op. cit. pp. 552 ff.

CHAPTER TWENTY-FOUR

1. Winston S. Churchill, *The Second World War*, vol. I (Cassell, 1948).

2. For an elaboration of this theme, see A. J. P. Taylor, *English History 1914–1945* (Oxford, 1965) ch. xv.

3. See, for example, for an excellent though fictional account, Duff Cooper, *Operation Heartbreak* (Pan Books, 1953).

4. Taylor, op. cit. p. 596.

CHAPTER TWENTY-FIVE

The student is in danger of being swamped by details as he reaches this nearly contemporary period of history. A lucid and stimulating survey is to be found in H. M. Pelling, *Modern Britain*, ch. 8 (Nelson, 1960), which I have found most helpful.

Brief Biographies

A small selection of brief studies of some of the interesting people who are mentioned in the narrative but not fully discussed there.

Sir John Anderson, Lord Waverley 1882–1958

Sir John Anderson was a distinguished civil servant who became a politician and an important statesman. He was Permanent Under-Secretary at the Foreign Office for ten years from 1922, and Governor of Bengal from 1932 to 1937. In 1938, he was taken into the Government as Lord Privy Seal and given responsibility for the vital work of preparing the nation's civil defences, especially against air attack. His name is therefore linked with air-raid precautions (A.R.P.) and especially with the Anderson type of air-raid shelter – a corrugated steel structure half-buried in back gardens all over Britain. He was Home Secretary from 1940 to 1941, Lord President of the Council from 1941 to 1943, and Chancellor of the Exchequer from 1943 to 1945. His political significance by this time may be judged from the fact that he was designated by Winston Churchill to become Prime Minister if both Churchill and Eden died.

See:
Sir J. W. Wheeler-Bennett, *Sir John Anderson*

William Maxwell Aitken, Lord Beaverbrook 1879–1964

Lord Beaverbrook was probably the most successful of all

L

the British 'Press Lords'. Scottish-Canadian by birth, his ownership of the *Daily Express* group of newspapers made him a millionaire and gave him great political importance. He was a skilled manipulator, exercising particular influence over Andrew Bonar Law. His inside knowledge of politics provided him with the material to become one of the most interesting historians of the period. His history is pungent and often one-sided, but is none the less important for that. He conspired against Baldwin and strongly advocated the cause of Empire. He was a friend of Churchill and a supporter of King Edward VIII. Churchill realised the possibilities of Beaverbrook's dynamism if it were channelled into politics, and appointed him Minister of Aircraft Production in 1940. He was brilliantly successful, and his contribution to victory in the Battle of Britain should not be underestimated. He became Minister of Supply in 1941; but this office brought him into conflict with Ernest Bevin, the Minister of Labour. The two men were incompatible in both temperament and technique. Beaverbrook left the War Cabinet in 1942: he was Lord Privy Seal from 1943 to 1945. After the war, the *Daily Express* continued its imperial crusade, and persisted in the use of the term 'Empire'.

See:

Lord Beaverbrook *Politicians and the Press; Politicians and the War; Men and Power; The Rise and Fall of Lloyd George*

Tom Driberg, *Beaverbrook* (an inadequate biography)

Ernest Bevin 1881–1951

Ernest Bevin was a titanic figure in the history of the Labour movement, and probably the greatest organiser and leader in the evolution of British Trade Unionism. Born in obscurity and extreme poverty, his social conscience first found expression in the chapel pulpit. He began his trade union career with the carters in Bristol and became prominent in the Dockers' Union, of which he was leader from 1910 to 1921. He achieved national fame with his presentation of evidence to the Shaw

Tribunal, which won him the popular title of 'the Dockers' K.C.' He inspired the foundation of the mammoth Transport and General Workers' Union and was responsible for much of the preliminary planning and organisation. He was General Secretary of the T.G.W.U. from its foundation in 1921 until 1940, when Winston Churchill, in one of his most far-sighted appointments, made Bevin Minister of Labour. He was thus responsible for the crucial work of organising and inspiring the nation's industrial effort for the remainder of the war. When Labour won the general election of 1945, Bevin resisted the temptation to be put forward as a rival for the leadership to Attlee, to whom he was loyal. Bevin was Foreign Secretary from 1945 to 1950, by which time he had virtually worked himself to death. His Foreign Secretaryship was distinguished by an earthy sincerity which won him wide respect, although he was not immune from prejudice, especially in his dealings with the problem of Palestine.

See:

Alan Bullock, *The Life and Times of Ernest Bevin*, 2 volumes to date

William Booth 1829–1912

William Booth was born in Nottingham, and became apprenticed to a pawnbroker. At the age of fifteen he experienced a religious conversion which dominated his whole life. In 1849 Booth moved to London and continued work in a pawnbroker's shop. By now he hated the work, but his family needed the money, and at least the job gave him an insight into the social and moral problems of penury. By 1852 he was preaching regularly in the Methodist New Connection. In 1861 he became an independent evangelical preacher. Three years later he instituted the Christian Mission in Whitechapel, using methods which later became familiar – open-air revivalist meetings, congregations housed in tents, and so on. The Salvation Army, with its military style discipline and organisation and its uncompromisingly evangelical and revivalist theology, was created in 1878. Scorned, ridiculed, and even prosecuted in the early days, the Salvation Army's banner of Blood and Fire carried its message of sin and redemption throughout London and the nation. It was probably the most decisive religious voice of its time, and its impact upon the social problems and religious apathy and ignorance was enormous, as was the influence of 'General' Booth's book *In Darkest England and the Way Out* (1890) From early ostracism, Booth became socially acceptable to upper-class philanthropists, and even enjoyed the patronage and encouragement of Edward VII.

See:

T. F. Coates *The Life Story of General Booth*
W. H. Nelson *General William Booth*
George Bernard Shaw, *Major Barbara* (1907)

Sir Edward Carson 1854–1935

Sir Edward Carson, a distinguished lawyer and dangerous political *prima donna*, was born and educated in Ireland. He played a leading part in the trial of Oscar Wilde, and became Solicitor General from 1900 to 1905. He was brought to the forefront of political life by his leadership of the resistance in Ulster to Irish Home Rule. He was prepared to go to the limit in marshalling the forces of Ulster, and in a theatrical gesture he was the first man to sign the Covenant, kneeling to do so. He was also closely involved in overthrowing Asquith, and was even regarded by some as a possible rival to Bonar Law for the leadership of the Conservative Party. He had become Attorney General in 1915, and was appointed First Lord of the Admiralty in 1917, in accordance with the bargain struck when Asquith was overthrown. At the Admiralty, Carson proved a conspicuous failure: he was removed, nevertheless remaining a member of the War Cabinet in 1917 and 1918. He was a Lord of Appeal from 1921 to 1929.

See:

Ian Colvin *Life of Lord Carson*

Denis Gwynn *History of Partition (1912–26)*
Ronald McNeill *Ulster's Stand for Union*

Austen Chamberlain 1868–1937

Austen Chamberlain, son of Joseph Chamberlain and step-brother of Neville, enjoyed a varied career in politics. He was Civil Lord of the Admiralty from 1895 to 1900. In 1900 he became Financial Secretary to the Treasury, and three years later, as part of Balfour's deal with Joseph Chamberlain he was promoted to the Chancellorship of the Exchequer. He was a member of the wartime coalition, and was Secretary for India from 1915 to 1917. In 1918 he became a member of the War Cabinet. He was Chancellor of the Exchequer in the post-war coalition until 1921, and was Lord Privy Seal from 1921 to 1922, during which time he was also Leader of the House of Commons. He was expected to become Chancellor again in 1924, but Baldwin appointed him Foreign Secretary, which office he held until 1929. In the National government of 1931 he became First Lord of the Admiralty.

See:
Austen Chamberlain, *Down the Years*
Charles Petrie, *Austen Chamberlain*

Lord Randolph Henry Spencer Churchill 1849–1895

Lord Randolph Churchill was the third son of the seventh Duke of Marlborough. He was an ambitious and vigorous politician and the inspiration of the four-man 'Fourth Party' which was intended as a ginger-group to liven up the Conservative opposition to Gladstone. Churchill was unscrupulous enough to make use of the Bradlaugh case to further these ends. He was Secretary for India in 1885 and 1886, and then, in July 1886, became the youngest Chancellor of the Exchequer since Pitt. Having captured the control of the Conservative Party organisation, he felt strong enough to challenge the

Cecils, but he overreached himself and pressed his budget proposals to the point of resignation. He foolishly gave the news of his resignation to *The Times* and was thus left totally exposed when, to Churchill's surprise, the resignation was accepted by Salisbury. Lord Randolph's political career came to an abrupt end, leaving his greatest claim to fame the fact that he was the father of Winston.

See:

Winston S. Churchill, *Lord Randolph Churchill*

Robert Rhodes James, *Lord Randolph Churchill*

Sir Edward Elgar 1857–1934

Elgar was the son of a Roman Catholic church organist in Worcester. He developed an interest in the violin, and he gained much of his early musical experience conducting local groups and arranging music for the brass band of a mental hospital. His marriage proved a decisive factor in his life: his wife strongly encouraged Elgar to develop his skill in composition. His first really distinguished composition, the *Enigma Variations*, came in 1899, followed in 1900 by *The Dream of Gerontius*, on the score of which Elgar wrote 'This is the best of me'. The next twenty years were Elgar's greatest creative period. The sublime *Introduction and Allegro* (1905) was followed by the *First Symphony* (1908), the *Violin Concerto* and the mature and moving *Second Symphony* (1911). *Falstaff*, a splendid portrayal in music of the many-sided Shakespearean character, appeared in 1913. The disillusioning impact of the first World War is apparent in the *'Cello Concerto* (1919), a work of intense and haunting melancholy. The death of Elgar's wife in 1920 removed his greatest inspiration, and he composed little of lasting significance during his last years. Elgar's music went out of fashion largely perhaps because he was too closely associated with the jingoistic words which became attached to his *Pomp and Circumstance* March as 'Land of Hope and Glory'. His work is now largely re-established, particularly through the enthusiasm of Sir John Barbirolli.

See:

Ernest Newman, *Elgar* (an early study)

Thomas Stearns Eliot 1888–1965

T. S. Eliot is an outstanding figure in the history of English literature, and a transforming influence upon modern poetry, drama and literary and social criticism. Born in the United States, Eliot settled in England in 1915 and spent eight years in the City before joining the publishing firm of Faber & Faber. He was already editing the literary quarterly review, *The Criterion*. *Prufrock and Other Observations*, his first volume of poetry, was published in 1917. *The Waste Land* his most revolutionary and important work, appeared in 1922 and reflected much of the sense of futility in the post-war world. A mellower attitude may be found in the later volume, *Four Quartets* (1944). Eliot is perhaps the only modern poet to have made an unquestionable success of drama in verse. *Murder in the Cathedral* (1935) is a most moving and powerful dramatisation of the conflict in the mind of Thomas Becket and the high drama of his martyrdom. *The Family Reunion* and *The Cocktail Party* are compelling excursions in verse into modern philosophical and social argument. As a literary and social critic, also, Eliot is highly influential. His *Essays* have been published in a collected edition, and his *Notes Towards the Definition of Culture* represents a serious contribution to modern thought.

See:

F. R. Leavis, *The Common Pursuit*

A. Tate (ed.), *T. S. Eliot, The Man and His Work*

R. Rees, *T. S. Eliot on Culture and Progress* (Journal of Contemporary History, vol 2 no. 2)

Herbert Gladstone 1854–1930

Herbert Gladstone, son of the great Gladstone, has his own claims to a place in the political history of his times.

It was Herbert who, in a moment of tactless, if understandable enthusiasm, let slip to the Press the secret of his father's conversion to Irish Home Rule in 1885. He served as Under-Secretary at the Home Office from 1892 to 1894, and as First Commissioner of Works in 1894 and 1895. His really significant role in politics, however, was as Liberal Chief Whip from 1899 to 1905, during which time he was the architect, with Ramsay MacDonald, of the agreements by which constituency Liberal parties left the L.R.C. candidates with a clear field in certain constituencies. Herbert Gladstone became Home Secretary from 1905 to 1910, and was Governor-General of South Africa from 1910 until 1914.

See:
Herbert Gladstone, *After Thirty Years*

Charles George Gordon 1833–1885

General Gordon was a professional soldier, who fought in the Crimea in 1855. Five years later he took part in the capture of Peking, and from 1863 until 1865 his exploits in China earned him the nickname 'Chinese' Gordon. He served in the Sudan from 1873 to 1876, and again from 1877 to 1880; but in spite of his great experience, he was a foolish choice on Gladstone's part for the evacuation of Egyptian forces from the Sudan. His orders were clear, but Gordon had little intention of obeying them. He paid for his determination to hold on to the Sudan with his life in 1885, when he was murdered in Khartoum. He also left Gladstone with an appalling burden of unpopularity. Gordon is one of the least definable characters in modern history.

See:
Lytton Strachey, *Eminent Victorians*
B. M. Allen, *Gordon and the Sudan*

Alfred Harmsworth, Lord Northcliffe 1865–1922

Northcliffe was the creator of the modern tabloid daily

newspaper, and was the archetype of the 'Press Lord', using his newspapers as a vast commercial enterprise and as a vehicle for his own political propaganda. *Answers* first appeared in 1888, in direct competition with George Newnes's *Tit-Bits*, which was the first example of spicy, racy journalism directed at the greatly increased reading public. Harmsworth bought the *Evening News* in 1894 and the *Daily Mail* began in 1896. By 1899 it was selling over half a million copies a day. In his search for readers, Harmsworth was unscrupulous, his reporters sometimes inventing stories if the real news did not seem to provide sufficient sensation. Harmsworth's power and prestige increased further when he bought *The Times* in 1908. His political influence was recognised during the first World War: in 1917 he led a British mission to the United States, and in 1918 he became director of British propaganda against the enemy.

Northcliffe's brother, Harold, Lord Rothermere (1868–1940) was also a power in both Press and politics. He was Director of the Army Clothing Department in 1916 and 1917, Secretary for Air in 1917 and 1918 and director of British propaganda to neutral countries in 1918. He took over the *Daily Mail* on the death of Northcliffe, and played a prominent part in the attempt to oust Baldwin from the leadership of the Conservative Party.

See:
R. Pound and G. Harmsworth, *Northcliffe*
E. Wrench, *Struggle*
Sir C. Stuart, *Secrets of Crewe House*; *Opportunity Knocks Twice*

Arthur Henderson 1863–1935

A much-loved and respected figure in the Labour Party, whose 'Uncle Arthur' he became, Arthur Henderson is perhaps most remembered for his tireless efforts in the cause of international disarmament. He was a cotton-spinner's son, born in Glasgow and brought up on Tyneside. Beginning working-life as an iron-moulder, Henderson entered politics through the trade union movement and the Wesleyan chapel. He was first elected to Parliament in 1903, when he won a famous three-cornered fight at Barnard Castle. He was secretary of the Labour Party from 1911 to 1934, and was Labour's representative in the wartime coalition. He was President of the Board of Education in 1915 and 1916, and a member of the War Cabinet from 1916 until he withdrew in 1917. He was Home Secretary in the first Labour government and Foreign Secretary in the second. He opposed MacDonald over the National government, but found an outlet for his political energy and sincerity in his dogged advocacy of international disarmament: he was President of the World Disarmament Conference from 1932 until 1935.

See:

M. A. Hamilton, *Arthur Henderson*

John Maynard Keynes, Lord Keynes 1883–1946

John Maynard Keynes was one of the greatest of all British economists, and exercised an unrivalled influence over the development of economic theory during the twentieth century. A Fellow of King's College Cambridge, whose finances he did much to restore, Keynes had wide cultural and artistic interests and connections, being closely associated with the famous 'Bloomsbury set'. He was an official at the Treasury from 1915 to 1919, and attended the Peace Conference. He came into prominence with his attack upon the settlement – *The Economic Consequences of the Peace*. During the 1920s he was developing his economic theories, and strongly attacked the basis of Churchill's return to the gold standard in *The Economic Consequences of Mr Churchill*. Lloyd George derived much of his programme for the 1929 general election – *We Can Conquer Unemployment* – from Keynesian theory and from Keynes' advice, whilst President Roosevelt's 'New Deal' in the United States, with its attack upon economic depression by vast programmes of public works, financed by the state from an unbalanced budget, was the greatest practical experiment in

Keynesian theory. In 1936 Keynes set out his *General Theory of Unemployment, Interest and Money*. He was chief adviser to the Treasury from 1940 to 1946; had he held such office ten years earlier, the modern economic history of Britain might perhaps have been different and happier.

See:
R. Harrod, *The Life of John Maynard Keynes*
H. Feis, 'Keynes in Retrospect', in *Foreign Affairs* (July 1951)
J. M. Keynes: note the works referred to above

Sir Herbert Kitchener, Lord Kitchener 1850–1916

Kitchener remains a controversial figure, especially now that time has dimmed the awesome effect of his pointing finger on the famous poster with its proclamation that 'Your country needs YOU!' Making his early military career in the Royal Engineers in 1871, Kitchener took part in the survey of Palestine between 1874 and 1878. He served in the Sudan during the ill-fated years 1883 to 1885. He was Sirdar of the Egyptian army from 1892 onwards, and won his most famous victory with the defeat of the Khalifa at Omdurman in 1898: his behaviour after the victory seems to have been unnecessarily brutal, and called forth the righteous indignation of the young Winston Churchill. After Omdurman, Kitchener's firmness, along with the diplomacy of the Government, brought about the withdrawal of the French force from Fashoda. Kitchener was Chief of Staff to Roberts in South Africa in 1899, and succeeded Roberts as Commander-in-Chief from 1900 until 1902. He was responsible for the effective, but ruthless and distasteful, campaign against the Boer guerillas, which involved the burning of farms and the rounding-up of the civilian population into concentration-camps. Kitchener was Commander-in-Chief in India from 1902 until 1909, when he was promoted field marshal, and British agent and consul-general in Egypt in 1911. Soon after war broke out, Asquith appointed Kitchener to the War Office. Kitchener was perceptive enough to prophesy and prepare for a long war, but he was regarded as something of a liability and there was intrigue against him. He was drowned in the cruiser *Hampshire* in 1916.

See:

P. Magnus, *Kitchener*

Sir G. Arthur, *The Life of Lord Kitchener*

George Lansbury 1859–1940

George Lansbury served as something of a patron saint to the Labour Party in the first half of the twentieth century. Moved by Christian convictions, his socialism was of an individual, instinctive sort, which was often unamenable to the restraints and disciplines – or even the loyalties – of a political party. Perhaps, therefore, his greatest work was in the context of local rather than national and international politics. It was in Poplar that he exercised his greatest influence. He was first elected to the Poplar Board of Guardians in 1892: in the working-class distress between the wars he became famous for what became known as 'Poplarism' – the deliberate flouting of governmental regulations limiting the amount of relief available to the unemployed. Lansbury became an M.P. from 1910 until 1912, and again from 1922 until 1940. He edited the ill-fated *Daily Herald* from 1919 until 1923, and then carried on the journalistic fight on behalf of the working class with his own *Lansbury's Labour Weekly*. He held office in the second Labour government as First Commissioner of Works, and then, with the débâcle in 1931, became the leader of the Labour Party. He was a convinced and lifelong pacifist, and so was in tune with the majority of the Party until he was brutally overthrown at the Labour Party Conference in 1935 by Ernest Bevin, who asserted that he had simply set fire to the faggots under Lansbury, who had been waiting for martyrdom for years.

See:

R. Postgate, *The Life of George Lansbury*

David Herbert Lawrence 1885–1930

D. H. Lawrence is probably the most important English novelist of the twentieth century, both for his impact upon the reading public and for his influence over later writers. Born in Eastwood, Nottinghamshire, he was the son of a miner. His mother obviously exercised a strong influence over his early life. Educated at University College, Nottingham, Lawrence gave up teaching to devote himself entirely to writing. The forceful, uninhibited approach of his early works made an immediate impression, with such novels as *The White Peacock* (1911), *Sons and Lovers* (1913) – unquestionably one of his finest achievements – and *The Rainbow* (1915). The influence of Freudian psychology, and of his own travels in New Mexico, Australia and elsewhere, became increasingly marked, as, for example, in *Women in Love* (1921) and *The Plumed Serpent* (1926). He also wrote many poems, and studies on psychoanalysis. His deep and abiding concern with the importance of sexual relationships in human life gradually led him into conflict with established social attitudes and with the law. A great deal less than justice is done to his personal and literary reputation by his association in the popular mind with the *cause célèbre* over *Lady Chatterley's Lover* – an inferior novel by any standards, and especially by comparison with Lawrence's own best work.

See:

F. R. Leavis, *D. H. Lawrence: Novelist,* and *The Common Pursuit*

Thomas Edward Lawrence 1888–1935

Lawrence of Arabia won a first-class degree in modern history at Oxford, and in 1910 he pursued his interest in Crusader architecture by touring Syria. From 1911 until 1914 he took part in the excavations of Carchemish. He became famous during the early stages of the First World War for his inspiration of the Arab revolt against the Turks. He won the confidence of the Emir Faisal, and seriously weakened the

Turks by attacking the Hejaz railway and threatening Medina. In August 1917 Lawrence won his greatest victory with the capture of Aqaba. In 1918, he entered Damascus ahead of Allenby, and held the city and maintained order until the arrival of the main British force. After the war, he attended the peace conference, and was employed in various capacities as an adviser on Arab affairs, but he was bitterly disillusioned over what he regarded as the betrayal of the Arab cause after the war, and sought to withdraw from public life. In 1922 he enlisted as an aircraftsman in the R.A.F., and later changed his name by deed-poll to Shaw; he was usually recognised as 'Lawrence of Arabia'. He died after a motor-cycle accident in 1935.

See:
Robert Graves, *Lawrence and the Arabs*
T. E. Lawrence, *Seven Pillars of Wisdom*, and *The Mint*

Alfred Milner, Viscount Milner 1854–1925

Milner had established a very high reputation as an administrator before he exercised his formidable influence in politics. He was under-secretary for finance in Egypt from 1890, until 1892 when he became Chairman of the Board of Inland Revenue. Probably his most significant period was as High Commissioner for South Africa from 1897 to 1905. Many of his ideas in dealing with the Boers were preconceived, and he was a very hard bargainer: he seems to have decided at an early stage that war was the most likely outcome of the British quarrel with Kruger, and his communications with the home government strongly indicate such an attitude. He was a member of the War Cabinet from 1916 until 1918 and served in the post-war coalition as Secretary for War in 1918 and 1919, and as Secretary for the Colonies from 1918 until 1921.

See:
A. M. Gollin, *Proconsul in Politics*
Lord Milner, *England in Egypt*

Sir John Simon, Viscount Simon 1873–1954

'Simon', declared Lloyd George, with characteristic malice but shrewd perception, 'has sat on the fence so long that the iron has entered into his soul'. A distinguished lawyer, Simon became a Liberal M.P. in 1906. He was Solicitor-General from 1910 to 1913, and Attorney-General from 1913 until 1915, when he became Home Secretary until 1916. He was famous for his pronouncement in 1926 that the General Strike was illegal. He led the group of Liberals who most wholeheartedly entered the National government in 1931, and who remained with the Government until they became virtually indistinguishable from Conservatives. Simon was an indecisive Foreign Secretary from 1931 to 1935 – a period when decisiveness in diplomacy was vitally needed. He was Home Secretary from 1935 to 1937, and Chancellor of the Exchequer from 1937 until 1940, when he became Lord Chancellor, an office which he held until 1945.

See:
Lord Simon, *Retrospect*

William Temple 1881–1944

William Temple was the son of Frederick Temple, Archbishop of Canterbury. He was educated at Rugby, and was a Fellow of The Queen's College, Oxford from 1904 to 1910, when he became Headmaster of Repton. In 1914 he became Rector of St James's, Piccadilly, and in 1919 a Canon of Westminster. He was Bishop of Manchester from 1921 to 1929, Archbishop of York from 1929 to 1942 and Archbishop of Canterbury from 1942 until his untimely death in 1944. William Temple was a scholar and a humanitarian, and his political views were radical and socialist. He was President of the Workers' Educational Association from 1908 to 1924. He was outspoken on the social problems of his time, and forcefully attacked governmental failure to deal with the moral degradation of unemployment during the 1930s. His theological and social thinking were alike progressive, and his death in 1944 was a great blow, for he had much to contribute to the national life in the post-war world: his national influence during a period of Labour government might have been particularly significant.

See:

William Temple, *Readings in Saint John's Gospel*; *Nature, Man and God*; *Christian Faith and Life*

F. A. Iremonger, *William Temple*

James Henry ('Jimmy') Thomas 1874–1949

J. H. Thomas was born in Newport, Monmouthshire, and began work on the railways as a cleaner, later becoming an engine-driver on the Great Western Railway. He became General Secretary of the National Union of Railwaymen in 1917 and held the office until 1931. He became an M.P. in 1910 and remained in the House of Commons until 1936. He played a prominent part in the negotiations over the General Strike, and was so strongly in favour of a settlement that some – especially the miners – thought he had betrayed the working-class cause. He was Colonial Secretary in both of the minority Labour governments. In 1929 he wanted the Foreign Office, but Ramsay MacDonald made him Lord Privy Seal with special responsibility for dealing with unemployment at which he was conspicuously unsuccessful. In 1930 he became the first holder of the office of Secretary of State for the Dominions. He was a strong supporter of the National government, and retained office as Dominions Secretary until 1935, when he once more became Colonial Secretary. He retired from public life in 1936, after letting slip some remarks which led to a betrayal of budget secrets. A controversial figure, and more popular outside than inside the Labour movement, he was caricatured by Low as 'The Right Honourable Dress Shirt'.

See:

J. H. Thomas, *My Story*

Herbert George Wells 1866–1946

H. G. Wells was born in Bromley, Kent, and was the son of a professional cricketer. His own early life was spent in the lower-middle-class surroundings which he was later to describe with such detail, irony and perception. He worked himself out of this environment and proceeded by scholarship to the Royal College of Science, and took a London University B.Sc. with first-class honours. After some experience as a schoolmaster, Wells took up journalism in 1893. He was earnestly progressive in outlook, and joined the Fabian Society in 1903. He was destined to become highly influential over radical opinion. His concern with social and political reform naturally marks much of his work. One of his earliest novels, *The Time Machine*, illustrates his interest in science-fiction, especially as a vehicle for social comment. *A Modern Utopia* (1905) serves a similar purpose. *Kipps* (1905) and *The History of Mr Polly* (1910) are his outstanding works set in the context of the lower middle class, whilst his most ambitious work was the *Outline of History* (1920). His idealism dampened into pessimism towards the end of his life, and his last work, *Mind at the End of its Tether* (1946) reflects pessimism bordering upon despair.

See:
H. G. Wells, *Kipps*; *The History of Mr Polly*; *Outline of History*

William Butler Yeats 1865–1939

W. B. Yeats was the son of a well-known Irish painter. His mother came from Sligo, an area which exercised a lasting influence over him. Yeats studied painting, but turned to writing, and produced his first volume of verse in 1889. He moved to London and described his experiences there, and indeed the whole first thirty years of his life, in his *Autobiographies*. From 1897 onwards he became interested in the Irish theatre, and, with Lady Gregory and others, was influential in the foundation of the Abbey Theatre in 1904. Yeats's own work for the theatre is technically highly imaginative, but very difficult to produce, and he is understandably famous as a poet rather than a playwright. In the early stages his poetry is elaborate, even pretty; but the development of his Irish patriotism transformed the man and his work. His form becomes austere and his message is characterised by a sort of fierce melancholy. Later still, his work becomes very difficult, its obscurity deriving from the growing complexity of the poet's own philosophy.

See:
W. B. Yeats, *Collected Poems* and *Collected Plays*
T. R. Henn, *The Lonely Tower*
A. Norman Jeffares and K. G. W. Cross, *In excited Reverie*

Select Bibliography

THE historical literature of the period is so vast that all that can be attempted here is to list, with comment, those works which have been especially useful in the preparation of the present volume, and which will prove richly rewarding to those readers who wish to follow up topics in which they are particularly interested. The fuller bibliography of the period may be found in the appropriate volumes of the *Oxford History of England* or in the admirable bibliographies prepared by the Historical Association.

GENERAL TEXTBOOKS

R. C. K. Ensor, *England 1870–1914* (The Oxford History of England, 1936).
A mine of information on the period: scholarly and lucid, but essentially a work of reference.

A. J. P. Taylor, *English History 1914–1945* (The Oxford History of England, 1965).
Characteristic of Mr Taylor at his best: provocative, witty, occasionally outrageous, but always stimulating.

É. Halévy, *A History of the English People in the Nineteenth Century*, 6 vols., 2nd rev. ed. (Benn, 1949–65).
Still probably the greatest general study of the period.
   vol. v, *Imperialism and the Rise of Labour* (1926).
   vol. vi, *The Rule of Democracy* (1932).

R. McKenzie, *British Political Parties*, 2nd rev. ed. (Heinemann, 1963).
A standard work on the subject.

C. L. Mowat, *Britain Between the Wars* (Methuen, 1955).
An indispensable work of reference and comment.

H. Pelling, *Modern Britain* (Nelson, 1960).
A masterpiece of compression and selection.

IMPORTANT BIOGRAPHIES, MEMOIRS, ETC.

G. E. Buckle (ed.), *The Letters of Queen Victoria* (John Murray, 1908).
A comprehensive and revealing collection.

Elizabeth Longford, *Victoria R.I.* (Weidenfeld & Nicolson, 1964).
An outstanding biography: thorough, perceptive and sympathetic, and spiced with much winsome anecdote.

Philip Magnus, *Edward VII* (John Murray, 1964).
A very readable, though perhaps over-indulgent, study.

Harold Nicolson, *King George V, His Life and Reign* (Constable, 1952).

H.R.H. The Duke of Windsor, *A King's Story* (Cassell, 1951).
A partial and moving piece of autobiography.

J. Wheeler-Bennett, *King George VI* (Macmillan, 1958).
A detailed and sympathetic account of 'George the Good'.

John Morley, *Life of Gladstone* (Macmillan, 1903).
The 'classic' life.

Philip Magnus, *Gladstone* (John Murray, 1954).
A more readable and perhaps more critical account than Morley's.

Roy Jenkins, *Sir Charles Dilke, A Victorian Tragedy* (Collins, 1958).
A vivid illustration of the power of 'scandal' in Victorian political life.

Robert Rhodes James, *Rosebery* (Weidenfeld & Nicolson, 1963).
A satisfying biography of a frustrating character.

Winston Churchill, *Lord Randolph Churchill* (Macmillan, 1906).
A work of filial piety and inimitable style.

Robert Rhodes James, *Lord Randolph Churchill* (Weidenfeld & Nicolson, 1955).
More perceptive, though less 'stylistic' than Winston Churchill.

Lady Gwendolen Cecil, *The Life of Robert, Marquess of Salisbury* (Hodder & Stoughton, 1921).
Splendidly detailed and balanced, but stops short at 1892.
J. L. Garvin, *The Life of Joseph Chamberlain*, vols. I and II (Macmillan, 1932–4).
Dull and uncritical, but has a monopoly of much vital information.
Julian Amery, *The Life of Joseph Chamberlain*, vols. IV, V and VI (Macmillan, 1951–69).
Takes over where Garvin leaves off.
Kenneth Young, *Arthur James Balfour* (Bell, 1963).
A work of great length but rather less historical depth, which fails in its attempt to make Balfour's personality attractive.
Philip Magnus, *Kitchener* (John Murray, 1958).
An important book, which reveals some unpalatable truths about a national hero.
Margot Asquith, *Autobiography* (Butterworth, 1920–2).
A fascinating insight into the high society of the period.
Roy Jenkins, *Asquith* (Collins, 1964).
An important and sympathetic study.
Edward Grey, *Twenty-Five Years* (Hodder & Stoughton, 1925).
An account of diplomatic tragedy, by one of the most attractive characters in modern British politics.
G. M. Trevelyan, *Grey of Falloden* (Longmans, 1937).
David Lloyd George, *War Memoirs* (Odhams Press, 1938).
Very one-sided, but far more important and more revealing about Lloyd George than any of the books written about him by other people. None of them does justice to its subject, but perhaps the most interesting are:
Malcolm Thomson, *Lloyd George* (Hutchinson, 1948).
Frank Owen, *Tempestuous Journey* (Hutchinson, 1954).
Robert Blake, *The Unknown Prime Minister* (Eyre & Spottiswoode, 1955).
Painstaking work of scholarship about Bonar Law.
G. M. Young, *Baldwin* (Rupert Hart-Davis, 1951).
A brief but moderately critical biography, which offended the Baldwin family.

A. W. Baldwin, *My Father, the True Story* (Allen & Unwin, 1956).
  The family's reply.
Raymond Postgate, *George Lansbury* (Longmans, 1951).
  An account of the patron saint of the Labour Party.
Julian Symons, *Horatio Bottomley* (Cresset Press, 1955).
  An enterprising study of one of the great rogues of the time.
Colin Cross, *Philip Snowden* (Barrie & Rockliff, 1966).
  As adequate a biography as can be expected, in the absence
  of documentary evidence. Certainly adds something to:
Philip Snowden, *Autobiography* (Nicolson & Watson, 1934).
Roy Harrod, *John Maynard Keynes* (Macmillan, 1951).
  A study of the man and of his epoch-making work.
Asa Briggs, *Seebohm Rowntree* (Longmans, 1961).
  An account of a pioneer of sociology.
F. A. Iremonger, *William Temple* (Oxford University Press,
      1948).
  The life and times of one of the great Christian leaders of
  modern times.
Duff Cooper, *Old Men Forget* (Rupert Hart-Davis, 1953).
  The autobiography of a politician of charm and courage.
Lord Citrine, *Men and Work* (Hutchinson, 1964).
  An autobiography which throws important sidelights on the
  development of the trade union movement.
K. Feiling, *Neville Chamberlain* (Macmillan, 1946).
  A thorough and painstaking effort, which fails to provide the
  material for Chamberlain's rehabilitation.
Winston Churchill, *My Early Life* (Odhams, 1947); *Thoughts
      and Adventures* (Odhams, 1947); *Great Contemporaries*
      (Odhams, 1947); *The World Crisis* (Thornton Butter-
      worth, 1927); *The Second World War* (Cassell, 1948–54).
  Churchill speaks for himself, as happily he is allowed to do in:
Randolph Churchill, *Winston S. Churchill*, vols. I and II (Heine-
      mann, 1966/7).
Lady Violet Bonham Carter, *Winston Churchill as I Knew Him*
      (Eyre & Spottiswoode/Collins, 1965).
  An affectionate, perceptive and often moving memoir.
C. R. Attlee, *As It Happened* (Heinemann, 1954).
  Attlee's natural reserve predominates, as it does in:

Francis Williams, *A Prime Minister Remembers* (Heinemann, 1961).

Alan Bullock, *The Life and Times of Ernest Bevin*, vols. I and II (Heinemann, 1960).
  A splendidly detailed and scholarly study of a titanic figure.

Michael Foot, *Aneurin Bevan* (McGibbon & Kee, 1962).
  One radical's warm appreciation of another.

Harold Macmillan, *Winds of Change* (Macmillan, 1966); *The Blast of War* (Macmillan, 1967).
  An illuminating insight into many personal and political facets.

SPECIAL STUDIES

Before 1914

J. L. Hammond, *Gladstone and the Irish Nation* (Longmans, 1938).
  A classic work of historical scholarship.

J. A. S. Grenville, *Lord Salisbury and Foreign Policy* (University of London Press, 1964).
  An important study, based upon much original research.

Elizabeth Longford, *Jameson's Raid* (Weidenfeld & Nicolson, 1960).
  An account and analysis of the ill-fated prelude to the Boer War.

A. Gollin, *Balfour's Burden* (Blond, 1965).
  A brilliant study, which throws much new light on both Balfour and Chamberlain in the context of the controversy over tariffs.

H. Pelling, *A Short History of the Labour Party* (Oxford, 1965).
  The standard work on the subject.

P. Poirier, *The Origins of the Labour Party* (Allen & Unwin, 1958).
  Usefully supplements Pelling.

J. W. Derry, *The Radical Tradition* (Macmillan, 1967).
  A scholarly work, which makes an interesting and stimulating blend of biography with historical and philosophical analysis.

Roger Fulford, *Votes for Women* (Faber & Faber, 1957).
A very readable account of the struggle for female suffrage.
Colin Cross, *The Liberals in Power* (Barrie & Rockliff/Pall Mall, 1963).
An excellent summary of the great Liberal administration of 1906–1916.
J. W. Derry, *Parliamentary Reform* (Macmillan, 1966).
A lucid brief account.

The Great War

C. R. M. F. Cruttwell, *A History of the Great War* (Oxford, 1936).
Still in many ways the standard work.
A. J. P. Taylor, *The First World War – An Illustrated History* (Hamish Hamilton, 1963).
J. Terraine, *Mons, Retreat to Victory* (Batsford, 1960).
Robert Rhodes James, *Gallipoli* (Batsford, 1965).
A. H. Farrer Hockley, *The Battle of the Somme* (Batsford/Pan Books, 1966).
All these books are profusely illustrated.
C. Barnett, *The Sword Bearers* (Eyre & Spottiswoode, 1963).
Four studies in high command during the Great War.
Barbara Tuchman, *August 1914* (Constable, 1962).
A study in depth and breadth.
Alan Moorehead, *Gallipoli* (Hamish Hamilton, 1956).
A critical account.
Duff Cooper, *Haig* (Faber & Faber, 1935).
A sympathetic biography.
L. Wolff, *In Flanders Fields* (Longmans, 1958).
Redresses the balance after Duff Cooper. Highly critical of Haig.
Robert Graves, *Good-bye To All That* (Cape, 1929).
One of the greatest and most moving of the memoirs of the war.
Siegfried Sassoon, *Memoirs of an Infantry Officer* (Faber & Faber, 1931).
A sensitive account of the impact of war.
See also the poetry of Wilfred Owen, Rupert Brooke, Siegfried Sassoon, etc.

Between the Wars

J. M. Keynes, *The Economic Consequences of the Peace* (Macmillan, 1919); *The Economic Consequences of Mr Churchill* (L. & V. Woolf, 1925); *General Theory of Unemployment, Interest and Money* (Macmillan, 1936).
  Examples of the impact of the thought of the most original economist of the age.
Lord Beaverbrook, *The Decline and Fall of Lloyd George* (Collins, 1963).
  Provides some fascinating insights from Beaverbrook's inside information.
Trevor Wilson, *The Downfall of the Liberal Party* (Collins, 1966).
  An important analysis of the collapse of the Liberal Party, making especially interesting use of the newspapers of the time.
Julian Symons, *The General Strike* (Cresset Press, 1957).
  A very readable account.
R. Bassett, *1931 Political Crisis* (Macmillan, 1958).
  A brilliant analysis, which goes far to dispel the illusion of a 'betrayal' of the Labour Party by MacDonald.
A. J. P. Taylor, *The Origins of the Second World War* (Hamish Hamilton, 1961).
  A highly controversial account.

The Second World War

Winston Churchill, *The Second World War* (Cassell, 1948–54).
E. L. Spears, *Assignment to Catastrophe* (Heinemann, 1954).
  An account of the ill-fated beginning to the Second World War.
P. Fleming, *Invasion 1940* (Rupert Hart-Davis, 1957).
  The challenges of 1940, and the responses by government and people in Britain.
Arthur Bryant, *The Turn of the Tide* (Collins, 1957); *Triumph in the West* (Collins, 1959).
  The diaries of Lord Alanbrooke.

C. Barnett, *The Desert Generals* (Kimber, 1960).
    A very controversial study, particularly critical of Mont-
    gomery.
J. Connell, *Wavell* (Collins, 1964).
    A sympathetic study of a scholarly soldier. See also:
J. Connell, *Auchinleck* (Collins, 1966).
Chester Wilmot, *The Struggle for Europe* (Collins, 1952).
    One of the earliest accounts of the military and diplomatic
    campaigns.
A. T. Harris, *Bomber Offensive* (Collins, 1947).
    Harris's own account of strategic bombing.
Viscount Montgomery, *Memoirs* (Collins, 1958).
Earl Alexander, *Memoirs* (Cassell, 1962).
    Personal recollections of two of the outstanding British
    generals.
D. Macintyre, *The Battle of the Atlantic* (Batsford, 1961); *The
    Battle for the Mediterranean* (Batsford, 1964).
    Important studies of the war at sea.
Evelyn Waugh, *Men at Arms*; *Officers and Gentlemen*; *Unconditional
    Surrender* (Chapman & Hall, 1952–61).
    A brilliantly satirical trilogy.

Since 1945

A. Shonfield, *British Economic Policy since the War* (Penguin, 1959).
    A critical and analytical survey.
The volumes (all published by Macmillan) surveying British
general election since the war are most valuable:
    R. B. McCallum and A. Readman, *The British General
        Election of 1945.*
    H. G. Nicholas, *The British General Election of 1950.*
    D. E. Butler, *The British General Election of 1951.*
    D. E. Butler, *The British General Election of 1955.*
    D. E. Butler and R. Rose, *The British General Election of
        1959.*
    D. E. Butler and A. King, *The British General Election of
        1964.*
    D. E. Butler and A. King, *The British General Election of 1966.*

Social History

C. Booth, *Life and Labour of the People of London* (Williams & Norgate, 1889–91).

B. Seebohm Rowntree, *Poverty: A Study of Town Life*; *Poverty and Progress* (Longmans, 1941).

W. H. Beveridge, *Unemployment* (Longmans, 1909).

Four cornerstones of the science of sociology.

W. Booth, *In Darkest England and the Way Out* (Salvation Army H.Q., 1890).

An insight into the mind and work of a great social reformer.

G. D. H. Cole and R. Postgate, *The Common People 1746–1946* (Methuen, 1932).

An historical survey.

S. J. Curtis, *Education in Britain since 1900* (Andrew Dakers, 1952).

The standard work.

F. Williams, *The Dangerous Estate* (Longmans, 1957).

E. Wrench, *Geoffrey Dawson and Our Times* (Hutchinson, 1955).

R. Pound and G. Harmsworth, *Northcliffe* (Cassell, 1959).

Three volumes illustrating the development of journalism in modern times.

W. Greenwood, *Love on the Dole* (Cape, 1933).

J. B. Priestley, *English Journey* (Heinemann/Gollancz, 1934).

Two outstanding studies of the social problems of the working class between the wars.

David Low, *Years of Wrath* (Gollancz, 1949).

A collection of the cartoons of an artist of genius.

Asa Briggs, *History of Broadcasting in the United Kingdom* (Oxford, 1961–5).

A detailed history of the development and organisation of a revolution in mass communications.

OTHER SOURCES

Journals, etc.

The recently founded *Journal of Contemporary History* has already produced some important papers and essays. The older-established *History Today* maintains a high standard of well-illustrated essays, many of them on the modern period. More academic are: the *Journal of the Historical Association, History*, and the *English Historical Review*.

Jackdaws (Cape) represent a splendid innovation in source material for the teaching of history. Three at least have so far been issued which are relevant to the modern period: *The Vote*; *Early Trade Unions*; and *Assassination at Sarajevo*.

Illustrations

The period is naturally very rich in illustrative material. *Picture Post*, founded in 1938, was an outstanding enterprise in pictorial journalism, and its collection of pictures is now incorporated in the Radio Times Hulton Picture Library, which is the best source of illustrations. The Imperial War Museum richly rewards the visitor, with its relics from both wars, its panoramas, and exhibitions from its three and a half million prints. The National Portrait Gallery houses the national collection of outstanding portraits.

Films

The Imperial War Museum has a collection of newsreels and war films from the two wars, whilst the National Film Library lends out news films which date back to 1895. The Rank Organisation and other groups lend 16-mm. and 32-mm. editions of outstanding films. Television has added to our material. B.B.C.'s series on *The Great War* and *The Lost Peace* are probably the outstanding achievement in this field to date. I.T.V.'s series *All Our Yesterdays* presents some very interesting material, sometimes spoilt by snide commentary.

Sound Recording

The archives of the B.B.C. represent a treasure-house for the modern historian. Some commercial companies have issued recordings of historic events. Decca, for example, has produced a set of Winston Churchill's speeches and readings from *The Second World War*: apart from the incidental music, the recording is a gem. The music of the period is by now well represented in the catalogues: the two greatest English works of the age are beautifully reproduced – Elgar's *The Dream of Gerontius* on E.M.I. and Britten's *War Requiem* on Decca.

Index